Mexican-Origin People in the United States

The Modern American West

Gerald D. Nash and Richard W. Etulain, Editors

Carl Abbott
The Metropolitan Frontier: Cities in the Modern American West

Richard W. Etulain
Re-imagining the Modern American West:
A Century of Fiction, History, and Art

Gerald D. Nash
The Federal Landscape: An Economic History of the
Twentieth-Century West

Ferenc Morton Szasz
Religion in the Modern American West

Oscar J. Martínez
Mexican-Origin People in the United States:
A Topical History

MEXICAN-ORIGIN

PEOPLE IN THE

UNITED STATES

A Topical History

❁

OSCAR J. MARTÍNEZ

❁

The University of Arizona Press

TUCSON

Oscar J. Martínez is the author of many works on the history of the
U.S.-Mexico borderlands, including *Troublesome Border* (1988) and
Border People (1994). He is Regents Professor of History at the
University of Arizona, where he has taught since 1988.

First printing
The University of Arizona Press
© 2001 The Arizona Board of Regents
All rights reserved

♾ This book is printed on acid-free, archival-quality paper.
Manufactured in the United States of America

06   05   04   03   02   01   6   5   4   3   2   1

Library of Congress Cataloging-in-Publication Data
Martínez, Oscar J. (Oscar Jáquez), 1943–
Mexican-origin people in the United States : a topical history /
Oscar J. Martínez.
p. cm. — (The modern American West)
Includes bibliographical references and index.
ISBN 0-8165-1179-9 (alk. paper) —
ISBN 0-8165-2089-5 (pbk. : alk. paper)
1. Mexican Americans—Southwest, New—History—20th century.
2. Mexican Americans—Southwest, New—Social conditions—20th
century.   3. Southwest, New—Ethnic relations.   4. Southwest,
New—Social conditions—20th century.   5. Southwest, New—
Emigration and immigration—History—20th century.   6. Mexico—
Emigration and immigration—History—20th century.
I. Title.   II. Series.
F790.M5 M37   2000
00-010291

British Library Cataloguing-in-Publication Data
A catalogue record for this book is available from the British Library.

To Mexican-origin people who, over the course of
many generations, have struggled for genuine inclusion in
U.S. society while making untold contributions to the
building of this country.

And to the youth of the new millennium:

Aim for the roses,
For success and fulfillment,
For dreams realized,
Unhindered by thorns.

CONTENTS

FIGURES

TABLES

ABBREVIATIONS

AFL	American Federation of Labor
AFWU	Arizona Farm Workers Union
ALRB	Agricultural Labor Relations Board
ANMA	Asociación Nacional México-Americana
AWOC	Agricultural Workers Organizing Committee
CDC	Community Development Corporation
CIO	Congress of Industrial Organizations
COPS	Communities Organized for Public Service
CSO	Community Service Organization
CUOM	Confederación de Uniones Obreras Mexicanas
EPCF	El Paso Community Foundation
EPISO	El Paso Interfaith Sponsoring Organization
FLOC	Farm Labor Organizing Committee
INS	Immigration and Naturalization Service
ILGWU	International Ladies Garment Workers Union
IRCA	Immigration Reform and Control Act
IWW	Industrial Workers of the World
LDF	Legal Defense Fund
LULAC	League of United Latin American Citizens
MALDEF	Mexican American Legal Defense and Education Fund
MAPA	Mexican American Political Association
MASRC	Mexican American Studies and Research Center
MAYO	Mexican American Youth Organization
MCOP	Maricopa County Organizing Project
MECHA	Movimiento Estudiantil Chicano de Aztlán
MELA	Mothers of East Los Angeles
NAACP	National Association for the Advancement of Colored People

NAFTA	North American Free Trade Agreement
NAWU	National Agricultural Workers Union
NFWA	National Farm Workers Association
NFWU	National Farm Workers Union
PASSO	Political Association of Spanish-Speaking Organizations
PCUN	Pineros y Campesinos Unidos del Noroeste
PLM	Partido Liberal Mexicano
SVEP	Southwest Voter Education Project
TELACU	The East Los Angeles Community Union
UCAPAWA	United Cannery, Agricultural, Packing, and Allied Workers of America
UFW/UFWU	United Farm Workers Union
UFWWS	United Farm Workers of Washington State
UMAS	United Mexican American Students
UTFW/TFW	United Texas Farm Workers
WFM	Western Federation of Miners

PREFACE

The historical literature on Mexican-origin people in the United States has expanded rather impressively in the past thirty years. Many books and a substantial number of articles on a multitude of topics are now available. What a difference there is between what college students can read now and what my generation had in the late 1960s as we struggled to learn basic Chicano/a history.

I remember in 1968 joining with fellow members of UMAS (United Mexican American Students) at California State University at Los Angeles to demand the creation of a Department of Mexican American Studies whose core curriculum would include a course in Chicano/a history. After some prodding, the university responded affirmatively, and the planning process began. It fell upon those of us interested in the history course to recruit an instructor. We were fortunate that Federico Sánchez, then a high school teacher in East Los Angeles (later to become a faculty member at California State University at Long Beach), agreed to take on the challenge, and in the spring of 1969 the course became a reality. Using Carey McWilliams' *North from Mexico* as our text and following a collective, research-sharing approach to discovery of knowledge, we plowed ahead in our quest to become better informed about our heritage. I have forgotten most of the courses I had as an undergraduate at Cal State, but not Federico's class. It turned into an exhilarating journey. Much of the information thrilled me and gave me pride, but what I learned about oppression and racism directed at Mexican-origin people made me angry. Those emotions drove my activism on campus and in the community during the halcyon days of the Chicano Movement. Such feelings also stimulated me to pursue further study and later, in my professional career, to make Chicano/a history one of my teaching fields and a major subject area for my research.

This book, then, is a product of decades of studying, teaching, researching—and living—many facets of the history of Mexicans and Mexican Americans. Along the way I have picked up a multitude of ideas and insights from community people, students, and colleagues. A collective thanks to all who have broadened my understanding of Chicano/a history. I have also benefited enormously from the prolific literature produced by historians and other social scientists, especially since the days of the Chicano Movement. I would like to express my heartfelt appreciation to all those *compañeras* and *compañeros* who have written the many excellent studies that now make it possible to write comprehensive topical and interpretive historical works, such as I have attempted here.

Gratitude is also due to many people in colleges and universities who have assisted me in identifying and accessing sources, including librarians at Arizona State University, California State University at Los Angeles, New Mexico State University, Texas Tech University, University of Alaska at Fairbanks, University of Arizona, University of California at Los Angeles, University of California at San Diego, University of New Mexico, University of Texas at Austin, University of Texas at El Paso, University of Washington, and Yale University. In particular, I thank my good friends Margo Gutiérrez, Mexican American and Latino Studies librarian/bibliographer in the Benson Latin American Collection at the University of Texas at Austin, and Christine Marín, curator/archivist in the Chicano Research Collection at the Arizona State University library, for generous and cheerful assistance beyond the call of duty. I am equally indebted to librarians at the Institute of Texan Cultures in San Antonio and the professional staffs of the public libraries in the following cities: Albuquerque, Anchorage, Atlanta, Denver, El Paso, Fairbanks, Fort Worth, Jacksonville, Los Angeles, Minneapolis, Modesto, Phoenix, San Antonio, San Diego, and Tucson. Among the libraries in these cities, the El Paso Public Library is unique in that it maintains a comprehensive and extremely helpful collection of published and unpublished works on La Raza, with an emphasis on Mexican Americans. Consequently I spent considerable time doing research in El Paso. Wayne Daniel and Mary Sarber, both now retired, kindly provided assistance while I worked in the La Raza collection.

Additionally, I would like to express my deeply felt appreciation to a number of people and institutions who supported the study financially and in other ways. The Ford Foundation and the El Paso Community Foundation (EPCF) facilitated some of the research in El Paso through their joint sponsorship of a borderlands project carried out by PROFMEX (The Consortium of Researchers on Mexico) during the early 1990s. I am especially grateful for the encouragement and support provided by EPCF president Janice Windle, EPCF executive vice-president Virginia Kemendo, PROFMEX president James W. Wilkie, and former PROFMEX director of programs David E. Lorey. At the University of Arizona, I received timely support from the History Department, the College of Social and Behavioral Sciences, and the Mexican American Studies and Research Center (MASRC). Summer grants awarded by Antonio Estrada and Adela de la Torre, former and current MASRC directors respectively, made travel to various locations possible at crucial times.

Finally, my heartfelt thanks to friends, colleagues, and associates who provided technical and editorial assistance. Ben Crowder of Ben's Custom Maps in Tucson took my basic map and diagram drafts and converted them to digital graphics. Among the people who offered advice and suggestions that led to many improvements are two anonymous readers, as well as Gerald D. Nash and Richard W. Etulain, editors of the University of Arizona Press series on the West in the Twentieth Century. Kirsteen E. Anderson patiently and skillfully edited the manuscript in preparation for publication.

INTRODUCTION

An image that remains firmly imprinted in my mind from my teenage years is the dramatic contrast between the most affluent and poorest neighborhoods in El Paso. As I delivered newspapers on my motor scooter to the opulent homes of the elite, I remember many meticulously manicured lawns and lush gardens. What struck me most was a row of rosebushes in one of the mansions that overlooked the city. In the spring all kinds of beautiful roses bloomed from those dazzling plants. The flowers glowed with rich and spectacular colors. I would stop often to feast my eyes and my senses.

What a difference between that scene and what I observed on the edge of town, literally on the rim of the desert, where recently arrived, downtrodden people from Mexico had founded new *colonias* and *barrios* (poor neighborhoods). On a lonely rosebush struggling to survive in the front yard of one of the unassuming homes appeared a few anemic and faded roses amidst small, dull, dry leaves tinged with brown and yellow. It seemed to me that abundant, menacing, sharp thorns overwhelmed the plant and prevented more flowers from blossoming. It was a wonder that anything grew there at all, given the aridity, the rocky soil, and the absence of nutrients for the plant.

The rosebush in the yard of that humble home is a metaphor for much of the historical experience of Mexican-origin people in the United States. For most Mexicans and Mexican Americans, roses, symbolizing the material benefits available to the American mainstream, have been in short supply; but thorns, representing prickly obstacles blocking both the growth and accessibility of those benefits, have been in abundance. Like the destitute homeowner who lacked the natural resources and other ingredients to make his rosebush produce plentiful, exquisite flowers, so too legions of underprivileged Mexican-origin people have faced many disadvantages inside their communities that have inhibited internal development comparable to that seen in privileged neighborhoods populated primarily by European Americans. Moreover, beyond their communities, people of Mexican extraction have encountered many other barriers and impediments in their quest to become successful in the larger world of American society.

In short, life in the United States for the masses of Mexicans and Mexican Americans has been anything but easy; by necessity these people have scraped, grappled, and jousted to make a place for themselves in the world of the mainstream population. Thus struggle, an overwhelming theme in the history of the group, is a major part of the story told in this book.

Another is change. Conditions have not remained static, and the passage of time has assuaged some of the hardships. Transformations have occurred whose impact has been deeply felt by the group. Mexican immigrants who arrived in the late twentieth century, for example, faced far better circumstances than those encountered by immigrants in the early 1900s. The economy of the United States in the post-1950 era differed greatly from the economy of the pre-1950 period. Opportunity for upward mobility, once rare, has become more accessible in recent decades, and racism, which once permeated the entire society, has declined substantially since the 1960s. To return to the metaphor, in the latter twentieth century a number of favorable elements decisively boosted the capacity of barrio rosebushes to produce more well-developed and beautiful roses.

In my own family history I have seen both struggle and change at work. My proletarian ancestors on my father's side began migrating from Mexico to the U.S. Southwest in the early twentieth century in search of work, enduring the discrimination common during that period. By the late 1950s my father, who had toiled for years as an undocumented worker, decided to move the family permanently to the United States. Both before and after the legalization of his immigration status, his story personified constant grind, instability, and disruption due to impermanence of employment and isolation from the mainstream population. In the process my mother coped with adversities and privations that are attendant to a life filled with uncertainties. Despite these antecedents, my siblings and I managed to break the cycle of chronic marginality and entered the middle class in the United States. We were fortunate to reach young adulthood precisely at a time of increased opportunity. Three of us earned university degrees (including two Ph.D.s) and became professionals. My own children, the next generation, are likely to do as well and probably better. The oldest one has recently earned an MBA and the next one is now in graduate school; two others are college undergraduates and the youngest is in high school. If they continue on their current path, all should be able to fulfill their aspirations.

The conditions faced by members of my immediate family today differ profoundly from those of my parents, grandparents, and great-grandparents. We, the luckiest generation so far, have been able to climb several rungs on the educational, occupational, and social ladders. Other relatives of mine, however, have had different experiences. They have not been as fortunate on the education and employment fronts and their circumstances remain modest. The history of my extended family, I believe, mirrors what has happened to Mexican-origin people on a grander scale. Some of us, whether because of luck, greater access to good schools and good jobs, support of others, individual effort, and whatever else, have been able to better our circumstances. But many others have not. The reasons for this uneven record are a primary concern in this book.

In some respects the history of Chicanos/as parallels that of other groups in the United States, especially that of people of color such as Native Americans and African Americans. Common denominators for these three Third World communities include being on the receiving end of extreme racism and enduring long-term marginality as a result of economic disadvantages rooted in colonial structures.[1] Still, significant differences remain. Whereas Native Americans as a population are indigenous to the United States, only a small percentage of Mexican-descent people today can make that claim, since the bulk of the group is of immigrant stock. Both Mexican-origin people and Native Americans lost much of their original land in the United States in the nineteenth century as a result of military conquest and fraud, but only Native Americans underwent relocation into reservations that resulted in pronounced isolation from the rest of society. In contrast to African Americans, the Mexican-origin population did not endure the degrading and destructive institution of slavery nor the extraordinarily high levels of post-emancipation violence and legal segregation directed against blacks in the South and other parts of the country. In these respects Mexicans/ Mexican Americans have fared better in U.S. society.

The pattern of similarity, qualified strongly by difference, applies as well to comparisons with European and Asian ethnic groups, whose presence in the United States is rooted in immigration. Mexicans, Europeans, and Asians have all faced discrimination as members of populations perceived as foreign or alien, and all have traveled the bumpy road to assimilation into the mainstream. Shared experiences are found especially within the ranks of the working classes across the ethnic spectrum, since all groups have had to contend with economic and social discrimination inherent in the capitalist system.

In other ways, however, the differences among Europeans, Asians, and Mexicans are profound. European immigrants, especially those from northern and western Europe, certainly stand apart in that over the generations they have endured less pernicious discrimination than immigrants from Third World areas, including Asians and Mexicans. European ancestry and white skin have been big advantages in American society, whereas skin hues and other physical and cultural features distinctly different from those of Europeans have been big disadvantages because of the existence of discrimination.

But it is in the realm of social origins where the divergence between Mexicans and both Europeans and Asians is most striking. The overwhelming importance of this factor has been greatly underappreciated by many scholars and commentators. Those immigrants who have entered the United States with valuable resources such as capital, a support network of affluent relatives, a high social standing, a college education, an urban background, professional job experience, and institutional savvy have had extraordinary advantages over immigrants who have originated in the bottom of the social order in their homelands and have lacked these crucial favorable circumstances.[2] Mexican immigrants fit into the latter category, deriving as they have largely from the proletarian sectors in their homeland. That means that historically far fewer Mexicans than Europeans and Asians have entered the United States with middle-class or elite antecedents.

The tidal wave of European immigration throughout the nineteenth and early twentieth centuries, probably made up mostly of lower-class people, nonetheless included significant numbers of skilled workers with experience in urban industries, as well as many people of higher social status with farming, business, professional, and skilled occupations.[3] By contrast, very few Mexican immigrants during that period had such backgrounds; most were agricultural workers. After 1920, as the U.S. Congress imposed immigration restrictions, middle-class individuals dominated the now drastically diminished but continuous European immigration stream. But impoverished Mexicans, unaffected by the quotas, continued to pour into the United States, except of course during the time of the Great Depression in the 1930s.

With respect to Asian immigrants, those who entered the United States before and during the age of restrictive laws against Asia (1882–1965) actually included significant numbers of farmers and merchants. And it is well known that since the elimination in 1965 of discrimination against Asian immigration, large percentages of such immigrants as the Japanese, Chinese, and Koreans have hailed from the most affluent sectors in their homelands and have brought with them extremely high levels of education and even capital, in many cases substantial amounts, to establish businesses.[4]

The rather small number of affluent and petite bourgeoisie Mexicans who have immigrated to the United States did so primarily in the 1910s and again in the 1980s and 1990s. In reality people of middle-class or higher status in Mexico have always been reluctant to emigrate because, despite certain frustrations with everyday conditions at home, life in Mexico *for them* historically has been much more comfortable and enjoyable than in the United States. Only in very recent years, with the advent of overwhelming problems associated with economic disasters, have changes in that pattern become apparent.

Another point to consider is that, over time, the return rate of privileged immigrants back to Mexico has been high. Among those middle-class families who arrived during the Mexican Revolution of the 1910s, for instance, many returned during peaceful interludes south of the border throughout that decade, during the 1917 draft scare at the time of World War I, during the U.S. economic crisis of 1921, and during the massive deportations and repatriations caused by the Great Depression. Specific information on return patterns for later periods remains scanty, but undoubtedly the rates for Mexicans have been higher than for other groups because of the ever-present anti-Mexican climate in the United States and the ease with which mobile immigrants can return home. In short, the traditionally small Mexican-origin middle-class pool in the United States has been drained to varying degrees on different occasions during the twentieth century. No other immigrant group has had a comparable experience.

Another historic factor for Mexican immigrants is that, as a result of geographic factors, before World War II the preponderant majority of the newcomers wound up in areas of the United States that offered working people rather limited opportunities for upward advancement. By contrast, as a consequence of their arrival on the East Coast, Europeans tended to settle in the regions of the country that provided the greatest opportunities, namely in eastern and midwestern industrial centers. Another reality is that Mexicans/Mexican Americans are the only group in American society to have experienced virtually uninterrupted absorption of large numbers of downtrodden immigrants from a neighboring developing country over the span of many generations.

The significance of all of this is that the degree of economic disadvantage has been much greater for Mexicans/Mexican Americans than for European or Asian immigrants. Since social and occupational backgrounds are decisive factors in shaping the destiny of immigrants, the origins of newcomers must always be kept in mind when interpreting how far they have progressed in their quest to achieve material success and social status in the United States. Mexican-origin people must be understood within the context of the unique historical forces and environmental conditions that have shaped their evolution, not against criteria that do not apply to them or are minimally relevant to their reality. Every group in American society has had its own historical trajectory, and while some generalizations across the ethnic spectrum are valid and appropriate, many others are not.

Yet it has long been customary for Americans both in and out of academia to make casual and simplistic comparisons about the ethnic experience. Frequently a level playing field is assumed to exist for all immigrant groups, without due consideration to varying social origins, unequal degrees of opportunities available in the United States, and different levels of exposure to discrimination. Cultural values are commonly—but emphatically erroneously—identified as the keys to success. Some groups are then credited with enlightened virtues and characterized as "progressive," while others are tagged with damaging stereotypes and labeled as "backward." Such judgments usually stem from one or more of the following: racial and cultural biases, myths, chauvinism, limited knowledge, or muddled understanding of multicultural history. In that vein, the record shows that people of Mexican origin have been interpreted negatively more frequently than positively by Americans. Even after decades of intensive multicultural education and public celebration of diversity, much still remains to be done to correct widespread ethnic misperceptions.

Significant variation is also apparent when the history of Mexicans/Mexican Americans is compared to that of other groups of Latin American origin. Broad unifiers for the Hispanic population as a whole include a common native language (Spanish), Hispanic culture, and for those with proletarian roots, the experience of working for wages and enduring deprivation. But the similarities among the different subgroups largely end there. Puerto Ricans, for example, are not immigrants in a technical sense because their island became a part of the United States through annexation in 1898. But they do have a history of migration and, like Mexicans/Mexican Americans, they are a predominantly working-class minority group. On the other hand, large-scale migration from Puerto Rico to the mainland is a post–World War II phenomenon, whereas Mexican immigration flows began in the nineteenth century. Furthermore, Puerto Ricans have settled predominantly in New York and other eastern areas, while Mexicans have settled primarily in the Southwest. The bulk of the Cuban American population is recently arrived as well, with the numerically significant immigration waves from Communist Cuba occurring in the 1960s and early 1970s. Most Cuban immigrants settled in Florida, with a large percentage making their home in Miami. Other Cubans migrated northward along the eastern seaboard and still others scattered throughout the United States. Significantly, unlike either Mexicans or Puerto Ricans, a sizable contingent of the Cuban newcomers originated in the elite and middle-class sectors in their homelands.

In contrast to other works that provide broad surveys and general interpretations of Chicano/a history,[5] here I have chosen to limit my coverage to processes, trends, and issues that have shaped social, economic, and political change during the twentieth century. Space limitations, as well as my own lack of expertise in cultural studies, prevent me from examining developments in important areas such as religion, philosophy, literature, folklore, art, music, sports, and pop culture. There is no question that Mexican-origin people have made enormous contributions in these fields.

Fortunately a growing literature now makes it possible for students to pursue humanistic knowledge pertaining to the Chicano/a experience on many fronts.[6]

I have utilized a topical approach for the book as a whole, but individual chapters adhere to a traditional chronological structure. Chapter 1 considers various aspects of population dynamics, including growth and settlement patterns. Chapter 2 provides an overview of Mexican immigration to the United States. Chapters 3 and 4 focus on social and cultural interaction with the mainstream population, emphasizing conflict, resistance to discrimination, and forms of adaptation. Chapter 5 discusses the participation of working-class Mexicans and Mexican Americans in the U.S. labor force, with an emphasis on employment patterns and union activity. Chapter 6 assesses the growth of the middle class and probes progress in general living conditions, employment, education, and business. Chapter 7 examines the various forms by which people of Mexican descent have expressed themselves politically, including involvement in community organizations and participation as voters and candidates for office. Chapter 8 summarizes salient historical points and offers reflections on issues of contemporary and future significance.

The focus of the book is on the twentieth century, although select pre-1900 antecedents are discussed where context pertaining to long-term trends is important. The rationale for emphasizing the twentieth century goes beyond the fact that this study is a part of a series of books on the history of the American West since 1900. The twenty million Mexicans and Mexican Americans living in the United States today are predominantly a product of post-1900 growth. One large portion of the contemporary population traces its presence here to migratory flows from Mexico between 1910 and 1930, an even larger immigrant contingent entered between 1940 and 1965, and the largest cohort by far arrived during the years 1965 to 2000.

An explanation is in order regarding self-referent terminology. I use "Mexican" to refer to Mexico-born individuals whose way of life reflects minimal Americanization. "Mexican Americans" or "Chicanos/as" are U.S.-born or Mexico-born persons with substantive levels of acculturation or assimilation into U.S. society. Since Chicano/a became widely used only after the mid-1960s, I have used it sparingly when referring to people who lived in previous periods. The descriptors "Mexican origin," "Mexican descent," "Mexican ancestry," "Mexican heritage," and "Mexican extraction" are interchangeable terms that include both Mexicans and Mexican Americans. I also make use of regional terms such as "Tejanos/as," "Nuevo Mexicanos/as," "Arizonenses," and "Californios/as." Many Nuevo Mexicanos/as have traditionally used "Hispano/a" and "Spanish American" as self-referents, and I have followed that practice here. Appellations such as "Latinos/as," "Latin Americans," and "Hispanics" are more comprehensive terms that include Mexican-origin people and other groups such as Cuban Americans, Puerto Ricans, and Central Americans. "Spanish-speaking" and "Spanish-surname" are two additional generic descriptors. Depending on the context and geographic location under discussion, I have used all these terms to refer to Mexicans/Mexican Americans. As for non-Hispanic whites, I opted for "European Americans" instead of the more common, but also more misleading, "Anglo Americans" (which wrongly implies that all non-Hispanic whites have their roots in Great Britain).

PART I

Natives and Immigrants

For centuries, we have been here, in El Norte de México,
long before it became the American Southwest.
Our ancestors explored and colonized these lands
long before the coming of the children of the pilgrims.

But the imposition of a border also made us immigrants.
And year after year many of us have crossed the line
into the United States, a country that we helped transform,
with cessions of territories and the sweat of our brow,
into the world's cornucopia, the land of economic dreams.

ONE

From Regional to National Minority

❖

Over the past four centuries, people of Mexican heritage have played a central role in shaping the destiny of many areas of the United States. Beginning in the 1520s, Spaniards and *mestizos/as* (people of Spanish-Indian parentage) penetrated the coastal zones, plains, mountains, valleys, and deserts of New Spain's northern territories to determine their potential for wealth and colonization. Permanent settlement of El Norte followed in subsequent centuries as a consequence of the early explorations. The colonizers settled mostly in California, Arizona, New Mexico, and Texas, relying on agriculture, stockraising, and mining for their livelihood. Remoteness, isolation, and frontier dangers undermined the development of industry, commerce, and external trade for many generations, however. Economic stagnation also inhibited the growth of the Mexican population during the decades preceding the U.S.-Mexico War of 1846–1848 and, with parts of California and Texas as exceptions, for many years following the establishment of the modern border in the 1840s and 1850s. As the American economy expanded and the need for labor increased in the latter nineteenth and early twentieth centuries, however, sustained cross-border migration boosted the Mexican-descent population throughout the United States and especially in the states bordering Mexico. Many of the patterns of growth that began then have continued to the present day.

The Nineteenth Century

At the beginning of the nineteenth century, California, Arizona, New Mexico, and Texas had a combined Spanish/Mexican population of more than 25,000 and an Indian population of 46,000. A climate of uncertainty prevailed throughout the region. Many settlers endured acute privation in daily living due to local underdevelopment and distance from the Mexican core. Situated at the edge of New Spain, they had to fend for themselves, producing the goods they needed for survival and acquiring whatever products they could through largely illegal trade with European Americans. Continuous attacks on towns, ranches, and farms by Apaches and Comanches posed a major danger. Large numbers of settlers perished fighting the Indians, while others suffered losses in stolen property. The conflict with Native Americans of course had its roots in the Spanish invasion of Indian lands and in the European effort to Christianize and "civilize" the indigenous peoples. A second danger stemmed from the continuing threat of invasion by aggressive foreign powers such as England, France, Russia, and the United States.

As a whole, the region played a peripheral role in the independence wars that swept Mexico in the 1810s. Nevertheless, the insurrection took a heavy toll in the form of a damaged economy and reduced protection from Indians. Texas suffered more than other areas, enduring some depopulation, trade disruption, food shortages, political instability, and hundreds of deaths directly related to the rebellion. When Mexico achieved independence in 1821, the new government faced a monumental task of nation building, and inevitably provinces distant from the core experienced neglect. Wishing to increase economic activity, *norteños/as* (northerners) expanded their trade with the European Americans who dribbled into Texas, New Mexico, and California during the 1820s and 1830s. In Texas, Mexico endorsed a plan previously approved by Spain to allow the entry of hundreds of European American families for the purpose of populating and developing that province. In the case of California, European American traders and trappers penetrated beyond the Sierra Nevada, establishing links with Mexican settlements on the coast, while ports such as Monterey and San Francisco carried on brisk trade with Yankee clippers.

The European American–led insurrection of Texas against the Mexican government in the 1830s ushered in the U.S.-Mexico War and profoundly changed the destiny of Mexicanos/as north of the Rio Grande. Texas became conflict-ridden once European American immigrants established numerical supremacy over the native Mexican population. By 1834 European Americans and their slaves outnumbered the Tejanos/as 23,700 to 4,000. In retrospect, Mexico regretted allowing so many foreigners to settle in Texas. In the early 1820s, however, permitting foreign colonization of sparsely populated and weakly protected frontier territories had made good sense. Spain and Mexico had both tried to induce more of their own residents in the heartland of Mexico to move to Texas, but the effort yielded unimpressive results. In the early nineteenth century, few people in the south felt a need to migrate northward. Further, interior Mexicans well understood the remoteness and dangers of El Norte. Most had no good reason to go so far and risk so much to make a new start in life. Prospective migrants could move to attractive areas within the heartland itself. Conversely, for the swelling numbers of European American farmers, ranchers, and entrepreneurs impelled by the pressures of U.S. westward migration, Mexico's far northern frontier offered great opportunities to obtain cheap land and conduct lucrative trade and commerce.

The successful Texan rebellion, the subsequent annexation of Texas to the United States in 1845, the invasion of Mexico by U.S. military forces in the U.S.-Mexico War, and the Gadsden Purchase in 1853 led to the detachment of one-half of Mexico's territories, including California, Nevada, Utah, New Mexico, Arizona, Texas, and portions of Wyoming, Colorado, Kansas, and Oklahoma. For those Mexicans residing north of the new boundary who desired to continue living in Mexican territory the only alternative became to move southward. In the post-1848 period, approximately three thousand Tejanos/as and Nuevo Mexicanos/as migrated to points in Tamaulipas and Chihuahua, retaining their allegiance to Mexico. Others unable or unwilling to move remained in their homes, placing their future in the hands of the U.S. government and those European Americans who migrated into the Southwest (see figure 1.1).

The importance of numbers in the rapid conversion of frontier Mexicans into a minority population cannot be overemphasized. In the case of California, within two years after the end of the war the native Californios/as went from constituting the predominant majority to comprising only 11

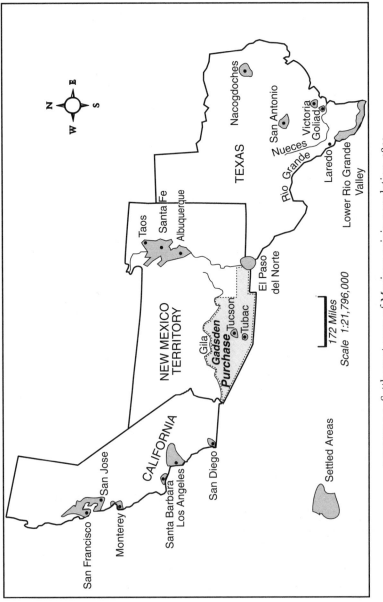

FIGURE 1.1. Settlement areas of Mexican-origin population, 1850.
(Based on Richard L. Nostrand, "The Hispanic-American Borderland:
Delimitation of an American Culture Region," *Annals of the Association of
American Geographers* 60, no. 4 [1970]: 645)

percent of the population. That percentage kept dropping as wave upon wave of European American immigrants headed to the Golden State. By 1900 Mexican-origin people made up only 1 to 2 percent of the state's 1.5 million people.

Throughout the West the expansion of mining operations, first in gold and silver and later in copper, attracted outsiders en masse. Another migration boom ensued during the 1880s when the arrival of the railroads solidified the economic links between the Southwest and the eastern United States and between the U.S. borderlands and northern Mexico. Agriculture and ranching, as well as urban industries and services, also grew in importance. Between 1850 and 1900 the combined population of California, Arizona, New Mexico, Colorado, and Texas increased from 407,000 to 5,358,000. The Mexican-descent population in the United States, which numbered between 86,000 and 116,000 in 1850, expanded to between 381,000 and 562,000 by 1900, with 98 percent residing in the preceding five states. At the turn of the century, Mexicans/Mexican Americans probably made up at least 7 percent, but not more than 10 percent, of the population of the Southwest.

Economic and Population Trends, 1900–1940

The first four decades of the twentieth century brought profound transformation to the southwestern United States, where most people of Mexican descent resided. Various basic industries substantially boosted their production as demand rose for raw materials and crops. Along the border with Mexico, agriculture assumed unprecedented importance in the region's economy, as new irrigation systems transformed deserts into croplands.

The surge began in 1902 with the passage of the federal Reclamation Act, which channeled public resources toward the construction of large water projects in arid zones. As a result, between 1900 and 1920 irrigated acreage in California, Colorado, New Mexico, and Texas rose from 3.3 million to 8.7 million acres. Desert areas such as the Imperial Valley of California, the Salt River Valley of Arizona, and the Rio Grande Valley of New Mexico and west Texas blossomed with new life. With water diverted from the Colorado River, acreage under cultivation in cotton, vegetables, fruits, and other crops in the Imperial Valley increased from 87,000 in 1910 to 385,000 by 1927. Following the building of Roosevelt Dam in 1911, farmers in the Phoenix area began cultivating hundreds of thousands of new acres of land, devoting much of it to cotton. In the Mesilla and El Paso Valleys, the new agricultural acreage made possible by the construction of Elephant Butte Dam in 1916 likewise induced large-scale crop production. California led the way in the expansion of commercial agriculture in the western United States. In Fresno County during the 1920s, the number of grapevines more than doubled and the amount of land devoted to cotton growing rose nearly tenfold. These and other agricultural initiatives propelled the Southwest into national prominence in the production of food products. By 1929, this region produced 40 percent of vegetables, fruits, and truck crops grown in the United States.

Mining constitutes another sector of the southwestern economy that experienced significant growth in the early twentieth century, with copper leading the way in areas of heavy Mexican/Mexican American settlement. In Arizona, copper production rose from 23 million pounds in 1883 to 719 million pounds in 1917. Mines and smelters at Bisbee, Morenci, and Douglas busily processed copper for use in the expanding electrical industry throughout the United States. Cities such as El Paso became binational mining centers, processing and shipping ores and selling supplies and services to mining companies and their workers. Infrastructure development accompanied the expansion of agriculture and mining, with railroad construction constituting the most important factor in linking the Southwest to the outside world.

In 1900 almost all U.S.-residing Mexicans and Mexican Americans lived in the Southwest. Established settlements in this region continued to grow from internal causes as well as immigration, while new communities sprang up in places that offered expanded economic opportunities. The influx of Mexican-descent people intensified during the 1910s and 1920s, when revolution and economic stress consumed Mexico. As time passed more and more immigrants headed to urban areas, where they swelled the population of countless places. Census data reveal that by 1930 more than half of the Mexican-origin population resided in cities.

In Texas, urban centers such as San Antonio and El Paso continued to attract immigrants who enlarged the number and percentage of the Spanish-surname population. By 1930 Mexicans/Mexican Americans made up more than one-third and one-half of the population in these two cities respectively. In California, the Mexican-descent population in Los Angeles exploded from 5,600 in 1910 to 97,000 in 1930. San Diego, Santa Barbara, San Jose, and San Francisco also became more Hispanicized during the period, although the numbers of Mexicans/Mexican Americans in these places remained far smaller than in Los Angeles.

In many communities, new barrios emerged out of labor camps initially established by industries that recruited workers of Mexican background, including agricultural companies, railroads, mines, smelters, factories, construction concerns, and shipyards. Settlements in Lubbock, Texas, serve as good examples of how agricultural and railroad camps eventually evolved into permanent barrios. The growth of cotton production and railroad construction and maintenance in the Panhandle of Texas in the 1890s necessitated labor, and migrants from both Mexico and New Mexico headed for Lubbock County. By 1909 the local railroad camps began to form the foundation of what would be dubbed Mexican Town. As railroad work became more dependable, families moved from the camps to more permanent structures. Simultaneously many cotton pickers who managed to make ends meet on a year-round basis in the Lubbock area joined compatriots who lived in Mexican Town. For years landless people from Roswell, New Mexico, moved back and forth between that community and the Texas Panhandle, and eventually many of them moved permanently to Lubbock.

The economic activities that spurred growth of the Mexican-origin population in the Southwest had the same effect in other sections of the country. Expansion of crops such as sugar beets, wheat, onions, potatoes, and fruits attracted fieldworkers to the Great Plains, the Midwest, and other areas. Laborers also found opportunities in railroad construction and maintenance, coal mines, oil fields, quarries, packinghouses, and factories. By the 1920s a large percentage of Spanish-speaking people had made the transition from constant migration beyond the border states in search of jobs to permanent settlement in those distant places.

Migration at the turn of the century spurred the formation of clusters of immigrants in eastern states such as Pennsylvania and New York. Additionally, increasing numbers of Mexicans settled in western states such as Nevada, Utah, Wyoming, Oregon, and Washington. Time and again migrant workers founded temporary settlements far from the borderlands that evolved into permanent colonias. Sixty families involved in the sugar-beet industry established a colony in Garland, Utah, in 1918; in subsequent years their numbers grew with the arrival of additional workers during the harvest season. In the Midwest, thousands of immigrants drifted from the sugar-beet fields in Minnesota's Red River and Minnesota River valleys into the city of St. Paul, where many found railroad work. Chicago also became a prime destination for immigrants, who "generally followed a northeast-ward drift from Mexico to Texas, then to farmwork in the Midwest, or to the packinghouses of Kansas City or to railroad track labor in various cities, and finally to the industrial areas of Chicago."[1]

New arrivals in crowded cities nearly always encountered the daunting challenge of finding a place to live. At various times in Gary, East Chicago, and Detroit during the 1910s, Mexicans lived in tents supplied by employers, in company barracks adjacent to noisy factories, and in other makeshift housing. Later many of the workers moved into boardinghouses, hotels, apartments, and flats, usually in the vicinity of their places of employment. Those with families and able to afford better housing settled in ethnically mixed, working-class neighborhoods.

One significant point about the story of Mexican migration beyond the Southwest is that it illustrates the readiness and determination of immi-grants to travel long distances and endure hardships in their tenacious search for a better life. The founding of permanent Mexican settlements on a large scale far from the border began when employers stepped up their efforts to import immigrant workers during the years of revolutionary up-heaval in Mexico. Steady expansion of agriculture spawned a system of labor recruitment within Mexico and along the Texas border, and gradu-ally a seasonal migration stream into many midwestern agricultural areas became institutionalized. Before long numerous channels led to countless centers that offered attractive job opportunities.

Mexican-descent people in old industrial cities tended to settle near their jobs in neighborhoods established by Eastern European immigrants at the turn of the century. As the number of Latinos/as grew, businesses and other institutions that served their needs sprang up, reinforcing the feeling of community. By 1920, almost three-quarters of the Mexican-origin popula-tion in the Midwest lived in urban areas. In some states even higher percentages prevailed, as was the case in Indiana, where more than 90 percent settled in Gary and East Chicago. A decade later, almost 70 percent of the Mexican/Mexican American population in Illinois lived in Chicago, and more than 60 percent in Wisconsin lived in Milwaukee.[2]

In Kansas, Hispanics of Mexican background tended to move constantly in search of employment. Many managed to find semipermanent jobs and stayed put for extended periods in camps on the edges of towns. Eventually people from these camps and other itinerant families found their way to Kansas City, Wichita, and Topeka, where employment could be found in railroad repair shops, meatpacking plants, and icehouses. A resident of Wellington, Kansas, recalled how various barrios got their names:

> Each Mexican community had its own affectionate name based on either the physical geography, the nature of the housing, or the nearby industry. For example, all of the railroad camps were known as La Yarda de Santa Fe or La Yarda de Burlington. The cement settlements were named after either the color of the housing or the building materials such as La Lata, La Plata, and the "yellow shacks."[3]

By 1930 the proportion of Mexican-origin people who resided outside the Southwest had risen to approximately 10 percent (see figure 1.2). Paul S. Taylor, an economist who conducted studies in various states, aptly described the widespread dispersal:

> The Mexicans are here — from California to Pennsylvania, from Texas to Minnesota. They are scattered on isolated sections along our Western railroads in clusters of from two to five families; they are established in colonies in the agricultural West and Southwest which form, in places, from one to two thirds of the local population. They have penetrated the heart of industrial America; in the steel region on the southern shore of Lake Michigan they are numbered in thousands; in Eastern industrial centers by hundreds. And they have made Los Angeles the second largest Mexican city in the world.[4]

It is not possible to know in precise terms the size of the Mexican-origin population during the first half of the twentieth century either on a regional or national basis because the U.S. Census Bureau collected and published very limited data pertaining to the group. But extant statistics on categories such as people born in Mexico, people of "Mexican stock" (meaning immi-

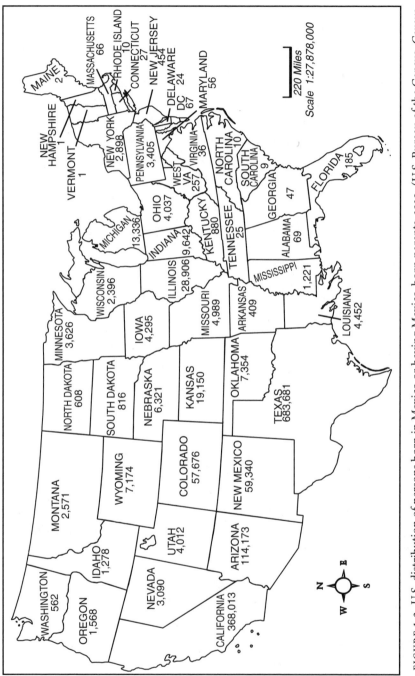

FIGURE 1.2. U.S. distribution of persons born in Mexico or having Mexico-born parents, 1930. (U.S. Bureau of the Census, *Census of Population, 1930*)

grants and U.S.-born persons of immigrant parents), and people classified by the Census Bureau as members of the "Mexican" race, that is, "persons born in Mexico, or having parents born in Mexico, who are not definitely white, Negro, Indian, Chinese, or Japanese," do permit reconstruction of a partial profile of the Mexican-descent population. As revealed in table 1.1, the highest figures nationally through 1940 derive from the designation for "Mexican stock." Almost 740,000 were so identified in 1920 and nearly 1.5 million in 1930. Given the fact that both the "Mexican stock" and "Mexican" definitions counted only immigrants and the first generation of U.S.-born Mexicans, census enumerators missed counting many members of the group. In New Mexico, the census reported only 59,340 "Mexican" people in 1930, but a local report based on the school population concluded that 202,709 "Spanish" (i.e., Mexican American) people actually lived in the state.[5]

The devastating effect of the Great Depression on the Spanish-speaking population can be gleaned by comparing data from 1930 and 1940 in table 1.1. The Census Bureau reported significant drops in the number of persons born in Mexico, from 640,741 to 377,433 ("Mexican stock"). A decline is also evident in the "Mexican" category and in the regional and national distributions. These figures confirm the departure from the United States of large numbers of both immigrants and U.S.-born persons of Mexican descent during the early 1930s, when economic and nativist pressures resulted in massive deportations and repatriations to Mexico. The exodus depleted many communities from coast to coast. Relying on sources other than the grossly incomplete census data, historians familiar with the period have estimated that between 500,000 and 1,000,000 people of Mexican origin left the country during the Depression. In the latter 1930s, however, as economic conditions improved and the demand for labor rose north of the Rio Grande, many of the deportees and repatriates returned to the United States.[6]

Economic and Population Trends since 1940

The U.S. recovery from the Great Depression triggered renewed immigration from Mexico and subsequent expansion of the Mexican-origin population. World War II, the Korean conflict, and the Vietnam War played enor-

TABLE 1.1 Select Data on Mexican-Origin Population, 1910–1940

	1910		1920		1930		1940	
	No.	%	No.	%	No.	%	No.	%
Total Mexican origin[a]	—	—	—	—	—	—	—	—
Total "Mexican stock" (MS)[b]	384,115	100.0	738,463	100.0	1,488,501	100.0	1,075,653	100.0
Born in Mexico	221,915	57.8	486,418	65.9	640,741	43.0	377,433	35.1
Born in United States	162,200	42.2	252,045	34.1	847,760	57.0	698,220	64.9
Total "Mexicans" (M)[c]	367,510	100.0	700,541	100.0	1,422,533	100.0	—	—
Born in Mexico	211,233	57.5	457,360	65.3	616,998	43.4	—	—
Born in United States	156,277	42.5	243,181	34.7	805,535	56.6	—	—
Total in Southwest	361,959 (MS)	94.2	673,938 (MS)	91.3	1,282,883[d] (M)	90.2	968,595 (MS)	90.0
Total outside Southwest	22,156 (MS)	5.8	64,525 (MS)	8.7	139,650[d] (M)	9.8	107,058 (MS)	10.0

Sources: U.S. Bureau of the Census, Censuses of Population, 1910–1940.

[a] Inclusive figures do not exist for these decades because the Census Bureau did not enumerate Mexican-origin people beyond those of foreign birth or foreign parentage. Thus, U.S.-born Mexican Americans of U.S.-born parents are missing from the data.

[b] "Mexican stock" was defined as individuals born in Mexico and U.S.-born individuals with one or two immigrant parents. These data include persons classified as "white."

[c] In 1930 the Census Bureau added the new racial category "Mexicans" to identify "persons born in Mexico, or having parents born in Mexico, who are not definitely white, Negro, Indian, Chinese, or Japanese." The 1930 published reports include retrospective numerical estimates of "Mexicans" in 1910 and 1920 based on the application of the 1930 definition to the non-racialized data collected in the previous two decades.

[d] 1930 "Mexican stock" enumerations for the states are not comprehensive; therefore, data on "Mexicans" are used for this year to calculate the Southwest/outside Southwest distribution.

mous roles in sustaining a prolonged cross-border flow as demand for labor kept rising in the Southwest and throughout the nation.

The emergence of the western United States as a prime military-industrial region fueled much of the economic growth that made possible the rise in population. Reacting to threats from Japan during the early 1940s, the federal government built many new military installations and expanded existing ones along the West Coast and in adjoining interior areas. New defense industries proliferated. The trend continued during the years of the Cold War (mid-1940s to late 1980s), with the result that cities adjacent to or near the border with Mexico achieved national and international prominence. Los Angeles, San Diego, Phoenix, Tucson, Albuquerque, El Paso, and San Antonio are examples of cities transformed into major metropolitan areas partly as a result of the federal spending sprees in the defense sector and in the construction of superhighways and other infrastructure. By the 1960s these urban centers had highly diversified economies, including manufacturing and service sectors that employed large numbers of low-wage workers.

Economic globalization also explains the transformation of the U.S. border region in the latter twentieth century, as corporations in such fields as electronics and textiles sought pro-business, low-wage, and warm-weather locales to reduce costs and remain competitive. These trends allowed the West and Southwest to reverse their long-standing nonindustrial, subservient status, becoming instead dynamic areas of growth and newfound prosperity.

The rising global demand for raw materials and foodstuffs after 1940 led to a significant expansion of mining and agriculture, two sectors that employ large numbers of Mexican Americans and Mexican immigrants. Mining areas in Arizona such as Bisbee, Clifton-Morenci, and Globe-Miami, as well as Silver City, New Mexico, led the way in expanding their resident labor forces, while ore processing centers such as Douglas, Arizona, and El Paso, Texas, provided opportunities in their smelters. But agriculture reigned supreme in the creation of jobs for the waves of low-skill Mexican and Mexican American migrants who fanned throughout the nation, with corporate-farming centers in California's Imperial and San Joaquin Valleys being the largest-scale employers of fieldworkers. Expanded capacity to

TABLE 1.2 Select Data on Mexican-Origin Population, 1950–2000

	1950a		1960a		1970b		1980		1990		2000c	
	No.	%	No.	%	No.	%	No.	%	No.	%	No.	%
Total Mexican origin	—	—	—	—	4,532,435	100.0	8,740,439	100.0	13,495,938	100.0	20,000,000	100.0
Born in Mexico	450,562	—	575,902	—	759,711	16.8	2,199,000	25.2	4,447,000	33.0	7,600,000	38.0
Born in U.S.	—	—	—	—	3,772,724	83.2	6,541,439	74.8	9,048,938	67.0	12,400,000	62.0
Spanish surname (Southwest)	2,281,710	—	3,464,999	—	—	—	—	—	—	—	—	—
Southwest	2,281,710	—	3,464,999	—	3,938,775	86.9	7,227,339	82.7	11,237,325	83.3	—	—
Outside Southwest	—	—	—	—	593,660	13.1	1,513,100	17.3	2,258,613	16.7	—	—

Sources: U.S. Bureau of the Census, Current Population Reports (1950–1990), and Census of Population: Persons of Hispanic Origin in the United States (March 1997).

a In 1950 and 1960, census data tracked individuals born in Mexico on a national basis and, for the Southwest region only, individuals of Spanish surname, regardless of country of origin. The "Spanish surname" category provides a reasonable estimate of the Mexican-descent population in the Southwest because in these decades the Hispanic population in that area was almost exclusively Mexican. Unfortunately, no Spanish-surname national data are extant.

b The category "Mexican origin" was introduced in the census beginning in 1970, encompassing people born in Mexico and people who trace their descent to Mexico. This allowed more accurate estimates of the total Mexican-origin population.

c Projected figures; the 2000 census was underway as this book went to press.

produce winter crops drove growers in the Lower Rio Grande Valley of Texas to hire more workers. Agricultural expansion also took place in Oregon, Washington, and Idaho, attracting large numbers of migrants to those states for the first time. States throughout the Great Plains and the Midwest also brought new land under cultivation and recruited additional field hands. Continuous migration of workers and their families in response to economic opportunity led to the founding of permanent settlements of Mexican-origin people in many new places and to significant increases in established Mexican-origin communities.

The expansion of the Mexican-origin population during the last five decades of the twentieth century was dramatic (table 1.2). In 1950, 2,281,710 persons of Spanish surname (a new census category applied regionally) resided in the Southwest and, although data are not extant, at least several hundred thousand more lived in other parts of the United States. In 2000, people of Mexican descent number approximately twenty million, reflecting decades of high birthrates and uninterrupted large-scale immigration from Mexico. The major role of the immigrant cohort in shaping the Chicano/a population is evident from the data. In the late twentieth century the Mexico-born expanded their numbers substantially, rising from 17 percent of the overall Mexican-origin population in 1970 to a projected 38 percent in 2000. The most striking example of the swelling of the immigrant cohort is found in California, where the Mexico-born population grew from 400,000 in 1970 to almost 2.9 million in 1990, an extraordinary increase of 700 percent.

Continuing earlier patterns, more than 83 percent of all Chicanos/as resided in the Southwest in the 1990s, with California and Texas having the largest concentrations. Areas within California that experienced particularly rapid growth included San Diego, the Los Angeles metroplex, the Bay Area, and towns and cities in the San Joaquin Valley. The booming economy in the Golden State continued to attract millions of immigrants as well as domestic migrants from both neighboring and distant states. In Texas, the Hispanic population grew dramatically along the border strip from El Paso to Brownsville, in San Antonio, in Houston, and in the Dallas–Fort Worth metroplex. Arizona, New Mexico, and Colorado offered fewer opportunities to newcomers and therefore experienced much less impressive gains, yet important urban centers in those states, such as Phoenix, Tucson, Santa Fe, Albuquerque, Las Cruces, Denver, and Pueblo, recorded significant expansion.

Los Angeles solidified its position as the U.S. capital of Hispanic America. By 1990, Latinos/as comprised 40 percent of the city's 3.5 million residents and 39 percent of L.A. County's 8.9 million population. In the 1980s alone, the number of Latinos/as in the city grew by 71 percent. People of Mexican origin constituted the bulk of the Latino/a population in Los Angeles, but the statistics also included Central Americans, Puerto Ricans, and Cubans. The extraordinary growth among Latinos/as is even more dramatic when measured in school enrollments. In 1990, Hispanics made up 63 percent of the student population in the Los Angeles Independent School District, compared to only 22 percent in 1970. By contrast, the white, non-Hispanic student population dropped from 50 percent to 14 percent during those two decades.[7]

Population gains experienced by cities often meant losses for rural areas. Such is the case in New Mexico where, beginning in the 1930s, Hispano/a-dominated counties in the northern part of the state lost a significant portion of their population to nearby Albuquerque and more distant urban centers in Colorado, Arizona, and California. At the height of the Depression, large numbers of Nuevo Mexicanos/as joined the migration stream of agricultural workers. Many never returned to their rural villages. As part of an official policy of resettlement for Hispanos/as who lived in overpopulated and economically stagnant areas, the federal government in the 1940s established vocational schools in Santa Fe, Albuquerque, and Las Vegas to provide training for rural workers who wished to enter the war industries in New Mexico and on the West Coast. Economically driven out-migration soon became institutionalized, and depopulation of mountain villages set in. The first waves of settlers in cities assisted family members and friends back home to make the same journey, establishing a system of chain migration that continued for decades. Mora County, for example, lost almost half its population between 1940 and 1960, while Sandoval County lost almost 40 percent during the 1950s.[8]

After 1940 large numbers of Mexican immigrants and native-born Chicanos/as joined existing labor migration streams and opened up new pathways into areas that until then had lacked people of Mexican ancestry. As in the early twentieth century, a large percentage of the migrants originated in the Texas-Mexico border region, from whence they scattered throughout the nation. The corridors leading to California, the Great Plains, and the Midwest continued to carry heavy traffic, while the Pacific Northwest became a new destination for an ever-increasing number of farmworkers. In Oregon and Washington, the influx of *braceros* (Mexican nationals under labor contract) during the 1940s engendered a parallel movement of Mexican American migrants, especially from Texas. By 1990 about 285,000 people of Mexican extraction lived in the northwestern states of Oregon, Washington, and Idaho (figure 1.3).

The post–World War II wave of Mexican-ancestry migrants who headed to the Midwest resembled the first wave that started in the 1910s, in that many of the newcomers originated in the same regions of Mexico and south Texas. Just as their predecessors had done, the newer arrivals held jobs in various places before finding a permanent home. Institutions that bound Mexican-origin communities together, such as businesses, churches, and clubs, had emerged in the cities during the first generation, but in smaller places such institutions did not appear until the 1950s and 1960s. By 1990, more than one million Mexicans and Mexican Americans lived in the following midwestern states: Illinois, Indiana, Iowa, Kansas, Michigan, Minnesota, Missouri, Nebraska, Ohio, and Wisconsin (figure 1.3).

During the last quarter of the twentieth century the eastern corridor of the United States attracted a large volume of Mexican-origin people. Most migrants, reflecting their humble origins, sought unskilled, low-paying jobs, but increasing numbers entered semiskilled and skilled occupations, while entrepreneurs founded businesses to meet the consumer and service needs of this population. By the 1980s, thriving Mexican colonias became part of the urban landscape in New York, New Jersey, Pennsylvania, Maryland, Virginia, North Carolina, Georgia, and Florida. These states had a combined Mexican-descent population of 441,000 in 1990 (figure 1.3).

Even the faraway states of Hawaii and Alaska attracted Mexicans and Mexican Americans in substantial numbers. Traditionally, only small numbers had ventured that far. By 1990, more than fourteen thousand people of Mexican extraction lived in Hawaii, and more than nine thousand resided in Alaska. Eager to avoid overcrowded urban centers in the mainland, La Raza's children migrated southwestward across an ocean and northwest-

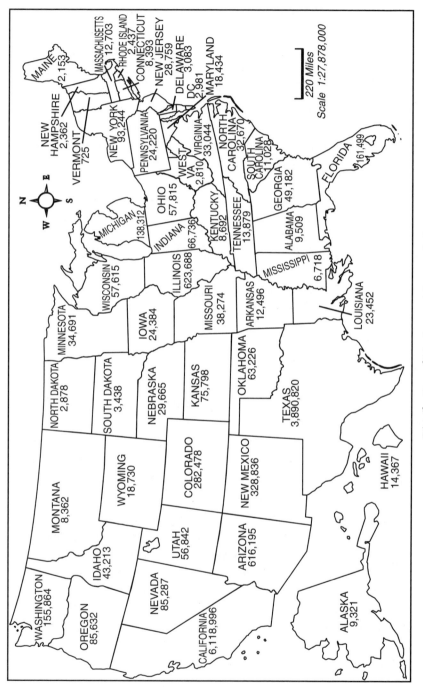

FIGURE 1.3. Distribution of Mexican-origin population, 1990.
(U.S. Bureau of the Census, *Census of Population, 1990*)

ward over half a continent hoping to find favorable conditions for a new start in the "last frontiers" of the United States.

On a visit to Alaska in 1999, I had the opportunity to chat with a number of Mexican immigrants who had settled in Anchorage. One meeting took place in one of the city's twenty-two Mexican restaurants. Rubén Mendoza R. and Rogelio Mendoza R., siblings in their thirties, related how they had migrated from Michoacán to work as waiters and cooks at Carlos' Fine Mexican Food, a thriving establishment in Anchorage owned by another Michoacaneco, Carlos Carrillo. The Mendoza brothers had gone to California first, but found that state "too problematic." The prospect of less job competition, higher wages, and a better family environment eventually lured them to Anchorage. Rubén arrived in the 1980s and Rogelio in the 1990s. Despite the remoteness and frigid winters, the economic and social advantages convinced the two brothers to settle in Alaska permanently. Other family members soon joined them. As is the case with large numbers of immigrants throughout the United States, the Mendoza brothers have kept in constant touch with relatives in Mexico by telephone and customarily travel to their homeland by air once or twice every year.

Conclusion

People of Mexican ancestry are both an old and a new group in U.S. society. Spanish explorations in the sixteenth century and the subsequent colonization of New Mexico, Texas, Arizona, and California established the foundations for the later demographic florescence of this ethnic population. With the creation of the border between Mexico and the United States in the mid-nineteenth century, a new process began. Mexicans who crossed the Rio Grande took on a new label, that of immigrants, and the Mexican-descent population became a mixture of the native-born and the foreign-born. Although the native-born outnumbers the foreign-born, the size of each group has varied over time. Large-scale Mexican immigration during the periods 1910 to 1930 and 1940 to the present has assured the continuous presence of a sizable foreign component in communities throughout the nation, especially in the last quarter of the twentieth century.

The Mexican-origin population remained highly concentrated in the Southwest for decades following its incorporation into the United States.

By the early twentieth century, however, Mexican Americans as well as immigrants began to migrate to the Northwest, the Great Plains, and the Midwest. Economic opportunity provided the impulse for this movement. In all parts of the country, large numbers of people gravitated toward the cities in search of industrial employment and social stability. The trend toward urbanization, first noticeable in the 1930s, continued unabated during the next seven decades. At the end of the twentieth century about twenty million highly urbanized Mexican-descent Americans lived in the United States. Members of the group could be found in every state of the union, although the Southwest remained the preferred place of settlement, with only about 17 percent living outside this region.

TWO

Contours of Mexican Immigration

❁

Between 1820 and 1996, nearly six million Mexicans immigrated legally to the United States, and millions more entered without documentation.[1] The overwhelming majority sprang from the ranks of the proletariat. This massive movement of people is, above all, a powerful manifestation of deep and long-standing cross-border interdependence and integration. Contrary to the popular perception that economically troubled Mexico is responsible for the exodus, the U.S. government and private-sector employers in many ways have participated directly and over an extended period of time in the wholesale uprooting from their homes of ordinary Mexicans, constantly luring them to the "land of opportunity."

The historical record reveals that since the late nineteenth century, Mexico has been pulled deeper and deeper into the orbit of the U.S. economy. The activity generated by foreign capital south of the border has triggered significant internal migratory shifts deep within Mexico itself, with sizable numbers of job seekers steadily heading northward toward American-dominated economic enclaves. Moreover, employers from the U.S. side constantly have utilized both informal and formal recruitment mechanisms within Mexico to draw labor into the United States. The foremost examples of U.S.-employer-initiated labor programs that have pulled large numbers of Mexicans to the United States are the guest-worker programs of World Wars I and II. Both functioned with the direct involvement of the U.S. government.

The level of cross-border movement has varied over time. A relatively small number of immigrants arrived in the United States prior to 1900, a larger flow occurred in the early twentieth century when a major revolution in Mexico triggered extensive uprooting and displacement, and the most voluminous cohort entered in the late twentieth century when recurring economic downturns in Mexico and a booming U.S. economy created powerful push-pull conditions. Historically the bulk of the immigrants have crossed the border in search of employment but, during select periods, a handful have sought political and even religious asylum in the United States.

The Mexican-origin population's contributions to the U.S. economy and U.S. culture parallel those of many other groups in society. In every section of the country, but particularly in the West and Southwest, Mexican workers have played prominent roles in the building of key rural and urban industries. Spanish and Mexican cultural influences — such as place-names architecture, art, music, and folkways — are ubiquitous in countless communities in the Southwest. Yet the positive aspects of Mexican immigration have gone largely unrecognized and unappreciated by mainstream Americans. For a variety of reasons, they have stigmatized Mexican immigrants and repeatedly turned against them during hard times. As the new millennium unfolds, Mexican immigration continues to be an acutely controversial issue, especially in the Southwest, the destination of most Mexicans.

Before 1900: A Steady Flow

Mexican immigration into what is now the United States can be traced back to the sixteenth century, when colonizers from the core of New Spain ventured northward in search of new lands to add to the expanding Spanish Empire. Eventually those migrations would result in the establishment of permanent settlements from California to Florida well before the American War of Independence. Prior to the U.S. invasion of the Southwest in the 1840s, Mexicans steadily moved into established communities in Texas, New Mexico, Arizona, and California, and that migration continued immediately after this area became a part of the United States in 1848. For example, thousands came across the border from Sonora and other parts of Mexico during the California gold rush.

Throughout the latter nineteenth century, Mexicans steadily entered the

Southwest in search of jobs. In Mexico the land policies of the Porfirio Díaz government, which favored monopolists, reduced the amount of land available to the *campesinos* (peasants). This played a major role in the displacement of people during the period. Additionally, demographic pressures and economic problems in the central plateau of Mexico drove thousands to areas in the north dominated by American companies. Once near the border, many workers eventually migrated to the United States, where higher wages prevailed.

Industries in the U.S. Southwest that required growing numbers of Mexican workers included agriculture, ranching, mining, and the railroads. Since immigration controls hardly existed along the border, American employers could readily tap into Mexican labor pools to satisfy their needs, and workers could cross the international line on their own impetus without much difficulty. Those laborers who worked on the railroad often traveled long distances into the interior of the United States, thereby pioneering new migration corridors for the waves of immigrants who would follow in later decades. Although hard data are not available, anecdotal evidence indicates that a substantial portion of the immigrants worked in the United States on a seasonal basis, returning to Mexico once the work ended. Many repeated that cycle year after year.

The overwhelming majority of the immigrants derived from the lowest social sectors of Mexican society, with perhaps the largest cohort of the downtrodden masses originating in the rural areas, where the oppressive hacienda system dominated the economy. Few of these immigrants could read and write. Lacking education and employment skills, they had no choice but to take back-breaking, low-paying, dead-end jobs. They lived their lives on the margins of society.

But the waves of Mexican immigrants also included some people of means who replicated the experience of privileged immigrants in general, using their social origins, family connections, wealth, education, and experience to do quite well in the United States. Three immigrant businessmen who settled in Tucson, Estevan Ochoa, Mariano Samaniego, and Leopoldo Carrillo, exemplify the positive experience of such select elite newcomers. All three enjoyed great success in their business operations and wielded substantial political influence. Ochoa served several terms in the Arizona territorial legislature and became mayor of Tucson in 1875.

More than 28,000 Mexicans registered as legal immigrants from 1821 to 1900, but many others remained uncounted because of the lax controls at the border. Census data on the foreign-born provide a better idea of the actual size of the immigrant community. Between 1850 and 1900 the Mexico-born population in the United States grew from 13,317 to 103,393.

1900–1930: Upsurge and Restrictions

The first three decades of the twentieth century witnessed the beginning of massive Mexican immigration to the United States, with nearly 728,000 legal immigrants and hundreds of thousands of undocumented people making their way across the border. Prolonged dictatorship and neglect of the masses, especially the landless peasantry, precipitated a revolution in Mexico in the 1910s that unleashed widespread destruction and displacement. Conditions were particularly critical in the countryside, where almost 90 percent of the population lived. Contemporary newspapers and official reports vividly depict great suffering created by continual crop shortages between 1914 and 1918, especially in the most embattled areas. This state of affairs proved to be a bonanza for U.S. employers who needed cheap labor. Now large numbers of desperate people could easily be lured to work in a variety of U.S. industries in both rural and urban areas.

Immigrants during the tumultuous 1910s generally may be classified into two categories: those who fled Mexico because of persecution or fear of violence, and those who escaped destitute conditions to seek economic opportunity in the United States; some, of course, entered the country for both these reasons. Political refugees, who constituted a small minority in the overall movement, crossed the border mainly during periods of violence, while impoverished refugees, whose numbers dominated the flow, emigrated throughout the entire decade. Many elite and middle-class Mexicans used the United States solely as a temporary refuge, returning to their homeland within a short time. But some from these sectors decided to stay permanently, making a living by establishing small businesses and, in the case of professionals, by rendering services to compatriots in immigrant neighborhoods.

While political stability began to return to Mexico in the 1920s, economic reconstruction lagged far behind, and large-scale emigration to the United States continued unabated. Balladeers chronicled the popularity of the United States as a destination during this period of prolonged hardship in Mexico. "If you could only see how nice the United States is," says a *corrido* (ballad). "That is why the Mexicans are crazy about it. I grant that Mexico is very pretty, but it's down and out; one works day and night and never ceases to be a *pelado* [penniless person]."[2]

The steady rise in the volume of Mexican immigration caught the attention of U.S. restrictionists, racists, and nativists, who made public pronouncements and applied pressure on the government to stop the flow across the border. For example, Samuel Bryan, a professor at Stanford University, warned in 1912 that the nation would pay a high price if immigration from Mexico continued.

> The evils to the community at large which their [Mexican immigrants'] presence in large number almost invariably brings may more than overbalance their desirable qualities. Their low standards of living and of morals, their illiteracy, their utter lack of proper political interest, the retarding effect of their employment upon the wage scale of the more progressive races, and finally their tendency to colonize in urban centers, with evil results, combine to stamp them as a rather undesirable class of residents.[3]

In the 1920s, opponents of Mexican immigration continued the assault during a highly charged debate over immigration quotas. Organized labor complained that Mexican workers depressed wages, degraded working conditions, and interfered with unionization efforts. Those concerned about social problems argued that Mexicans did not have the capacity to assimilate, and racists centered their attacks on alleged detrimental consequences of biological mixture. Congressman John Box of Texas warned that the "illiterate, unclean, peonized" Mexicans had a very casual attitude toward interracial miscegenation, and could be expected to mix freely with Indians, African Americans, and whites. "Such a situation," Box stated, "will make the blood of all three races flow back and forth between them in a distressing process of mongrelization."[4] A businessperson from Arizona, referring to Mexicans as "a horde of semibarbarous Indians," wrote to the White House expressing alarm over "social and moral ravages" unleashed on the country by their presence. "Do we need to re-convey to Mexican barbarism . . . and thereby submerge and . . . destroy . . . for all time white civilization?" [5]

The inflammatory rhetoric of the anti-Mexican forces, however, could not overcome the lobbying power of southwestern corporations and growers, who needed a steady supply of immigrant workers, and the flow across the border continued. Employers won their first victory during World War I, when they persuaded the U.S. government to suspend restrictionist provisions in the Immigration Law of 1917, including the new head tax, literacy requirements, and time limits on labor contracts. Additionally, the U.S. government assured Mexican nationals that they would not be inducted into the U.S. military. Such a guarantee became necessary after many Mexicans returned to their homeland as a result of the illegal conscription of thousands of their countrymen by U.S. Selective Service boards eager to channel foreigners into military service.

To ensure a steady flow of labor, the Department of Labor established the Temporary Admissions Program of 1917, a guest-worker arrangement that allowed more than 80,000 Mexicans to work in agriculture, on the railroads, and in the mines. Employers requested workers through the Bureau of Immigration or the U.S. Employment Service, agreeing to pay employees the prevailing wages and to deposit a portion of their pay in postal bank accounts for withdrawal when the workers left the country. Employers bore the responsibility for recruiting the workers, transporting and housing them, and providing acceptable working conditions. The government intended to suspend the Temporary Admissions Program at the end of World War I, but proponents lobbied successfully for extensions until 1921, when the economic expansion precipitated by the war ended.

After years of sustained demand for their services, workers suddenly faced layoffs and depressed living conditions. Economic pressures precipitated by the 1921 crisis and an increasingly hostile environment drove large numbers of Mexicans back to their homeland. Tragically, many people were stranded in the United States as employers failed to provide transportation back to Mexico. Reports from across the country that year described deplorable conditions faced by thousands of destitute Mexicans, including 800 in the Phoenix area, 1,700 around Kansas City, and 12,000 in Fort Worth.

Worsening conditions prompted the U.S. government to impose quotas and administrative restrictions on immigration. But once again employers in the Southwest, with the assistance of elements in American society sympathetic to Mexico, prevented diminution of Mexican immigration by convincing Congress to exclude Latin America from the quotas. The Immigration Act of 1921 provided for a yearly quota of 387,803 for the Eastern Hemisphere, with a 3 percent limitation on immigration from any country based on the number of people from each nationality living in the United States as of the federal census of 1910. A second law in 1924, reflecting rising and widespread sentiment against the waves of eastern and southern Europeans who had arrived at the turn of the century, reduced the annual quota to 186,437 and the nationality limitation to 2 percent of the 1890 census. The law also allotted 86 percent of the annual quotas to northwestern Europeans and reaffirmed the extant ban on Asian immigration. In addition to introducing quotas, the restrictive laws of the 1920s toughened qualitative requirements for prospective immigrants and strengthened enforcement at the border. After 1924, responsibility for the apprehension of undocumented immigrants fell on the shoulders of a new agency, the Border Patrol. The administrative restrictions of the 1920s slowed down but did not stop Mexican immigration.

1930–1940: Pressure and Repatriation

The Great Depression that began in 1929 deepened the opposition to immigration and spawned a movement to rid the nation of foreigners. Mexicans became the principal target of the attacks, leading to massive deportations and repatriations. Thus in the 1930s between half a million and one million Mexicans departed the United States.[6] Reflecting the overall composition of the Mexican-origin population, most of those who exited hailed from the working class. But many families of higher social status also left, depleting an already small Mexican/Mexican American middle class and elite sector.

In the initial stages of the Depression, deportations and threats of deportations impelled thousands of Mexicans, especially in Texas, to return to Mexico. By 1931 the deportation campaign had spread nationwide. The publicity surrounding the deportation drives increased hostility toward foreigners among European Americans and intensified fears among Mexicans themselves, precipitating massive "voluntary" departures. Gradually local officials took the initiative to implement orderly repatriation campaigns, and the federal government, wishing to maintain an amiable relationship with Mexico, assumed a low profile in the process. Ad hoc arrangements soon evolved into an institutionalized system whereby officials from various levels of the U.S. bureaucracy worked with the Mexican consuls to provide transportation for Mexicans to the border, where they became the responsibility of the Mexican government.

The trauma unleashed by deportations and repatriations touched Chicano/a communities everywhere. Sweeps and raids by immigration agents and local police heightened nativism and encouraged private citizens to attack Mexicans directly. Extreme hostility flared up in the workplace in states and cities that passed laws prohibiting the hiring of non–U.S. citizens in publicly financed projects. Although such statutes applied to all aliens, in the Southwest they were clearly directed against Mexican immigrants.

Not surprisingly, violation of civil and human rights became commonplace and included harassment, intimidation, illegal arrest and imprisonment, separation of families, and expulsion. Some of the worst incidents occurred in 1931, as the following examples illustrate. In Los Angeles, the police rounded up hundreds of Mexicans in La Plazita Park, subjecting them to humiliating interrogations and detentions. In El Paso, Mexicans repeatedly experienced job discrimination and attacks by the press and public officials. One Mexican woman who had resided in the United States for fifteen years was deported along with her children, two of whom were U.S.-born, because health officials claimed she had syphilis. It did not matter that she had legal papers and that her blood test had proved negative. In Malakoff, Texas, a bomb destroyed a Mexican labor center, while signs warned Mexicans to leave town. In Terre Haute, Indiana, a large mob bullied Mexican railroad workers, forcing them to vacate their jobs in order to make them available to Americans.[7]

Anti-immigrant hysteria in Colorado turned ugly in 1935 and 1936 when Governor Johnson ordered "alien" sugar-beet workers out of the state and imposed a blockade on the southern border with New Mexico to prevent the entry of indigents. Armed National Guardsmen stopped and searched trains, buses, and cars, making sure that only those travelers carrying sufficient money or able to demonstrate a means of support passed through. Spanish Americans from New Mexico, long accustomed to migrating back and forth across the state line, understandably reacted with indignation to the governor's policy. Officials apparently ended the blanket blockade sometime in 1936, but in 1939 they once again prevented Mexican sugar-beet workers from entering Colorado. Other states, including California, also temporarily closed their borders to both immigrants and to displaced farmers and farmworkers from the dustbowl areas of the American Great Plains.

The anti-immigrant pressures created painful dilemmas and predicaments for many families. One woman from Long Beach, California, recalled the agony of deciding whether to stay in the United States or depart for Mexico, as her foreign-born father wished.

> Each night the family would gather in the kitchen, kneel on the bare wooden floor, join hands and pray together. . . . Mom and I went to talk to the local priest to determine if we could be forced to leave, that is to be repatriated. He advised us that since five of the six children were born here and were American citizens by birth, we could not be forced to leave. . . . Mom prayed for a better day so we stayed.[8]

Understandably, deportees and repatriates often developed bitter feelings toward the United States because of the callous treatment they received. In 1932 a young Mexican woman from Indiana summed up common sentiments: "[The United States] is my country but after the way we have been treated I hope never to see it again. . . . As long as my father was working and spending his money in Gary stores, paying taxes, and supporting us, it was all right, but now we have found we can't get justice here."[9] Middle-class entrepreneurs likewise developed great resentments when they were forced to depart the United States, leaving behind businesses built and nurtured with care over a period of years. Professionals and skilled craftsmen abandoned their careers, facing great uncertainty in Mexico.

U.S. officials escorted deportees and repatriates across the boundary and turned them over to Mexican officials, who had the responsibility of meeting their immediate needs, arranging for transportation to their places of destination, and beginning the process of reintegration into Mexican society. The Mexican government waived customs regulations and allowed migrants to import personal belongings and occupational tools. Mexico also provided employment assistance and offered land to those who wished to go into farming. Despite good intentions, however, the Mexican government could not deliver on many of its promises, and the returnees suffered many hardships in Mexico.

Problems began immediately upon crossing the border, as swelling numbers of migrants figured out the next move. Many families ran out of money at the border as they waited for the erratic government-sponsored rail transportation, and they had no choice but to seek assistance from seriously strained local charities. One eyewitness described a poignant scene in Ciudad Juárez:

> On both sides of the street in front of the immigration office were parked the cars of homesick Mexicans . . . most of them battered Fords. . . . Loaded in the cars, upon the running boards, on racks behind, on bumpers in front, and even on the tops, was a motley and ill-arranged display of every conceivable thing which a family might collect as part of a housekeeping equipment. There were beds, bedsprings, mattresses, washtubs, cooking utensils, washboards, trunks, cots, tents, tent poles, bedding; and atop one of the loads was a crate of live chickens.[10]

About 80 percent of the *repatriados* (repatriates) headed to small towns and villages throughout Mexico, 15 percent to the cities, and 5 percent to newly established agricultural colonies.[11] Because of the scarcity of employment opportunities and the resentment expressed by many local people against the newcomers, adjusting to their new surroundings was extremely difficult for most migrants. Mexicans often labeled the repatriados as *agringados* (Americanized) and told them they did not belong in Mexico. In the case of the agricultural colonies, some proved successful, but most languished because of remote locations, poor soil, water shortages, inadequate startup funds, insufficient support mechanisms, and unfavorable markets for the crops.

A 1933 letter sent by the Mexico City–based La Unión de Repatriados Mexicanos to *La Opinión*, a Spanish-language newspaper in Los Angeles, described the hardships plaguing repatriates. La Unión bitterly stated that repatriates "had returned [to Mexico] only to die of hunger and to inspire pity at the doors of charitable organizations, where they receive only one meal a day." [12]

Some of the blame for the misfortunes encountered by the repatriates lay with the inefficiency of the Mexican government, but most of the problems stemmed from shortages of resources during a period of great economic difficulty in Mexico. Throughout the repatriation movement, various Mexican agencies worked diligently on both sides of the border to facilitate the deportees' return to their homeland and reincorporation into Mexican society.

By the mid-1930s the harsh reality of life in an impoverished Mexico began driving desperate repatriates back to the United States, but many, even those born north of the border, encountered difficulties recrossing the border at a time when the U.S. Immigration Service exercised strict control over immigration. The U.S. Catholic Welfare Conference stepped in to help the migrants, with mixed results. Large numbers who could not re-enter legally because they lacked birth certificates and other papers instead waded across the Rio Grande or walked across the desert into the United States.

1940–1965: Resurgence

Immigration restrictions eased substantially when World War II created serious labor shortages in the United States. Americans now welcomed the returning repatriados as well as first-time entrants. The demand for Mexican workers continued beyond 1945 as the Cold War, the Korean conflict, and intervention in Vietnam spawned a steady expansion of the U.S. economy. Consequently, from 1940 to the mid-1960s Mexican immigration in the United States rose substantially; close to 400,000 Mexicans immigrated legally as permanent U.S. residents while an undetermined number crossed the border without documentation.

Mexican men entered the United States in large numbers as part of a guest-worker program that began in 1942, shortly after the United States became involved in World War II. At the time, serious shortages of workers, especially in agriculture, had created a crisis for the national economy. Accordingly, the two countries signed a bilateral agreement known officially as the Mexican Farm Labor Supply Program and informally as the Bracero Program. The U.S government assumed primary responsibility for recruiting and transporting male workers from Mexico to the United States and back home again when their contracts ended. Employers took on the obligation to pay fair wages and provide adequate working and living conditions. The pact excluded women because Mexico feared they would be subjected to unacceptable treatment and abuse at the hands of greedy employers and sundry predators.[13]

The 1942 agreement continued in force until the end of 1947, when the U.S. Congress allowed the legislation to expire because wartime labor shortages no longer existed. About 220,000 braceros participated in the program during that five-year period. For the next four years, an informal and somewhat chaotic system governed the labor flow. Despite the fact that employers who desired braceros had to recruit them with only limited assistance from the two governments, more than 200,000 contracted workers entered the United States during this period. More than twice that number, however, crossed the border without documentation. Significantly, the U.S. Immigration Service intermittently facilitated labor recruitment by allowing employers to contract undocumented workers directly from detention centers in the Southwest. The procedure of turning apprehended "wetbacks" into legal braceros became known as "drying out."

When the Korean conflict broke out in 1950, the U.S. government showed renewed interest in large-scale labor importation. Mexico, wishing its workers to have greater protection abroad, suggested a return to a formal arrangement. In 1951 the two countries enacted the Migratory Labor Agreement. This new Bracero Program functioned until 1964, facilitating the signing of almost 3.5 million bracero contracts.[14]

The Bracero Program in its various incarnations stirred controversy in both countries for more than two decades. Labor unions in the United States charged bitterly that braceros displaced U.S. workers and depressed wages and working conditions. South of the border, many activists complained about the discrimination and exploitation suffered by braceros in the United States, while agricultural interests blasted the government in Mexico City for helping foreign employers take away their laborers. The strongest promoters of the Bracero Program were of course U.S. growers, its primary beneficiaries. They contended that the United States needed braceros because Americans would not perform hard agricultural work for modest wages. Support for the program in Mexico rested primarily with ordinary people in need of employment and with the government, which saw the remittances sent back home by braceros as an important source of foreign exchange earnings for the nation.

The tension arising out of the importation of workers into the United States at times damaged official relations between the two governments. For example, an impasse in negotiations over wages and working standards triggered a diplomatic incident in El Paso–Ciudad Juárez in October 1948. Large numbers of hopeful braceros had gathered on the Mexican side waiting for official approval to cross the boundary. Cotton growers from El Paso and the surrounding area stood ready to transport the workers to the fields. Mexican authorities, however, withheld permits pending resolution of the dispute. U.S. immigration officials, facing pressure from Texan employers and having been given the green light from Washington, then unilaterally allowed the anxious and hungry workers to enter the United States. In an unprecedented move, Border Patrol officers in effect acted as labor recruiters, "arresting" the undocumented workers momentarily and then quickly "paroling" them to anxious U.S. growers who then rushed them to the cotton fields. One week and seven thousand illegal entrants later, the Immigration Service shut the gates again. The incident caused an international furor and prompted the Mexican government to end temporarily its participation in facilitating bracero labor for U.S. employers. Mexico demanded and received an official U.S. apology for subversion of established procedures and breach of existing agreements.

A similar incident occurred along the California border in January 1954, during another breakdown in Bracero Program talks. At that time about 3,500 Mexicans were permitted to cross illegally into the United States to satisfy labor demands. Incredibly, Mexican police officers tried physically to prevent many from crossing, while the U.S. Border Patrol extended a helping hand. U.S. immigration officials also emptied detention centers, took the undocumented detainees to the border, and instructed them to put a toe on the Mexican side to satisfy technical requirements of departure and legal entry, and turned over the newly certified braceros to U.S. growers. Mexico protested, but within a short time negotiations resumed and the Bracero Program got on track again.

While most braceros worked in the Southwest, significant numbers went to the Northwest, the Great Plains, and the Midwest. Between 1943 and

1947, most of the nearly 47,000 braceros in Idaho, Oregon, and Washington performed farmwork, but some were recruited for other tasks, including assisting the National Forest Service to put out forest fires. During the same period, more than 28,000 braceros worked in agriculture, railroad maintenance, and industry in Ohio, Indiana, Illinois, Michigan, Wisconsin, Minnesota, Iowa, Missouri, Nebraska, and Kansas. Chicago became a major recruitment and distribution point for braceros during the crucial war years from 1943 to 1945.[15]

In his classic book *Merchants of Labor*, Ernesto Galarza details many abuses suffered by braceros during their work stints in the United States. Complaints registered by workers included "underemployment, unsatisfactory earnings, [questionable] deductions from wages, poor food, excessive charges, improper records, substandard housing, unnecessary exposure to hazards and occasional physical mistreatment."[16] Employers and compliance officers routinely ignored the complaints or failed to follow up with concrete solutions, prompting individuals and groups of braceros to engage in work stoppages and even to desert their contracts. In 1946, twenty-four farmworkers in Millington, Michigan, left their jobs and walked to Detroit seeking the assistance of the Mexican consul. Their grievance centered on low wages and improper payroll deductions. Two years later a crew in Akron, Michigan, also quit their jobs and traveled to Detroit seeking assistance.[17]

In addition to mistreatment in the workplace, braceros had to contend with discrimination in the communities where they worked. Many establishments posted "No Mexicans, White Trade Only" signs in an effort to keep braceros away. Many Mexicans reported verbal abuses, false arrests, and physical attacks. Historian Erasmo Gamboa cites a case in Medford, Oregon, where "a Mexican national was attacked in public 'without provocation' and severely injured by five young men. After the assault, the battered man was arrested on a charge of being intoxicated. During the arraignment, the judge acknowledged that 'those who made the attack should have been arrested instead.'"[18]

In the case of Texas, deeply rooted anti-Mexican racism and grower disdain for official wage and employment guidelines prompted the Mexican government to exclude that state from participation in the Bracero Program from 1942 to 1947. The ban forced employers to find alternative sources of cheap labor, and they resorted to recruiting undocumented workers without much difficulty. In 1947 Mexico attempted to manage the flow of workers into Texas by allowing the reentry of expelled illegals as contracted braceros but, as Otey M. Scruggs writes, the majority of Texas growers "chose to ignore the new management, and many of those who had their workers 'legalized' failed to comply with the terms of the contract. . . . As long as they could obtain wetbacks, they could ignore braceros, whose use required the farmers' acquiescence in conditions of employment which they detested."[19]

In the late 1940s and early 1950s the number of undocumented migrants entering the United States rose dramatically. Whereas in 1946 the Border Patrol apprehended about 91,000 persons, by 1949 it detained nearly 279,000, and by 1953 apprehensions had jumped to more than 865,000. As pressures mounted to stop the flow of undocumented migration, the U.S. government in 1954 launched a well-publicized, military-style campaign popularly known as Operation Wetback. Aggressive raids and dragnets conducted by mobile immigration forces resulted in the apprehension, expulsion, and voluntary departure of hundreds of thousands of Mexicans. General Joseph M. Swing, the Immigration and Naturalization Service (INS) commissioner, assured the nation that "The so-called wetback problem no longer exists. . . . The border has been secured."[20] The INS "victory" of the 1950s lasted but a short time, however; undocumented immigrants would cross the boundary in even larger numbers in subsequent decades.

With few exceptions, during the bracero era the Mexican government cooperated with the United States to facilitate the flow of contract labor and ease legalization of undocumented workers in the custody of the INS. Officials in Mexico City felt uncomfortable and embarrassed about the disadvantaged situation faced by masses of illegals, much preferring that they cross the border with legal protection. In 1951 in Brownsville, Texas, a zealous and paternalistic Mexican Public Health official communicated such a message to a group of detained undocumented workers about to be airlifted to Mexico by the INS:

> I am charged to tell you that you have committed a great sin in coming to this country without being asked for, without being needed here. The Government of Mexico is disgusted, fed up with this clandestine business of you,

its citizens, going to the United States just because of a fancy. All this for the mirage of the dollar. . . . What have you gained here? Nothing. Nothing but sorrowful illusions. And why has this come to pass? Because you have been deceived by rumors. . . . Now I beg you, in the name of our country, in the name of Mexico, I beg you not to return in this clandestine manner. . . . Do not continue to make yourselves warehouses full of cheap Indians. You should be ashamed of yourselves, abandoning your homes, traitors to your Mexico. Mexico is esteemed and loved in the world, and you are making a bad example of this situation. . . . If you come back legally contracted you will enjoy the rights of all men living under the eye of Jesus Christ. . . . The worker is always welcome here if he is legally documented. The man who comes here otherwise is distrusted. He who comes legally is trusted. They tell him, "Come in, señor." That is what the United States is now doing: deporting you out of here so if you come back they can say to you, "Come in, good Mexicans, to work." [21]

This remarkable statement reveals a profound lack of understanding of the forces that compelled Mexicans to enter the United States without documentation. Many immigrants simply could not meet the bureaucratic requirements for legal entry or lacked the resources to travel to the designated recruitment centers. Official hurdles and delays in obtaining certification routinely discouraged many workers. Finally, American employers, who resented government interference in their affairs, frequently advised workers, including certified braceros, to bypass the legal apparatus in favor of undocumented entry. In short, the Bracero Program actually reinforced a long-standing system that encouraged and facilitated illegal migration into the United States.

1965–2000: Expansive Immigration and Renewed Restrictionism

In the mid-1960s several developments combined to create ripe conditions for accelerated Mexican immigration to the United States. The termination of the Bracero Program in 1964 left hundreds of thousands of former participants and their families stranded throughout northern Mexico, especially along the border. Years of employment in the American economy had fixed their economic orientation away from their homeland and many, if not most, ex-braceros eventually found a way to reenter the United States. The Bracero Program had primed undocumented immigration, especially to areas where growers had long preferred unregistered workers. Thus a vast pool of potential immigrants consisting of former braceros, undocumented persons, and individuals seeking legal permanent residency in the United States congregated in the Mexican border region. A new surge in cross-border migration ensued.

After years of debate, the United States passed a landmark immigration law in 1965 that abolished the racist national-origins system first established in the 1920s and reaffirmed in 1952. Nondiscriminatory hemispheric and country quotas now guided immigration policy. The new quotas allocated 170,000 slots annually for the Eastern Hemisphere and 120,000 for the Western Hemisphere, with a per-country limit of 20,000. Later Congress replaced the hemisphere-based quotas with a worldwide ceiling of 290,000 and increased the per-country quota to 26,000.

Whereas the U.S. government sought to restrict immigration with the new numerical limitations, the law actually stimulated the entry of foreigners in unforeseen ways. Few unskilled and low-skilled workers could obtain the required, stricter labor certification from the U.S. Department of Labor, driving many of them into the undocumented migration stream. Another key provision in the 1965 law pertaining to family reunification made it easier for U.S. citizens and immigrants already residing in the United States to bring in their relatives, because close kin such as children, spouses, and parents were exempted from numerical restrictions. Subsequent exemptions and amendments allowed Mexicans and other nationalities, particularly Asians, to enter the United States in numbers far above the country quotas every year. Between 1981 and 1996, approximately 3.3 million Mexicans entered the United States legally.[22]

Undocumented migration continued to grow as a result of tougher entry requirements for ordinary workers and despite the increased enforcement capacity of the Border Patrol. Taking select years as examples, apprehensions of Mexicans without papers numbered 202,000 in 1969, 989,000 in 1979, 831,000 in 1989, and 1.6 million in 1996. The INS estimated that 2.7 million undocumented Mexicans resided in the United States in 1996.[23]

After the 1960s a higher proportion of both legal and illegal immigrants sought urban jobs rather than agricultural work, and many more became permanent residents, rather than temporary settlers, in the United States. Mexicans also found their way to practically all corners of the country. Ever-increasing numbers of Mexicans headed beyond the Southwest "to cultivate mushrooms in Pennsylvania, build offices in Atlanta, milk cows in Idaho, harvest tobacco in North Carolina, slaughter pigs in Iowa, manicure lawns in New Jersey, wash dishes in Michigan, clean fish in Maryland, and bale hay in South Dakota."[24] The scale of the dispersal is reflected in the opening of new consulates by the Mexican government in unexpected cities such as Honolulu, Anchorage, Buffalo, and Charlotte.

The high levels of undocumented immigration after the 1960s triggered yet another heated national debate in the United States. Restrictionists, including labor unions, population control groups, and environmentalists made familiar arguments about negative economic impacts, overcrowding in the cities, and potential ecological disasters. Immigration supporters, led by national Hispanic organizations with newly acquired political influence, refuted those charges and argued that immigrants actually made significant contributions to American society. The controversy spawned an avalanche of studies by the government, academic researchers, and sundry interest groups to determine the economic and social impact of immigrants. In general, those opposed to immigration marshaled evidence to show that immigrants were predominantly harmful in a variety of ways, and those supportive of immigration produced data that showed they were predominantly beneficial. The most objective researchers concluded that immigrants contributed more to U.S. society than they took from it.[25]

While academics and others debated the impact of immigration, the charges leveled against immigrants in the media and the political arena swayed public opinion in the direction of new restrictionism. An old remedy, that of penalizing employers who hired undocumented workers, gained momentum in Congress and, in 1972 and 1973, the House passed legislation calling for fines and jail sentences for employers. Business groups and Hispanic organizations pressured the Senate to reject both bills, however. In 1977, President Jimmy Carter proposed an immigration plan that included employer sanctions and amnesty for undocumented immigrants already residing in the United States. Carter's plan generated intense debate but no concrete legislation.

The controversy raged into the 1980s, prompting Congress to create a national commission that made sweeping recommendations for new legislation. After several failed attempts, a historic bill became law in 1986, the Immigration Reform and Control Act (IRCA). Apart from allocating more resources to the INS and reimbursing states for immigration-related expenses, IRCA established a system of penalties for employers who knowingly hired undocumented workers; granted amnesty to undocumented persons who could prove they had lived continuously in the United States since before January 1, 1982; allowed growers to continue hiring foreigners contingent upon nonavailability of domestic labor; and granted foreign farmworkers temporary resident status and eventual permanent amnesty if they could prove that they had lived in the United States for at least three years and had worked in agriculture at least ninety days in each of those years.

The amnesty provisions of IRCA had a significant impact on the Chicano/a community, as Mexicans accounted for more than 70 percent of the approximately 2.7 million people who legalized their status. Adding a new, sizable cohort to the permanent Mexican-origin population in the United States, amnesty immigrants left their shadowy existence and participated more visibly in community life; they also emerged from an economic underworld and openly joined the Chicano/a labor force. By the mid-1990s, many of them had become U.S. citizens and began voting in local and national elections, thus strengthening Hispanic political power.

In the short term, the deterrent mechanisms introduced by IRCA diminished the flow of undocumented immigrants into the United States, but by the early 1990s the levels of apprehensions by the Border Patrol resembled those of the pre-IRCA period. The 1986 law clearly failed in its highly publicized objective of stopping surreptitious immigration. A major loophole allowed continued hiring of illegal workers because employers had the obligation to check documents but not to verify their authenticity. Soon after the passage of IRCA counterfeit immigration documents became widely available, and workers easily acquired whatever identification cards employers asked of them. In Los Angeles, acute competition among counterfeiters drove down the price of green cards and Social Security cards by half in the five years following IRCA's enactment. One raid in 1991 in a predominantly Chicano/a neighborhood yielded 250,000 fake documents with an estimated value of nearly $8,000,000; they included green cards, Social

Security cards, U.S. and Mexican birth certificates, and California automobile registration forms.[26]

As predicted by Hispanic groups opposed to employer sanctions, IRCA led to increased hiring discrimination against Mexicans and other Latin Americans "suspected" of being illegal aliens. A study by the U.S. General Accounting Office in 1990 revealed that 10 percent of employers surveyed admitted to some form of bias against "foreign-looking" or "foreign-sounding" workers. Another 14 percent said the law prompted them to hire only those workers born in the United States and to avoid hiring anyone with temporary work eligibility documents.[27]

Frustrated by the failure of IRCA to stem the flow of undocumented immigration, the U.S. government turned to other strategies. The INS strengthened the infamous Tortilla Curtain (a border fence constructed in key urban areas in the 1970s) and reinforced extant walls on the border. New barriers went up, including formidable corrugated steel walls along the San Diego–Tijuana sector and the Arizona-Sonora border. More television cameras and electronic sensors guarded strategic points in the border cities, while powerful stadium lights illuminated the all-important Tijuana–San Diego crossing. The INS also increased the size of the Border Patrol and assigned more helicopters, land vehicles, and other equipment to border duty.

The greater presence and assertiveness of border law enforcement agents became dramatically clear in El Paso–Ciudad Juárez in 1993 with the implementation of Operation Blockade. Immigration officials sought to stop immigrants from crossing the Rio Grande with an overwhelming show of force, positioning personnel and vehicles along the riverbank at close proximity to each other around the clock. When critics spoke out against this military-style campaign, the authorities changed its name to Operation Hold the Line in an effort to soften the image of the new approach to halting unwanted immigration. Statistics confirm that the blockade in El Paso achieved its intent. Few immigrants could penetrate the line. In the first five months of the operation, Border Patrol apprehensions declined by 73 percent in comparison to the same period a year earlier. According to media accounts, most El Pasoans, including Mexican Americans, strongly supported the blockade, but residents of neighboring Ciudad Juárez made their outrage known in street demonstrations, international bridge shutdowns, and boycotts of U.S. stores. Many would-be immigrants simply headed to other less patrolled urban centers or to remote, unpopulated desert areas to cross the border. Nogales, Arizona, for example, experienced an acute rise in the apprehension of undocumented crossers after the enactment of the El Paso blockade.[28]

The debate over immigration reached a crescendo in California in 1994 as voters overwhelmingly approved Proposition 187, which denied welfare, health, and education benefits to undocumented persons and increased penalties for document fraud. Sponsors of the initiative installed a large billboard on Interstate 10 near the Arizona border that sarcastically welcomed motorists to California, "The Illegal Immigration State." The sign warned visitors not to "let this happen to your state." Although most Latinos/as opposed Proposition 187, more than two-thirds of the European American electorate voted for it, as did majorities in the African American and Asian American communities. The issue became highly politicized when Governor Pete Wilson, seeking to boost his chances for reelection, assumed the role of leading political spokesman against immigrants. Many Chicano/a and Latino/a organizations held lively forums and loud demonstrations in the months before the election, but their pleas failed to convince the non-Hispanic electorate majority to reject Proposition 187.

The controversy over immigration raged on in California throughout the late 1990s. On the defensive, Latinos/as fought back with increasing assertiveness and sophistication. Immediately after the passage of Proposition 187, the community filed a lawsuit to stop implementation, and in 1995 a federal judge struck down the portions of the law that denied public services to undocumented immigrants. In 1996, a follow-up California initiative dubbed Save Our State, which sought to deny citizenship to the U.S.-born children of undocumented mothers, failed to qualify for the ballot. California's Latinos/as scored other victories in 1998, when they forced the removal of the offensive anti-immigrant billboard on Interstate 10, and most significantly in 1999, when they pressured Governor Gray Davis to abandon any further court proceedings on behalf of the state's effort to preserve core sections of Proposition 187. The only portions of 187 that remained in effect pertained to penalties for the manufacture and use of fraudulent immigration documents.[29] The burial of Proposition 187 marked one of the most significant political victories ever achieved by Latinos/as in the Golden State.

Meanwhile, in Washington Congress followed the lead of the anti-foreigner electorate in California by passing new legislation to further restrict immigration and to reduce benefits for immigrants. The Illegal Immigration Reform and Immigrant Responsibility Act of 1996 significantly expanded the enforcement capacity of the INS, increased penalties for smugglers and producers of fraudulent documents, mandated automatic deportation of immigrants with criminal records, and granted states the authority to deny services and benefits to undocumented people. Another law, the Personal Responsibility and Work Opportunity Reconciliation Act, created major new restrictions on health, social security, and welfare entitlements formerly extended to legal immigrants. Although Congress subsequently restored some of the lost benefits, these laws spawned profound insecurity among immigrants and aroused the ire of immigration and civil-rights advocates. The fear of losing entitlements drove large numbers of legal immigrants to become U.S. citizens, a welcome development in Latino/a communities long characterized by low naturalization rates.

The recent backlash in the United States against immigrants, especially incessant negative publicity and incendiary statements by political leaders and commentators, has had the effect of intensifying the dangers faced by newcomers. Among the outrageous rhetoric was a comment made by one of Atlanta's most popular radio disk jockeys, who suggested in 1995 that Mexicans seeking to enter the United States without documentation should be shot with machine guns placed in guard towers at the border. "Take a few out coming across the river [and] we'll take care of this illegal immigration problem," he said. "We'll just dump the bodies back across the other side of the border."[30] Unfortunately some members of the law enforcement community, including agents of the Border Patrol, share that aggressive mentality, with tragic consequences. Numerous immigrants have been shot to death at the border in recent years, and many others have been subjected to other forms of physical violence. In one widely publicized incident in 1996, as television cameras rolled from a news helicopter hovering above, sheriff's deputies viciously clubbed two immigrants while others ran for cover following a dramatic chase on a California highway.[31]

One result of the hostility against immigrants is that they have been compelled to go deeper underground in order to avoid detection. That inevitable response has made them more vulnerable to exploitation and abuse by unscrupulous predators and abusive employers. Across the country many immigrants live in squalor and work in substandard conditions in farms, poultry plants, construction sites, and other businesses where the work is arduous and the pay is low. Two recent chilling cases of extreme exploitation occurred on the East Coast. In 1997 New York authorities freed some sixty undocumented Mexicans, most of them deaf-mute, from virtual slavery. Their "bosses" had housed them in two overcrowded, wretched apartments and forced them to beg and sell trinkets in the subways and streets. The following year federal officials in Florida broke up a slavery ring of twenty Mexican women who had been forced into prostitution. The women, some as young as fourteen, had been lured from Veracruz, Mexico, by the promise of domestic and service jobs in the United States. For two years the women had no choice but to work in makeshift brothels catering to farmhands to pay off the $2,000 smuggling fees.[32]

By far the most catastrophic recent development is the sharp rise in the number of deaths among undocumented immigrants seeking to cross the border. Because of tougher enforcement in urban zones at the international line, more and more would-be immigrants have attempted their entry into the United States in unpopulated, remote, and dangerous areas. Between 1993 and 1996 nearly 1,200 border crossers lost their lives as a result of drownings, accidents, exposure, and homicide. "It's as if a plane crashed on the border every year and nobody noticed," commented one of the researchers who compiled the grim statistics contained in a report entitled "Death on the Border."[33]

Conclusion

Mexican immigration to the United States is an increasingly significant story that continues to unfold into the present, reshaping the Chicano/a population and constantly capturing the attention of the dominant society. This human movement began shortly after the creation of the border in 1848 when interdependence between northern Mexico and the U.S. Southwest emerged as a significant trend. With the passage of time, Mexico's economy as a whole has become closely tied to that of its powerful neighbor, triggering a protracted and ever-expanding flow of laborers to areas in Mexico dominated by foreign capital and to sections of the United States in need of cheap labor. The most pronounced cross-border flow of the nineteenth century commenced in the 1880s, when growing opportunities in the Southwest in agriculture, ranching, mining, and the railroads lured thousands of campesinos and wage laborers from Mexico's interior. One of the most significant factors driving emigration from Mexico during the period was the depressed conditions in rural communities caused by demographic pressures and shortages of agricultural land.

The devastation wrought by the Mexican Revolution in the 1910s significantly enlarged the immigration stream. Fortunately for those uprooted from their homes in Mexico, the domestic troubles coincided with a boom in labor demand in the U.S. borderlands arising primarily from the development of large-scale commercial farming. During World War I, the U.S. government passed the first law to restrict Mexican immigration. Yet acute labor needs forced a modification of the law and movement across the border continued, some of it under the auspices of the century's first guest-worker arrangement, the Temporary Admissions Program of 1917. In the 1920s Mexican immigration continued unabated because of the persistence of economic distress south of the border and the success of U.S. employers in persuading Congress to exclude Mexico and other Latin American countries from the restrictive quotas imposed by the Immigration Acts of 1921 and 1924. Nevertheless, the debate over quotas elicited extremely negative portrayals of Mexicans from those who opposed their presence in the United States. At that time anti-Mexican racism reached its apogee.

The Depression years have appropriately been called a "decade of betrayal."[34] When a sagging U.S. economy no longer needed foreign cheap labor, Americans pressured Mexicans into leaving the United States in staggering numbers—from 500,000 to 1,000,000. Many of the deportees and repatriates, including U.S. citizens victimized by unfortunate circumstances, suffered greatly from social rejection and economic deprivation in Mexico. Eventually, as demand for cheap labor rebounded north of the border, most of the repatriados found their way back to the United States.

A new wave of massive immigration began during the World War II period and continued through the 1990s, as interdependence deepened between the United States and Mexico. Major innovations in handling the flow included the Bracero Program of 1942–1964 and the amnesty provision of the Immigration Reform and Control Act of 1986. In the 1990s the debate over control of undocumented immigration and benefits given to immigrants, both illegal and legal, reached new heights. Anti-foreigner sentiment became deeply entrenched in California and in other states, precipitating punitive electoral referenda and new restrictionist legislation at the federal level. Immigrants became pariahs. The nation took a drastic turn toward conservatism, and attempts to impose strict limits became the prevailing trend. Yet despite all of this, Mexican immigrants continued to arrive in the United States in ever-increasing numbers, proving that the powerful forces of supply and demand still reigned supreme in shaping human migration.

Determination and perseverance are apt characterizations of the responses of generations of Mexicans in the United States to the multiple challenges they have confronted. Unlike other immigrant groups whose numbers have included high percentages of well-educated, skilled, and professional people, Mexicans for the most part have originated in the bottom socioeconomic sector in their homeland. Over time the number of middle-class or elite Mexicans who have immigrated permanently to the United States has been strikingly small. Thus, historically, Mexican immigrants as a group have started life in the United States as seriously marginalized people. Theirs is an epic story of struggle which has surely resulted in frustration and even failure for many. But just as surely many have experienced fulfillment and success. That theme is taken up in chapters 7 and 8.

While acknowledging the prevalence of working people in the historical stream of Mexican immigration, one interesting development over the last two decades is the increasing numbers of middle-class and elite Mexicans who have made the United States their new home. In comparison to the prodigious numbers of well-to-do immigrants who arrived from Asia during the same time span, the number of affluent Mexican immigrants remains modest indeed. But from the internal perspective of the Chicano/a community, the infusion of even a minute number of higher status Mexican nationals is of significance. Available evidence suggests that the latest influx of privileged Mexicans has been greater than in prior periods, such as during the years of the Mexican Revolution, and that the newest movement is much more permanent. What accounts for this new trend? The collapses of the Mexican economy during the 1980s and 1990s top the list of motivating factors. Middle-class Mexicans in general have suffered acute job losses and devastating declines in their standard of living, while portions of the elite sector have seen part of their wealth dissipate with chronic devaluations of the national currency. Another factor is instability produced by powerful forces that have rocked the Mexican political system since the early 1980s. The impact of this small but well-educated and economically well-off cohort of immigrants on the greater Chicano/a community is not yet clear. It certainly merits close attention in the years ahead.

PART II

The Scourge of Racism

We welcomed the children of the Pilgrims,
and we got along just fine—at first.
But more and more strangers from the East poured in,
and soon, they, the new majority, became the insiders,
and we, transformed into a minority, became the outsiders.

It was not easy to be both Mexicans and Americans.
Duality spawned ambivalence and many dilemmas.
We had no choice but to fashion our own identity.

Though we looked like Mexicanos and Mexicanas
from the land of the Aztecs and the Zapotecs,
living in the United States made us
different from them, and they from us.

But because we looked alike,
the Americanos saw us as one and the same.
Simple-minded lumping and labeling
erased roots and distinctions.

We sought to explain ourselves to the Americanos.
We tried to learn English, to fit in, to integrate.
But most of them built steely walls around their world,
and used their power to keep us in ours.

THREE

The Legacy of Oppression

❁

In its relations with people of color, the dominant society in the United States until recent decades utilized ponderous and systemic violence, racism, and discrimination as devices for exerting control and domination. The Mexican/Mexican American generations of the nineteenth and early twentieth centuries lived that tragic experience. This lamentable history is painful to acknowledge because this country since its founding has professed equality for all as a fundamental tenet of life in a democratic society. The historical record, however, is clear and eloquent. Scores of people labeled as "undesirables," "aliens," and "foreigners" endured denigration, physical attacks, exclusion, and segregation during the worst of times. To some extent these maladies are still with us today. Fortunately, however, they are no longer so thoroughly woven into the fabric of our society and institutions as they once were.

As unpleasant and uncomfortable as they may be, these aspects of human relations in the history of our nation must be faced squarely by anyone earnestly desirous of achieving a fuller understanding of the historical condition of Mexican-origin people and other minority groups. Accordingly, this and the chapter that follows consider the phenomenon of oppression during those periods in history when institutional racism played a very influential role in shaping majority-minority relations. The effects of such behavioral patterns on contemporary relations are addressed as well. Mexican/Mexican American resistance to subordination is of course central to the story and, while that theme is developed here, it receives much more attention later in the book, specifically in the chapters on labor (chapter 5) and politics (chapter 7).

Violence

Violence is an old theme in the often strained relationship between Mexicans/Mexican Americans and European Americans. It dates back at least to the 1830s, when the Texas rebellion against Mexico relentlessly polarized one group against the other. Warfare made life extremely uncomfortable for Tejanos/as, a group that had been relegated to numerical minority status and subjected to discrimination. As the conflict with Mexico raged, Tejanos/as felt entrapped in a no-win situation. Staying loyal to the motherland meant arousing the ire of the Texan rebels, and embracing the insurrection invited attack from the Mexican military. Neutrality was not practical because strong suspicions prevailed among both sides that nonalliance really meant solidarity with the enemy. Thus, many Tejanos/as who professed neutrality suffered persecution from both sides. This hostile and dangerous climate transformed Tejanos/as into outcasts and foreigners in their native land. Then in the 1840s ethnic strife escalated again when the United States invaded the northern Mexican frontier during the U.S.-Mexico War of 1846–1848. Mexicans in Texas as well as New Mexico and California endured battles, military occupation, death, injury, property loss, and sundry dislocations and discomforts. In short, the Texas rebellion and the war against Mexico had a devastating effect on Mexicans in the Southwest. Even more distressing was the new political, economic, and social order under which they had to live after the creation of the new border.

In effect, frontier Mexicans became a colonized group, having undergone foreign conquest and subordination within the American system. The degree of colonization varied according to place, social class, generation, and place of birth. But few Mexicans and their U.S.-born descendants escaped its bane. Elites lost wealth, power, and influence. At the lower end of society, the poor endured economic marginality, including lower wages than their European American counterparts, substandard working conditions, and few opportunities for upward advancement. Segregation, poverty, poor education, and discrimination relegated most people of Mexican extraction to subaltern status.

Oppression perhaps ran deepest along the border, where recurring international incidents spawned extreme nationalism and nativism among European Americans. Three examples of violent confrontations suffice to illustrate the highly charged environment in which the border Mexican-origin population lived. The first is the Cart War of 1857, during which jealous European American businessmen attacked Tejano teamsters who dominated trade from San Antonio to the Texas coast. Seventy-five people died in these assaults. A second instance of violent conflict occurred in the Texas Lower Rio Grande Valley. In retaliation for abuses perpetrated on Mexican-descent individuals by the European American power structure, Juan Nepomucena Cortina led a series of raids on European American–controlled settlements in 1859–1860. Twenty-three people died in these disturbances. A third clash occurred in 1877 in the El Paso area, where Mexican Americans joined with Mexican nationals in a rebellion against obnoxious European American politicians and unprincipled profiteers intent on taking over local communal salt mines. Several clashes produced numerous deaths and destruction of property. Many Mexican Americans accused of perpetrating the violence took refuge in Mexico. Among historians, this incident is popularly known as the El Paso Salt War.

Although not as intense and prolonged as the disorders in the borderlands, conflict in other areas also took a heavy toll. In northern California during the gold rush, native Californios/as and immigrants from Sonora were driven from the goldfields by angry mobs intent on keeping "foreigners" from sharing in the bonanza. In Southern California in the 1850s, violent confrontations referred to as race wars broke out repeatedly, leading to numerous deaths. Injustices perpetrated by law enforcement officials and the courts against the poor triggered many incidents as well as banditry, a form of resistance used by a number of individuals intent on striking back at European American oppression. Best known among the so-called social bandits of the nineteenth century are Tiburcio Vázquez and Joaquín Murieta. Tragically, the bandits' activity often unleashed indiscriminate retaliatory violence by European American lawmen, and many innocent people perished.

In the twentieth century, the border region once again took center stage in ethnically related lawlessness and violence involving both Mexicans and Mexican Americans. During 1915–1916, hundreds of raids associated with the Plan of San Diego broke out in the Texas Lower Rio Grande Valley. This plan called for an uprising in the Southwest, the creation of an independent state that might later be annexed to Mexico, and the liberation of African Americans and Native Americans from European American domination. Evidence suggests that insurrectionist elements involved in the Mexican Revolution may have played a central role in the authorship of the plan and may have used the raids to their advantage in dealing with the U.S. government. Regardless of the origin of the plan and its multiple intents, there is no question that many border Tejanos/as who had grievances against the European American power structure made their discontent felt through participation in the raids. These disturbances had a catastrophic effect as they engendered brutal repression by Texas Rangers, sheriffs, and vigilantes. Hundreds of people died, mostly poor Mexicans and Chicanos/as caught in the crossfire, while untold numbers of terrified victims had no choice but to flee their homes.

Official violence directed at Mexican-origin people went beyond the ruthless activities of roguish law enforcement personnel in the turbulent border region. Throughout the country, Mexican immigrants were more likely to face flagrant violations of civil rights, trumped-up arrests, prejudiced courtrooms, unmerited convictions, harsh sentences, police brutality, inhumane treatment in prison, and too often, unjustified capital punishment. The authorities could get away with such abuses partly because a belief prevailed in American society that Mexicans had a predisposition for criminal activity. Many European Americans sustained the racist premise that the Indian blood that ran through the veins of Mexicans made them naturally irrational, confrontational, and prone to committing crimes. Some even thought of Mexicans as closer to animals than to humans. The acceptance of such attitudes in turn often encouraged civilians, including employers, to impose their will on Mexicans through the use of force. Historian F. Arturo Rosales has painstakingly researched incidents of civilian violence toward Mexicans in the United States during the first third of the twentieth century, successfully documenting ninety-five such encounters in Texas and sixty-nine additional ones in other parts of the country.[1] Undoubtedly many more incidents occurred, but no one ever bothered to report them.

By the 1930s the nature of ethnic relations began to change as instability associated with revolutionary activity and lawlessness in the borderlands subsided and modernization set in throughout the Southwest. Deep-seated differences continued to exist and racial confrontations surfaced repeatedly, but large-scale violent encounters, the pattern during preceding generations, became less common. Henceforth group physical violence would manifest itself primarily in clashes between community residents and the police, between workers and employers during heated labor strikes, and in sporadic racial riots. During periods of heightened animosity toward minorities and immigrants, however, Mexican-origin people still encountered violent mob actions.

The two best-known street disturbances during the past two generations in which Mexican ethnicity played a central role occurred in Los Angeles. In the summer of 1943, in an incident known as the Zoot-Suit Riots, European American servicemen assaulted young Chicanos, beating them and stripping them of their clothing. Motivated by prejudice, the Los Angeles Police Department labeled the "zoot-suiters" as the perpetrators of the violence and arrested many of them. Three decades later, in 1970, the police unleashed a wave of violence when they broke up a large demonstration against the Vietnam War known as the Chicano Moratorium. In the rampage that followed, officers killed popular journalist Rubén Salazar and injured many demonstrators.

Over time the border zone has remained the most violence-prone area, continuously witnessing attacks and confrontations, often of a deadly nature, between law enforcement agents and border crossers. Illegal trade, including drug trafficking, accounts for a portion of the violence, but for generations thousands of migrant workers have been killed, raped, robbed, and harassed by both lawmen and criminals. On the border and throughout the United States, police brutality and unequal treatment in the judicial system continue as serious problems to the present day.

Attitudes and Images

Violence against Mexican-origin people is rooted to a significant degree in negative attitudes of European Americans toward people of color. The legacy of antagonism can be traced to English antipathy toward Spain during the sixteenth century, evolving from there into acute U.S. disdain toward

Mexico during the nineteenth and twentieth centuries. The historical record makes it clear that European Americans have viewed Mexicans and Chicanos/as in highly disparaging terms, with books, magazines, newspapers, movies, and television being major venues for popularizing unflattering images and degrading stereotypes.

In the nineteenth century, many European American explorers, adventurers, soldiers, traders, merchants, trappers, travelers, novelists, reporters, and freelance writers found much that they disliked about Mexico's northern frontier. These observers characterized the mestizo population as vastly inferior to white Americans and commented extensively on the "backwardness" of Mexican culture. Reflecting the religious intolerance of the age, they also heaped substantial criticism on Catholicism and its "priest-ridden" system. The literature that depicted Mexicans in exaggeratedly pejorative terms is a direct reflection of U.S. ethnocentrism and feelings of superiority promoted by the ideology of Manifest Destiny. That imperialist dogma impelled Americans to pursue territorial conquests aggressively and to seek the spread of "civilization" among "barbarians" and "savages." In his study of attitudes in nineteenth-century Texas, historian Arnoldo de León points out that ethnocentric European Americans viewed Mexicans as inferior, labeling them as docile, ignorant, decadent, mediocre, indolent, immoral, hedonistic, cruel, vindictive, and bloodthirsty.[2]

Manifest Destiny continued to influence many writers into the twentieth century, although some post-1880 authors broke with tradition and instead romanticized and mythologized the Spanish period in the Southwest, especially in California. The revisionists distorted reality by ignoring the causes of inequities in Spanish/Mexican society and characterizing life in the missions and haciendas as idyllic, serene, picturesque, and carefree. Gallant Spanish *caballeros* and beautiful, rich *señoritas* spiced their stories. In the process of romanticizing the elite Californios, such writers downgraded ordinary mestizos/as. Spaniards, no doubt because of their European origins, were elevated to a higher plane, but Mexicans, as descendants of Indians, continued to be depicted as ignorant, backward, and lazy people.

By 1900 the image of Mexicans and Mexican Americans as an inferior population was well established in the United States. Sharing the prejudices that prevailed in the dominant society, many European American scholars simply followed the popular view in writing about Mexico and the Southwest. Some expressed extremely racist opinions. For example, Samuel J. Holmes, a zoologist at the University of California, argued in the 1920s for an immigration policy that excluded Mexicans because "[they] do not measure up to the average level of our own American stock." Asserting that Mexicans were at the intelligence level of the American Indians and consequently far below that of European Americans, he warned that growth of the Mexican population in the United States would mean racial "degeneracy."[3] Holmes was only one of many scholars who subscribed to the racist theory that the purity of the American Anglo-Saxon stock was endangered by non-Nordic "races." Madison Grant of the New York Zoological Society and psychologists William McDougall of Harvard and Carl C. Brigham of Princeton likewise believed that the Nordic "race" was superior to all others and that indiscriminate mixing would bring about "mongrelization."[4]

European American sociologists and anthropologists perpetuated negative characterizations of Mexican-origin people in countless community studies undertaken from the 1920s to the 1960s. Villagers and barrio residents emerged from this research as people hopelessly trapped in backwardness by their alleged stubborn adherence to traditional, unprogressive values and self-destructive behavior. Ascribed traits included lack of ambition, non-success orientation, superstition, complacency, irrationality, and fatalism. In a study published in 1954, sociologist Lyle Saunders wrote that "whereas it is the belief of [European Americans] that man has an obligation to struggle against and if possible to master the problems and difficulties that beset him, the Spanish-speaking person is more likely to accept and resign himself to whatever destiny brings him." Likewise anthropologist William Madsen wrote in 1964: "Fatalistic philosophy produces an attitude of resignation which often convinces the Anglo that the Latin lacks drive and determination. What the Anglo tries to control, the Mexican-American tries to accept. Misfortune is something the Anglo tries to overcome and the Latin views as fate."[5]

Scholars from other disciplines took the model of the unprogressive Mexican for granted and further spread damaging stereotypes. In a widely used textbook first published in 1956, historian Ray Allen Billington belittled Spanish colonization in the Southwest, characterizing it as far inferior to the settlements established by European American pioneers. To Billington, the European American "frontier technique" emerged victorious because "cocksure pioneers . . . emphasized the role of the individual in the subjugation of nature," while Spanish/Mexican frontiersmen allegedly subordinated themselves to the crown and the church.[6] Another textbook author, western historian W. Eugene Hollon, implicitly portrayed Spaniards and Mexicans as lethargic and unimaginative in their search for precious metals in Mexico's northern frontier: "Although the Spaniards and Mexicans wasted three centuries in a search for gold in the Southwest," wrote Hollon in 1961, "the Anglo-Americans found it within a year after the conquest."[7] Another example of simplistic stereotyping is political scientist Edward Banfield's explanation for powerlessness in the Mexican American community. "Perhaps the Latins' most serious handicap is their persistent attachment to Mexican, rather than North American, cultural standards. Among other things, this leads them to be satisfied with things as they are."[8]

Among the venues for propagating negative images of ethnic minorities, none has been more powerful than the movie industry. Except for short interludes, throughout the twentieth century Hollywood systematically and routinely portrayed Mexicans and Mexican Americans in blatantly derogatory stereotypes. This sordid history began in the days of silent films with the introduction of the "greaser" character, a swarthy, dishonest, corrupt, conniving, incompetent, and sleazy individual. The widespread appearance of this distasteful personage is revealed in the following film titles: *The Greaser's Gauntlet* (1908), *Ah Sing and the Greaser* (1910), *Tony and the Greaser* (1911), *The Greaser and the Weakling* (1912), *The Girl and the Greaser* (1913), *Bronco Billy and the Greaser* (1914), *The Greaser's Revenge* (1914), *Bronco Billy's Greaser Deputy* (1915), *The Greaser* (1915), and *Guns and Greasers* (1918).

Although Hollywood studios stopped using the offensive epithet "greaser" in movie titles after 1918, the characterization lived on for decades afterward. Mexican-origin people routinely appeared on the screen as bandits, villains, murderers, thieves, thugs, muggers, kidnappers, gangsters, drunkards, sneaks, cheats, clowns, buffoons, and naïve, shallow lovers. In the development of greaser characters as well as other more benign portrayals of Mexicans and Mexican Americans, Hollywood commonly used racial mixture as a metaphor for depravity and roguery, as the following film titles reveal: *The Octoroon* (1909), *The Half-Breed's Foster's Sister* (1912), *The Half-*

Breed's Sacrifice (1912), *Half-Breed's Treachery* (1912), *The Half Breed* (1916), *The Quarterbreed* (1916), and *Mixed Blood* (1916).

Men have dominated the unsavory greaser and mongrel characters, but plenty of women have appeared on the silver screen in degrading roles as well. Scores of films have included downtrodden and ignorant Latinas as peripheral characters. For example, cantina dancers and prostitutes have abounded in movies about the Mexican Revolution or in American westerns set in the border region. One of the most popular characters is the Hispanic "dark lady," also known as the "spitfire." Historian Juan R. García summarizes the unique appeal of this character to American audiences:

> Raised from a minor role to star billing . . . , the Mexican spitfire often displayed a broad mix of emotions on the screen. She usually possessed a fiery temper, great courage, and deep passion with a heavy dose of unreasonableness. Ultimately, however, her erratic behavior was designed to endear her to audiences, especially when her tantrums led to amusing difficulties with the English language.[9]

Shortly after the introduction of the greaser and other objectionable characters, the Mexican government as well as members of the Mexican American community in the United States expressed indignation at the racism perpetuated by Hollywood. In 1913 Mexico criticized a film about the Mexican Revolution, and during World War I residents of Tucson, Arizona, blasted the Douglas Fairbanks studio for portraying Mexico as a country populated by thieves and cutthroats. In the 1920s the Tucson newspaper *El Mosquito* angrily accused Paramount Pictures of reneging on previous promises to stop degrading Mexicans. The reason for *El Mosquito's* outburst was the release of *A Mexican Port in the Pacific*, which featured prostitutes, drug users, and other contemptible characters. In the Midwest, activists expressed similar outrage with Hollywood, arguing that the despicable images on the screen promoted American antagonism toward Mexico and Mexicans who lived in the United States. Critics of Hollywood cheered in 1922 when Mexico finally banned the screening of U.S. films that degraded Latinos/as. A prominent Mexican moviemaker posed the following questions to U.S. readers of the magazine *Moving Picture World*: "How would Americans like to see films made by [Mexico] where the American was always the scoundrel whose villainies were his downfall? Or to see pictures where one Mexican star would sneeze and twenty-three Americans would fall dead, which is about the average number killed by the American star in such cases."[10]

Hollywood responded to the boycott and its attendant negative publicity by abridging the negative characterization of Mexicans. In the late 1920s, greaser-type characters appeared less frequently on the screen. The new-found sensitivity faded within a few years, however, and Hollywood returned to business as usual.

Lamentably many Latino/a actors have made themselves available to play denigrating roles out of economic necessity and because positive roles for Mexicans and Mexican Americans have been in short supply in Hollywood. During the 1930s and 1940s, for example, actor Leo Carrillo repeatedly played the role of the "greaser gangster," a sinister, bungling character not to be taken seriously. Carrillo's ugliness and treacherousness on the screen differentiated him from European American actors who played gangster roles such as James Cagney and Edward G. Robinson. Cagney and Robinson were commonly portrayed as intelligent, classy, sophisticated, and charming, albeit evil. One of Carrillo's notorious movies is *The Girl of the Rio* (1932), in which he played a rich, cowardly, obnoxious, drunken villain named Señor Tostado. Not surprisingly, *The Girl of the Rio* elicited strong disapproval from the Mexican government, which resented Carrillo's loathsome character as well as the portrayal of other Mexicans in the movie as hustlers, corrupt officials, and stupid-looking bystanders. Hollywood not only ignored the protest, it produced a sequel, *In Caliente*, featuring the usual deviants and buffoons.

During World War II Hollywood made another turnaround and began portraying Latinos/as more positively. A number of films featured Latin American historical heroes and included stars from south of the border. The change apparently stemmed from pressure by the U.S. government, which at the time sought a closer relationship with Latin America through the Good Neighbor Policy. Hollywood films deemed offensive by Latin Americans had constituted an obvious impediment to that goal. Thus in the spirit of "good neighborliness" and antifascism, Warner Brothers produced *Juárez* (1939), an epic film that celebrated beloved Mexican President Benito Juárez's ouster of Austrian Emperor Maximilian and restoration of a democratic republic during the 1860s. In the years following the making of *Juárez*, the Latin image on the screen improved. Simplistic and stereotypical caricatures were toned down. But they did not disappear.

In the 1960s violence became a staple theme for Hollywood, and repackaged "greasers" made their return to the big screen. Latin American bandits and criminals appeared in many spaghetti westerns and movies about drug trafficking. To film historian Allen L. Woll, "a new set of rules governing the portrayals of Latin Americans seem[ed] to be in effect": Extreme and mindless violence, incompetence, and ridicule became standard themes once again.[11] Woll concluded that Hollywood made few improvements in its portrayal of Latinos/as during the Civil Rights era. By contrast, other ethnic groups witnessed significant advances:

> Blacks have graduated from their janitorial jobs and now portray doctors, lawyers, and physicists. The American Indian is no longer the barbarous villain who attacks helpless white settlers. . . . Only the Latin American has missed the cultural reorientation of the films of the past decade [mid-sixties to mid-seventies]. . . . The Latin has remained a rapacious bandit or an object of ridicule. Even more degrading is the fact that a Latin is rarely able to portray his own race in leading film roles.[12]

With the proliferation of cable television since the 1980s, both old and recent movies that contain negative Hispanic images have been made accessible to mass audiences. Film scholar Alfred C. Richard Jr. notes that on one day alone in 1993, cable companies in the northeastern United States showed ten films containing offensive material.

> The images shown included a sadistic Hispanic killer, super Anglo heroes saving a South American revolution, a slimy Latin dictator, a hot blooded and unfaithful *puta* [whore] who kills her husband, a singing Mexican stereotype down under, Spaghetti Western Mexicans at their despicable best, Anglo fun and danger across the border, [and] a sadistic, Nazi loving incestuous Paraguayan mother and son."[13]

The persistence of negative Hispanic stereotypes in films has been balanced to at least a small degree by greater sensitivity and even-handedness in some sectors of the industry. In recent years some Hollywood studios have made a number of films featuring positive aspects of the Latino/a way of life, and a few Hispanic actors and actresses have become well known to mainstream American audiences. Some Mexican Americans have also become producers and directors, assuring greater authenticity in story lines and character presentation. Among some of the best of the recent movies about Mexican Americans are *La Bamba* (1987), *The Milagro Beanfield War* (1988), *Stand and Deliver* (1988), *Mi Familia/My Family* (1995), and *Selena* (1996). Yet even well-known Chicanos/as in Hollywood have succumbed to Tinseltown pressures to make movies about deviancy and pathological behavior in minority communities. Edward James Olmos, for example, came under heavy criticism for directing and starring in *American Me* (1992), an extremely violent film about drugs, prison life, and the Mexican Mafia.

Television has been another influential vehicle in shaping the image of Hispanics in the United States and, as with Hollywood movies, the record is highly unsatisfactory. Researchers S. Robert Lichter and Daniel R. Amundson found that during the 1950s and early 1960s groups such as Hispanics, African Americans, and Asians were largely ignored by the industry. European Americans comprised about 90 percent of all the characters. "Just one character in fifty was Hispanic, fewer than one in a hundred was Asian, and only one in two hundred was black." Not surprisingly, Hispanics played predominantly negative roles. For example, while pioneering Latino/a characters on popular shows such as *The Cisco Kid* and *Zorro* actually played "positive and even heroic characters, they were often outnumbered by evil and frequently criminal Latino adversaries. . . . For most Hispanic characters, life consisted of lounging in the dusty square of a sleepy Latin town, waiting for the stars to come on stage." [14]

In the realm of television advertising, many companies in the 1960s used stereotypical Hispanic characters such as revolutionaries, bandits, buffoons, and loafers to sell everything from potato chips to deodorants. Perhaps the most offensive caricature was the Frito Bandito, who spoke heavily accented English, dressed like a sloppy revolutionary, and stole Frito-Lay chips. Another bandit-like, overweight figure starred in Arid deodorant commercials that presented him as the ultimate odor test. And in a cigarette ad, a sluggish-looking revolutionary would put off going to war until "mañana," only after he had finished smoking an L&M. These nauseating commercials prompted many protests from Mexican American organizations, and eventually television stations across the country took them off the air. Yet offensive commercials resurface from time to time. In 1998, fast-food chain Taco Bell introduced a Chihuahua that keeps asking for tacos in heavily accented English. Competitor Jack in the Box responded with its own commercial satirizing the Taco Bell dog and rebuking him for eating beans. The audience is made to understand that the dog has "smelled up" the place.

In the late 1960s television programming became more socially inclusive as a result of pressures generated by the Civil Rights Movement. Members of minority groups gained greater visibility on prime time shows, and new sit-coms featured minority themes. In contrast to African Americans, however, Hispanics had limited success in finding acceptance for shows based on Latino/a casts. *Chico and the Man* (1970s) and *A.K.A. Pablo* (1980s), both of which focused on humorous situations in the Mexican American commu-nity, constitute two exceptions. Yet these shows had short lives. A significant step forward occurred when Hispanic actors played leading roles in success-ful shows such as *CHiPs* (late 1970s–early 1980s) and *Miami Vice* (1980s). In the case of *Miami Vice*, the strong detective played by Edward James Olmos projected a positive image, but unfortunately a plethora of other Hispanic characters did not. "Trafficking in human misery made these [*Miami Vice* Hispanic] characters rich enough to own cities and sometimes even small countries. They were among the nastiest criminals on TV in the 1980s." [15] In the 1990s television continued to portray Latinos/as in disparaging terms, but not as frequently as in previous years.

Perhaps the most serious problem with television is the continuing rela-tive invisibility of Hispanics in network programming. The National Coun-cil of La Raza has documented a severe and chronic underrepresentation in entertainment programming since the start of the television age. From 1955 to 1992, the "proportion of Hispanics on television . . . actually *de-creased* from about 3 percent to around 1 percent." By contrast, women and African Americans increased their visibility substantially. Another survey in 1999 confirmed the underrepresentation. Latinos/as still made up only 1 percent of major characters on network television. Outraged by the lack of progress, a coalition of Latino/a organizations called for a boycott of all network shows and products of corporate sponsors.[16]

Given the long-standing and widespread stereotypical portrayals and underrepresentation of Latinos/as in literature, movies, television, and the news media, it is hardly surprising that public surveys have consistently placed the group near the bottom of the ethnic hierarchy. One such survey conducted in 1989 ranked Hispanics forty-ninth in perceived social standing among fifty-eight ethnic groups.

Semi-legal and De Facto Discrimination

Influenced by pervasive negative racial attitudes, early on the European American power structure actively promoted physical segregation of Mexican-origin people. Policymakers already inclined to keep the races apart derived legal and moral justification from the 1896 *Plessy v. Ferguson* ruling by the U.S. Supreme Court. The Plessy decision, which legalized segregation of blacks under the "separate but equal" notion of racial coexistence, intensified the segregation of other nonwhite minorities. Thus racist officials conveniently labeled dark-skinned mestizos/as as Indians or blacks, making it easier for developers, real estate agents, and landlords to exclude them from European American neighborhoods. Barrios populated exclusively by Mexican-origin people proliferated in countless urban centers, usually in isolated peripheral zones or in undesirable central areas that adjoined industrial plants or railroad yards.

Housing segregation during the 1920s in Gary, Indiana, as documented by historians Neil Betten and Raymond A. Mohl, typified conditions in many communities:

Although Mexicans might rent apartments or buy substandard homes at exorbitant rates on the south side, it was practically impossible to rent in "better" parts of Gary. "On the north side they will not rent to Mexicans," said a Mexican immigrant. . . . Another Gary Mexican told how he could rent only after passing as a non-Mexican. In another case a fair-complexioned, light-haired Mexican steel worker with an Anglicized name arranged to buy a home in the middle-class Tolleston district. When the real estate agent saw his darker wife and children and realized they were Mexicans, he refused to complete the transaction. However, if the worker had provided the agent with a sizable bribe and agreed "to deny my Mexican nationality," a deal could have been made. The agent felt that, if he could claim the family was Spanish rather than Mexican, he would not violate the unwritten local codes of his profession. Such housing discrimination continued at least into the late 1940s.[17]

During World War II, housing segregation in Los Angeles kept many Mexican Americans from obtaining well-paying jobs in defense industries because they were forced to live too far from the factories. Communities such as South Gate, Pico Rivera, Maywood, and Vernon, where many defense plants were located, had housing covenants that prohibited the selling of homes to dark-skinned minorities. Even in the absence of racially exclusive covenants, Mexican-descent people still found it very difficult to move to desirable neighborhoods because banks routinely denied them home loans. "Thus, when the war came along," writes historian John H. M. Laslett, "very few Mexican Americans were in a position to apply for high-skill, high-wage jobs in the shipbuilding, aircraft, or munitions industries located far from Central and East L.A., even if they had not been excluded on racial grounds [by the employers]."[18]

Public facilities such as hotels, restaurants, theaters, and barber shops routinely banned Mexicans and Mexican Americans or channeled them to locales set aside for nonwhites, typically the least desirable sections in the buildings. Businesses often posted signs on doors or windows stating "No Mexicans Allowed." Hospitals kept dark-skinned mestizos apart from white patients. One of the most pernicious practices was to allow nonwhites the use of recreational centers or permit them to participate in recreational activities only on select days. Many swimming pools reserved the day before the scheduled changing of the water for minorities. In Phoenix, swimming pools and dance halls followed the "Mexican day" custom, while the major local newspaper sponsored separate picnics for white, black, and Mexican-origin children. In Garden City, Kansas, only whites were permitted to use the large swimming pool situated close to the barrio, prompting some of the youth to find surreptitious ways to enter the pool. "As we were not allowed to use the pool at any time," recalled a resident of the town, "there were many nights we would climb the fence to sneak a swim, only to be interrupted by our local police department who gave us chase out of the pool." This cat-and-mouse game inevitably led to some arrests.[19]

Even churches practiced segregation. The Catholic Church and Protestant denominations understandably provided separate facilities or separate services for non-English-speaking members, but ascribed or assumed language and cultural differences were often used as excuses to keep Mexicans and Mexican Americans apart from European Americans. Not surprisingly,

"Mexican churches" sprouted throughout the land. Wherever worshipers of Mexican background attended the same churches as European Americans, custom often required that the former sit in the back pews. St. Mary's Church in Phoenix is a good example of imposed segregation and the hurtful consequences for minority parishioners:

> For thirteen years, 1915 to 1928, Mexican families endured the "basement" experience at St. Mary's. Masses, weddings, baptisms, funerals, and other church functions remained in the basement for them. Mexican American Adam Diaz later recalled attending services at St. Mary's as a child; especially vivid was his first communion. The Mexican children waited in the basement for the bishop from Tucson to finish serving the Anglo children upstairs; they could hear the lovely organ music. The wait seemed eternal to Diaz, but eventually the bishop came down and quickly gave the Mexicans communion. The Mexican children were then taken upstairs to leave. "That's when we saw the beautiful tables of food that the nuns had laid out, but they wouldn't let us stay or take part. It was for the Anglos." Mrs. Diaz took the Mexican children home and gave them refreshments, but the episode upset the parents, who became more determined to overcome the discrimination and segregation they and their families were experiencing.[20]

The story of the "forty blond babies" is perhaps the most poignant incident pertaining to religion and discrimination in the Southwest during the early twentieth century. One day in 1904 Father Mandin, a new priest in Clifton, Arizona, announced to his predominantly Mexican and Mexican American congregation that many children from New York were available for adoption. The parishioners enthusiastically expressed desire to adopt "blond" babies, and the priest wrote back to the foundling home transmitting that sentiment. Shortly thereafter forty small children, accompanied by a European American nun, arrived in Clifton-Morenci. The nun was shocked to learn that most of the adoptive parents were of Mexican extraction, whereupon she unsuccessfully attempted to stop the delivery of the children. After much argument, the nun agreed to go along with the original arrangement and, with some exceptions, the adoptive parents took their new babies home and celebrated the occasion. When the European American community in Clifton learned that Hispanics had "bought" European American babies, a rude mob forcibly took the children from their new parents and placed them in "proper" homes pending a permanent solution. At Morenci, pressure exerted by European American residents prompted Father Mandin to retrieve the children from the Mexican/Mexican American homes as well. Apparently twenty-one of the children were then taken from Arizona, but nineteen remained in the hands of the European American community. The foundling home in New York then attempted to recover the remaining children, but the European American "foster parents" had already initiated legal adoption proceedings. The case went before the Arizona Supreme Court and the U.S. Supreme Court, and both institutions upheld the adoption of the children by the European American parents. For the Spanish-speaking people of Clifton-Morenci, this was a tragic event not only because they lost the children, but because they were viciously maligned and degraded as unfit parents by their European American neighbors, the press, and the courts.

The labeling of Mexican and Mexican American adults as inferior and deficient human beings naturally carried over to their children, who early on became acquainted with discrimination in the schools sustained by an injurious system of segregation that lasted until the mid-twentieth century. "Although there were no laws that mandated the practice of segregation," writes education historian Gilbert G. González, "educators did invoke the state power granted to school administrators to adapt educational programs to the special needs of a linguistically and culturally distinct community." [21] School districts justified the creation of separate "Mexican schools" on the grounds that these would be beneficial to students of Latin American heritage who lacked a satisfactory command of the English language. Often educators pointed out as well that poor Mexican-origin students felt uncomfortable going to school with more affluent European American students. On the surface such arguments seemed reasonable. Yet in many school districts racism and economic greed were the prime motivating factors for segregation.

El Paso is a good example of racist attitudes put into practice in education. Several educators interviewed by economist Paul S. Taylor in the 1920s elaborated on prevailing attitudes toward students of Mexican descent. The El Paso superintendent of schools confided that European Americans wanted "to separate the Mexicans," and some wanted them to remain uneducated. "They [European Americans] want the $15 per capita tax and then don't want the Mexicans to go to school. With seventy-seven Mexican children in one of our districts about $185 a month is paid for teachers' salaries, [while] $1,100 a month goes to the teachers at the American School with about fifty-three pupils." The principal of El Paso's Bell School stated that the majority of the Mexican/Mexican American students "seem to want to study for white-collar jobs when they are not well fitted for them. They [Mexican/Mexican American children] are all right at learning by rote but not at reasoning." [22] The superintendent of schools at the nearby rural community of Clint, Texas, commented: "From the farmer's point of view education may spoil labor. We need somebody to do the labor . . . Mexicans are regarded as a servant class. The compulsory attendance law is not enforced. No one is interested in enforcing it." [23]

A survey conducted in the 1930s revealed the existence of segregation in 85 percent of the school districts in the Southwest. The degree of segregation ranged from extreme in south Texas, where students usually remained apart in all the grades, to mild in some of the small districts in California, where segregation was present only in select elementary grades. Along with isolation from European Americans, segregation for Mexican-descent students typically meant having substandard facilities and inferior instruction. Moreover, constant turnover among teachers who resented being assigned to "Mexican schools" proved seriously disruptive to the educational process in countless communities.

Bigotry became especially pernicious during World War II, when Mexican Americans continued to feel maligned by the dominant society despite the fact that many made the ultimate sacrifice on behalf of their country. It was difficult to reconcile fighting for freedom abroad and encountering the kind of discrimination found in areas like the south plains of Texas. A sign in a Lubbock barber shop read, "No Dogs Allowed, No Mexicans Allowed." [24] A restaurant owner in Levelland broke a bottle on the head of a young Chicano who wanted to buy cigarettes, and local officials in Big Spring and Lamesa refused to allow migrant cotton pickers the use of local toilet facilities. After the war, Pauline R. Kibbe, the executive secretary of the Texas Good Neighbor Commission, published a mind-boggling laundry list of racist practices throughout Texas, including discrimination in business, amusement establishments, housing, employment, and education. Kibbe included "terrorism on the part of law enforcement officers and others" on her list.[25]

Segregation reached such absurd proportions that some communities in Texas maintained separate funeral homes and cemeteries for European Americans and people of Mexican descent. The most widely publicized incident involving this type of segregation is the denial in 1948 of funeral services to Félix Longoria, a soldier killed in the Pacific, by a European American funeral director. Following a storm of controversy Longoria was finally buried in Arlington National Cemetery. In 1951 *Look* magazine reported that in one town bigoted European Americans even "partitioned the local pet cemetery into two parts — one for pets of Anglos and the other for those of Latins."[26]

By midcentury Mexican American organizations became sufficiently strong to begin forcing large-scale change through the courts and in the halls of Congress. It is important, however, to recognize the early struggles that ordinary Mexicans and Mexican Americans waged against the racism directed at them. From the beginning, brave individuals fought back with whatever means and tools they had at their disposal, often enlisting the help of Mexican consulates. Protests against school segregation, for example, occurred in San Angelo, Texas, in 1910; in Santa Paula, California, in 1914; in Argentine, Kansas, in 1924, and in San Bernardino, California, in 1929. Mexican-origin parents also won legal victories against school districts in Tempe, Arizona, in 1925, and in Lemon Grove, California, in 1930. But some of the most far-ranging successes occurred during the period of the GI generation, when World War II and Korean War veterans and other community leaders aggressively challenged the policies of school districts throughout the Southwest. In the 1947 *Mendez v. Westminster* decision, a federal court ordered the desegregation of schools in the Westminster School District and other districts in Southern California. The following year another federal court enjoined four school districts in Texas from segregating students of Mexican extraction. These and other court cases litigated by Mexican American organizations provided key precedents for the historic 1954 Supreme Court ruling that finally ended racially motivated school segregation nationwide.

With the passage of civil rights legislation by the U.S. Congress during the 1960s, racial discrimination declined, but de facto residential and school segregation has continued and in some cases has grown worse. Mexican-origin people have remained highly concentrated in barrios in cities such as Houston, San Antonio, El Paso, Denver, Tucson, Phoenix, and Los Angeles. Commonly inner-city neighborhoods suffer from poverty, substandard housing, inferior schools, and a host of social problems, including high crime rates. A recent study undertaken by researchers at Harvard University reported that segregation among Hispanic students has increased significantly, with the average percentage of European Americans attending predominantly Hispanic schools dropping from 35.5 in 1980 to 30.6 in 1997. White flight from central urban areas to the suburbs explains much of the growing ethnic imbalance in public education.[27]

In assessing segregation, we must not overlook causes that are not racial in nature. A significant part of today's residential segregation is due to structural inequalities in society that affect all people concentrated at the bottom of the social order. Additionally, large numbers of poor immigrants from Mexico have been pouring into inner-city neighborhoods for many decades, reinforcing ethnic concentration. It must also be recognized that over the last few decades many upwardly mobile individuals have moved out of impoverished barrios and into mixed middle-class neighborhoods. Yet it must not be forgotten that the lingering effects of past racial discrimination continue to play a role in the segregation and marginality of minorities, including Mexicans and Mexican Americans.

Conclusion

Conflict between Mexican-origin people and European Americans has a long history. Serious discord first erupted in the 1830s when waves of European American immigrants overwhelmed the small Mexican community in Texas and imposed a system of subordination on the local people. A decade later ethnic friction intensified as the United States military invaded the entire Mexican northern frontier during the U.S.-Mexico War. U.S. annexation of Texas in 1845 and absorption of other Mexican provinces per the Treaty of Guadalupe Hidalgo in 1848 transformed the people of those areas into "foreigners in their native land." Violence, attitudinal racism, and discrimination became key instruments in maintaining the conquered population in an inferior status.

The patterns established during those early years remained in place for generations, surfacing in exaggerated form during periods of intense polarization. At the time of the Mexican Revolution, pronounced anti-Mexicanism in south Texas led to indiscriminate attacks on Tejanos/as and Mexicanos/as. Hundreds of innocent people perished or fled the area as vigilante groups and Texas Rangers terrorized many Spanish-speaking communities. In Mexico and in U.S. border towns with large Mexican colonias, deeply antagonistic feelings toward the United States resulting from these and other events spawned assaults on European Americans. As discussed in the previous chapter, during the Depression of the 1930s the majority population labeled Mexican-origin people as undesirable foreigners who did not deserve to live in the United States. Firings, layoffs, threats of deportation, media propaganda, and other pressures led to a mass exodus to Mexico, a truly devastating blow to the Chicano/a community.

Antipathies toward Mexican-origin people, at both the institutional and individual levels, declined slowly as the decades passed. Changes for the better occurred especially rapidly during the 1960s. While negative attitudes and the system of oppression have not yet disappeared, institutional racism began to unravel in the 1970s as Chicano/a organizations aggressively fought exclusion and bigotry on many fronts and as the U.S. government implemented a legislative agenda long demanded by civil rights organizations, particularly those in the African American community. These significant developments are addressed in chapter 7.

FOUR

Identity and the Struggle for Integration

❀

Mexican-origin people have been able to maintain their ethnic distinctiveness and cohesion in the United States largely because their culture has been constantly reinforced by continuous migratory streams from Mexico. All the same, they have made a determined effort to harmonize their lives with those of the dominant white European American population. The desire to belong, to be recognized, and to be counted as full-fledged members of the American mosaic has been consistently strong over the generations. Racism and other institutional impediments, however, have made genuine participation and inclusion elusive goals for large numbers of Mexicans and Mexican Americans. Overcoming the stigma constructed by society in being "Mexican" has been a major challenge. In this chapter we turn our attention to issues pertaining to identity, especially the ambivalence felt by many people sandwiched between two countries and two cultural traditions. The changing nature of the impulse toward integration is examined in three major areas of interaction with the mainstream population: naturalization, military service, and intermarriage.

Ambivalence

Uncertainty over racial, ethnic, and cultural identity is one of the major costs of the long struggle waged by Spanish-speaking people for acceptance by the European American majority. Labels imposed upon Mexicans and Mexican Americans, such as "greasers" and "foreigners," and the characterization of their way of life as "backward" have had devastating effects. So too has the pressure to shed Hispanic cultural traits and give up the Spanish language in the interest of assimilation. Yet many who have acquiesced and followed that strategy in the pursuit of incorporation into the mainstream have encountered rejection. Elements in the dominant society, especially prior to the 1960s, made it known that people of Mexican extraction were unworthy of assuming first-class citizenship. Powerful mixed messages and contradictory forces, then, have created inner strife among many people who have strained to become Americans in the face of disdain and discrimination.

Sadly, for many Mexican-origin people the pursuit of integration has been accompanied by denial of their heritage. This behavior is well illustrated by scorn for the term "Mexican." Such repudiation stems from the pronounced negative connotation "Mexican" has had in the United States. Long ago Mexican-origin people learned that by blurring, minimizing, or obliterating their Mexican genetic and cultural inheritance, they could receive better treatment from European Americans. Thus began the practice of passing as Spanish rather than Mexican. By calling themselves Spanish, defensive Mexican Americans sought to "purify" their blood, "whiten" their appearance, and "Europeanize" their heritage. Later, other terms such as Latin, and more recently Hispanic, came into vogue as substitutes for Mexican.

New Mexico offers the most compelling example of the denial of Mexican identity. Apparently after World War I increasing numbers of Hispanos/as replaced the term "Mexican," the most commonly used self-identifier up to that point, with "Spanish" or "Spanish-American." Both of the latter terms had been used by previous generations. Anthropologist Nancie L. González attributed the upsurge in affinity for the Spanish appellation to a growing feeling among Hispanos/as that identification with Mexico lowered their social status within the dominant society. As hundreds of thousands of poor and often illiterate Mexican immigrants entered the United States in the 1910s and 1920s, European Americans tended to view the entire Mexican-origin population as alien, ignorant, and downtrodden. Lacking an understanding of the centuries-old presence of Hispanos/as in New Mexico and predisposed to stereotyping on the basis of race and ethnicity, European Americans seldom made a distinction between natives and newcomers, assigning inferior status to both. "In effect," wrote González, "the New Mexican, perceiving himself in danger of being pushed down . . . , fought back by making scapegoats of his foreign cousins. Thus . . . [Hispanos/as could say to European Americans], 'You don't like Mexicans, and we don't like them either, but we are different. We are Spanish-American, not Mexican.'" González pointed out that the rejection of the term "Mexican" was strongest among middle-class and elite Hispanos/as who wished to disassociate themselves from the social characteristics and problems common to working-class Mexican immigrants.[1]

The embracing of Spanish identity among sectors of the Mexican/Mexican American population was not confined to New Mexico, of course. As reported by economist Paul S. Taylor, in Colorado's South Platte Valley during the late 1920s, the local Spanish Americans claimed "superiority to the Mexicans . . . on the grounds of superior language, education, cleanliness, and culture." Taylor noted that even children felt obliged to make pernicious distinctions. One example involved several Spanish American boys saying to their scout leader, "Don't call us Mexicans. Don't confuse us with 'greasers.'"[2] Similar attitudes were found among many Californios/as, Arizonenses/as, and Tejanos/as.

The repudiation of Mexican identity deeply disturbed officials in Mexico, who responded by launching initiatives through Mexican consulates designed to foster pride in and loyalty to the motherland. In the 1920s and 1930s consular authorities created honorary commissions to give legitimacy and visibility to elite immigrants who promoted Mexican patriotic activities and also sponsored libraries and schools for the study of the Spanish language and Mexican history and culture. Shortages of funds undermined these projects, however, and led to rather modest results.

Race as a concept is key to understanding the problem of identity. Given the widespread belief in the United States of the superiority of fair-skinned people over dark-skinned people, many Mexicans and Mexican Americans vigorously asserted that they belonged to the white race and should be so classified. In the 1930s the League of United Latin American Citizens (LULAC) led the fight to reverse a growing trend in federal, state, and local bureaucracies to classify Mexican-origin people as nonwhite. The U.S.

Census Bureau viewed the group largely as a non-Caucasian population and encouraged their classification as colored. Many communities in Texas followed the Census Bureau's lead, designating dark-skinned mestizos as colored in birth and death records. In Wharton County, Texas, election officials wrote "colored" on poll tax receipts. LULAC and other organizations saw in the reclassification effort a great potential for intensifying segregation and discrimination against the Latino/a community. Leaders feared the kind of treatment accorded African Americans, whose marginality derived from a system of de jure discrimination based on their status as a "colored" or "black" race. By the end of the decade the voices of opposition in the Mexican/Mexican American community had succeeded in stopping the reclassification scheme, and the authorities once again identified members of the group as white in official documents.

In everyday life, however, European Americans continued to view Mexican-origin people as a non-Caucasian population. This elicited considerable indignation among Mexican American veterans of World War II and the Korean conflict and others involved in community activism. In a 1965 article that formed part of a series on conditions among Latinos/as in San Antonio, *San Antonio Evening News* writer Manuel Ruiz Ibañez, after interviewing more than one hundred people, reported that Mexican Americans found the denial of the designation white just as "aggravating" as the discrimination practiced against them. One interviewee expressed a common complaint:

> A man born in Germany, Ireland, England or any other European country comes to the United States and is immediately recognized as American after becoming naturalized. Yet we are not considered as just plain Americans, despite the fact that we were born here and in many cases come from families which have lived here for several generations. Many of us are descendants of men and women who were here way before any Anglos ever set foot on this land, but still we are designated as "Mexicans." [3]

One of the most tragic consequences of the stigma attached to the label "Mexican" in the United States is the shame and sense of inferiority felt by many people so identified. Sociologist Ozzie G. Simmons documented such feelings among residents of south Texas during the early 1950s. "The Mexican ambivalence about equality with Anglos," wrote Simmons, "is reflected in the constraint, lack of poise and self-assurance, and general sense of discomfort that characterizes the behavior of Mexicans of all classes when they participate in informal social situations with Anglos." [4] One Mexican American businessman saw the root of the problem in the racial brainwashing that had gone on for generations:

> The trouble with the Mexican people is that 50 to 60 percent of them have an inferiority complex. The Anglo Americans think they're superior and have been telling us that for so long that half the [Mexican] people actually believe they're inferior. Once in awhile I believe it myself because I have heard it so often. From the time we are knee high, we hear we're inferior, so we can't help believing it. The only way to overcome it is to tell ourselves we're not inferior, and then go out and prove it. [5]

It is clear that fear of racial discrimination drove large numbers of Mexican-origin people to demand being classified as white. And yet, paradoxically, in order to obtain legal relief from discrimination, beginning in Texas in the 1950s, civil rights organizations carried on a legal struggle to convince the courts that Mexicans and Mexican Americans constituted an ethnically and linguistically distinct, and implicitly "nonwhite," group within the population. In 1954, in *Hernández v. Texas*, the U.S. Supreme Court affirmed that interpretation, opening the door to the filing of discrimination lawsuits based on Mexican ethnicity. Up to that point educational and legal institutions had turned racism on its head for malevolent purposes. For example, courts had justified exclusion of Mexican Americans from bodies such as juries on the grounds that since members of the group were officially white, their total absence from all–European American juries, including those panels charged with judging Hispanic defendants, was legally nondiscriminatory. In later years, in the course of extensive civil rights litigation, the Mexican American Legal Defense and Education Fund (MALDEF), led the effort to institutionalize the legal principle of ethnic distinctiveness for the Mexican-origin population. Eventually the "white" designation became less of a concern as racism declined in the United States. Nevertheless, high percentages of Mexican Americans have continued to insist that they are as white as European Americans.

Another highly significant issue related to identity is the uneasy relationship that has existed between U.S.-born Mexican Americans and immigrants. The newcomers have been accused of competing for scarce jobs, driving down wages, and making unionization more difficult. Half a century ago, LULAC publicly called for a halt to Mexican immigration, including guest workers, arguing that the constant influx of cheap labor from Mexico undercut the material advancement of earlier immigrants and made it much more difficult for Mexican-origin people to become integrated with the dominant society. Professor and activist George Sánchez loudly denounced the U.S. government for failing to stop the continuous flow of undocumented workers, whom he perceived as causing great displacement among native-born workers. Sánchez shared the opinion held by other leaders that large-scale surreptitious immigration had a harmful effect on assimilation:

> From a cultural standpoint, the influx of a million or more wetbacks a year transforms the Spanish-speaking people of the Southwest from an ethnic group which might be assimilated with reasonable facility into what I call a culturally indigestible peninsula of Mexico. The "wet" migration tends to nullify processes of social integration going back 300 or 350 years, and I would say at the present time has set the whole assimilation process back at least twenty years.[6]

The deep divisions over Mexican immigration continued into the late twentieth century. In 1984, when the national debate over immigration legislation intensified, polls by the Southwest Voter Registration Project revealed that 60 percent of Hispanic voters in Texas favored sanctions against employers who hired undocumented workers. "We don't get along with Mexicans," confided a Chicano from Los Angeles to a journalist in 1986. He disdainfully accused immigrants of bringing down the neighborhood and of "taking money out of our pockets" by abusing the welfare system. Other Mexican Americans interviewed blamed "undocumented workers for lower salaries and the loss of jobs [and] the overcrowding of schools and health clinics."[7] In Arizona, the cultural chasm between the two groups recently exploded into gang warfare in urban barrios and triggered rioting in the state's largest prison. A third-generation Mexican American woman from Phoenix characterized some of the cultural traits and living arrangements of the immigrants as "disgusting," while a Baptist minister complained about the immigrants' taste in music and food preparation techniques, as well as their habit of disposing of "the innards of goats" in trash cans and "stinking up the alley."[8]

The persistent negative characterization of immigrants has understandably aroused the ire of the newcomers. In the 1920s and 1930s, nationalistic exiles and refugees who had departed Mexico during the turbulent 1910s and had vigorously promoted loyalty to the motherland and adherence to Mexican culture blasted Mexican American leaders who advised their followers to forget Mexico and concentrate on becoming Americans. When Mexican Americans demeaned Mexico, the immigrants responded with insults of their own, referring to the disparagers as *pochos* and *cholos*, meaning people whose way of life had been corrupted by a freakish mixture of Mexican and American cultural traits. Many immigrants believed that Americanized Mexican Americans had acquired abhorrent social attitudes and values, including arrogance, laziness, and immorality.[9] One of the popular corridos of the period denounced Mexican Americans who denied their heritage:

> . . . Many Mexicans don't care to speak
> The language their mothers taught them
> And go about saying they are Spanish
> And deny their country's flag.
>
> Some are darker than black tar
> But they pretend to be Saxon;
> They go about powdered to the back of the neck
> And wear skirts for trousers . . .
>
> My kids speak perfect English
> And have no use for our Spanish
> They call me "fader" and don't work
> And are crazy about the Charleston.
>
> I'm tired of all this nonsense
> I'm going back to Michoacán. . . .[10]

The divergent perspectives held by the native and foreign-born people of Mexican origin have become more pronounced in recent decades in areas that have large concentrations of undocumented people. California is the state where immigrants have been placed most on the defensive. Yet they have not passively borne the attacks against them. They have defended themselves loudly and have even participated in public demonstrations.

A major source of friction is language, as suggested previously. But the problem of language has reached far beyond the Mexican/Mexican American population because of the long-standing opposition among European Americans to the widespread use of Spanish in the United States. The view of the dominant society—that to be of Mexican extraction is to be inferior—has extended to language as well. Speakers of Spanish have been perceived as inferior to speakers of English. Even a portion of the Mexican-origin population has internalized that perspective.

Until the 1960s, schools commonly punished children for speaking Spanish. Officials pointed to the need to learn English as the reason for inflicting sanctions. Tragically, the children interpreted the speaking of Spanish as a form of negative behavior on their part. That experience took a heavy toll on their identity and self-esteem. The advent of bilingual education in the 1970s introduced a more enlightened approach to the issue of language, but the program has been continually plagued with many problems, including lack of resources, teacher shortages, inadequate training of teachers, improper use of teaching techniques, and hostility on the part of the European American majority. Opposition to bilingual education reached a crescendo in 1998 with the passage of Proposition 227 in California. This measure called for the dismantling of bilingual education in the state. Voters approved the initiative by a margin of 69 percent to 31 percent. Hispanic voters, however, opposed it by a ratio of 2 to 1. Though Latino/a organizations immediately challenged Proposition 227 in the courts, bilingual education has already suffered substantial damage. Most likely other states will pursue similar initiatives, and the U.S. Congress may well cut off federal funding in the near future.

Opposition to bilingual education goes hand in hand with recent efforts to make English the official language of the United States. Groups such as U.S. English and English First have campaigned hard to convince a large portion of the American public that the use of languages other than English fosters fragmentation in the country and threatens political stability. Led by California, seventeen states and dozens of cities and towns had declared English as their official language by 1990, sending a message to Hispanics and other language-minority groups that they should rid themselves of their native tongues as quickly as possible. In 1999, however, supporters of "English only" suffered a major defeat when the U.S. Supreme Court refused to overturn a decision by the Arizona Supreme Court that had declared that state's 1988 "English only" ballot initiative unconstitutional. This development produced a sigh of relief in the Hispanic community nationwide.

Ironically, language bashing in the United States has coincided with a recent significant rise among Latinos/as of mastery of the English language and participation in European American culture. Numerous polls and studies show that immigrants are eager to learn English and that they take advantage of every opportunity to do so. By the third generation, very few people of Mexican descent actually use Spanish as their primary language. One study found that 84 percent of Hispanics in the Rocky Mountain region reported English as their usual language. From these and other data the author concluded that "Spanish as a dominant first language is rapidly disappearing in the United States." Another researcher who studied language use in Southern California concluded "that were it not for new arrivals from Mexico, Spanish would disappear from Los Angeles nearly as rapidly as European languages vanished from cities in the East." [11]

In short, the experience among people of Mexican extraction regarding acquisition of the English language is not much different from that of other immigrant groups in American society. Spanish does not pose a threat to English because in each generation most of those Hispanics who use Spanish as their usual language, an unmistakable minority of the Latino/a population, eventually shift to English. Immigrant children in particular learn English very quickly. Either the dominant society is unaware of these trends or chooses to ignore them. Whatever the case, it is clear that many attacks on Latinos/as and their native language have their roots in prejudice and fear.

Paths to Integration

NATURALIZATION

Until the second half of the twentieth century, very few Mexican immigrants desired to become U.S citizens. In 1920, only 5.5 percent of Mexicans eligible for citizenship became naturalized, compared to 49.7 percent of all other immigrants.[12] Such rates held steady for decades.

It is clear that discrimination played a major role in the reluctance of

Mexicans to legally embrace the United States as their country in place of their beloved homeland. For years, the decision to grant or deny the privilege of citizenship rested with state and court officials, leaving much room for abuse because of the widespread sentiment that Mexicans did not deserve that honor. A large percentage of Mexicans actually could be legally excluded on the basis of race, since the Naturalization Law provided that only white immigrants qualified for citizenship. Although officials did not always abide by that interpretation, it did create a legal limbo that lasted until 1952, when a new Immigration and Naturalization Act finally ended such discrimination against nonwhite immigrants.

Over the years Mexican immigrants have cited both loyalty to their homeland and adverse treatment in the United States as the major reasons for rejecting naturalization. An immigrant who had lived in the United States for a quarter century cited his abiding attachment to Mexico in an interview in the 1920s: "I would rather cut my throat before changing my Mexican nationality. My country is before everything else."[13] The indignation felt by Mexicans over rejection by Americans and the effect of this feeling on naturalization rates are acutely evident in responses given during that era by two students asked to explain why so few Mexicans became citizens:

> What good would it do us? The Americans wouldn't treat us any better if we did. They say we are black, they call us Indians, Greasers, Cholos, and getting naturalized wouldn't make us any different.
>
> A Mexican who becomes an American citizen is looked upon [by other Mexicans] as a renegade, a traitor, and since the Americans also look down on him, he is like a "man without a country." . . . In some places they will not allow us in theaters, barber shops and other public places. Does treatment like that make us want to be citizens?[14]

Immigrants also rejected naturalization because they did not wish to lose the protection accorded them by Mexican consulates. Often diplomatic officials from Mexico constituted the only recourse available for getting relief from abusive U.S. employers and discriminatory institutions such as the police and the schools. Clearly this constituted a powerful incentive for Mexican immigrants to retain their nationality. In addition, the desire to keep the rights and privileges of Mexican citizens, especially remaining eligible for all manner of employment in their homeland, being able to own property along the coast and on the border, and being able to invest without restriction prompted many to shy away from U.S. naturalization.

As the decades passed, conditions changed and naturalization rates slowly went up. By the 1970s and 1980s, the percentage of naturalized Mexican immigrants had risen to 11.5 and 18.6 respectively. Still, such rates lagged behind those of other immigrant groups. In the 1990s, two developments caused a dramatic surge in applications for U.S. citizenship submitted by Mexicans. First, the growing anti-immigrant movement in California and in the U.S. Congress threatened to eliminate or drastically diminish social benefits for both undocumented and legal immigrants. At the peak of the anti-foreigner hysteria, the application rate for naturalization climbed by nearly 500 percent in Los Angeles. Some 1.3 million immigrants from many countries applied for citizenship in 1996, and that figure rose to 1.5 million in 1997. Mexicans headed the parade. Soon an underfunded and understaffed U.S. Immigration and Naturalization Service faced a mammoth backlog of petitions awaiting attention. Los Angeles led the nation in the number of unprocessed applications.

Second, a Mexican law enacted in March 1998 for the first time permitted dual citizenship for Mexicans living abroad. A long-held wish among immigrants finally came true. Acquiring U.S. citizenship would no longer cancel out their Mexican nationality. It would now be possible to retain sentimental loyalty toward Mexico and safeguard material interests located south of the border while simultaneously becoming citizens of their country of residence. Not surprisingly, large numbers of eligible individuals eager to formalize the coveted dual citizenship status stampeded government offices in both countries.

Thus, a threat to personal well-being emanating from the United States and an act of inclusiveness originating in Mexico changed the citizenship landscape for Mexican immigrants. Without a doubt the yearning to make their voices heard in the United States through the ballot box at a time of intense xenophobia constituted another reason for the extraordinary rise in applications for U.S. naturalization among Mexicans.

MILITARY SERVICE

The historic struggle among people of Mexican origin to gain acceptance in the United States is also reflected in the pains they have taken to prove their patriotism to their adopted land. The issue of loyalty first surfaced in the 1830s and 1840s, when the Texas rebellion and the U.S.-Mexico War inevitably created deeply conflicting feelings among Mexicans in the borderlands. Members of the generations that endured invasions of their homelands in particular harbored hatred for the United States, while others who witnessed post-1848 American aggressions toward Mexico could not help but sympathize with their brothers and sisters south of the Rio Grande.

As time passed, however, the relationship between the two countries improved, new generations of U.S.-born Mexican Americans emerged, and strident attitudes and intense ambivalence became less pronounced. Yet European Americans continued to raise the issue of patriotism. When the Spanish-American War broke out in 1898, rumors circulated that people of Spanish/Mexican origin would not support it or volunteer to fight against their cousins from Spain. In the case of New Mexico that assumption had some truth, as many Hispanos/as remained indifferent to the conflict or maintained a neutral stance because of divided loyalties. Isolation from the mainstream society, cultural and language differences, and lack of clear incentives constituted additional reasons for the low enlistments of Hispanos/as in the military. The Nuevo Mexicano/a elite, however, voiced loud support for the war. This is reflected in speeches of leaders as well as editorials in Spanish-language newspapers.

Questions about patriotism surfaced anew in the 1910s when relations between the United States and Mexico deteriorated. Anti-Mexican feelings rose among European Americans as Mexican revolutionaries persecuted U.S. citizens in Mexico and raided U.S. border towns. Simultaneously, many Mexicans and Mexican Americans cultivated anti-U.S. sentiments as a result of repeated American interventions in Mexico's political affairs and military invasions of Mexican soil. More than likely most Mexican-origin people in the United States simply shrugged their shoulders and quietly supported their adopted country. Others, however, feeling a need to reassure skeptical European Americans, took a public stance against Mexico. In 1914, for instance, following the U.S. invasion of Veracruz, hundreds of Mexican Americans in El Paso volunteered to patrol poor neighborhoods near the international line to deter possible subversion among recent Mexican immigrants or infiltrators who might surreptitiously cross the Rio Grande. In an extraordinary mass meeting in the El Paso Courthouse, one hundred "Spanish Americans" pledged their readiness and guaranteed the willingness of five hundred others to serve in whatever capacity their country dictated:

> While we are called Mexicans, we are not. We are Americans, born and brought up under the Stars and Stripes and as loyal to it as any other American. Many people in this city have said that we would rise up and incite riots in this city if President Wilson was forced to land American troops or blue-jackets on Mexican soil, but quite the contrary we are ready to shoulder a rifle and march in the ranks with the American soldier who is of Anglo-Saxon or Celtic origin.[15]

World War I in particular posed a dilemma for Mexican immigrants recently arrived in the United States. Many felt ambivalent about lending military service to a country that discriminated against them personally and constantly bullied the land of their birth. Consequently an undetermined number of men, including naturalized U.S. citizens, departed the United States to avoid conscription. The drafting of thousands of Mexican nationals in 1917, including workers in the country only temporarily, gave a powerful impetus to the exodus. During the war years representatives of the Mexican government intervened repeatedly with local draft boards and the military itself to rescue Mexican citizens entangled by the system and in danger of winding up on the European front. Interestingly, draft boards assumed Mexican men to be U.S. citizens and therefore draftable if they could not readily prove their Mexican nationality with certified birth certificates.

The exodus of 1917 caused by the draft scare prompted the authorities, the newspapers, and ordinary Americans once again to express doubt about the loyalty of Mexican-origin people. In reality, members of the group volunteered for military service during the war at a rate proportionately higher than that of other ethnic groups. Hispanos made up 65 percent of the volunteers and draftees from New Mexico, including forty-one men from Chimayo, an isolated community that counted only 129 households in 1910. Large numbers of Spanish-speaking individuals saw combat in Europe and many received fitting recognition for their valor. For example, Mexico-born Marcelino Serna, from El Paso, earned many decorations, including the Distinguished Service Cross and medals of high distinction awarded by the English, French, and Italian governments.

The pattern set by Mexican Americans during World War I of eagerly serving the country became even more pronounced during World War II. Possibly up to 500,000 Chicanos/as saw duty in the various branches of the military, with high percentages winding up on the front lines and carrying out the most hazardous missions. "We believed that by joining the service, we could lay to rest the idea that Mexicans were disloyal to the United States," stated one veteran. "We wanted to prove that while our cultural ties were deeply rooted in Mexico, our home was here in this country."[16] The dedication and valor demonstrated by the Mexican American GIs of the 1940s is reflected in their seventeen Congressional Medals of Honor, the most earned by one ethnic group. Tragically many paid the ultimate price in proving their loyalty, dying in disproportionate numbers on the battlefield. Between 50 and 75 percent of the war casualties whose home was in south Texas had Spanish surnames, prompting attorney Alonso S. Perales to question whether racist military leaders deliberately assigned Mexican-origin servicemen to highly hazardous duty as a way of getting rid of them permanently. Perales also wondered if many European Americans in south Texas were avoiding military service or were simply given safer jobs away from the front. Another indication of overrepresentation in dangerous areas is the fact that Spanish-surname soldiers made up more than 25 percent of the prisoners of war on the infamous Bataan Death March.[17]

One of the least-known chapters of Mexican American history is the contribution of women to the war effort in the 1940s. Although the number of Chicanas on active duty appears to have been small, their contributions in the world of work proved significant. They took on a variety of jobs in the regular economy as well as the defense industries. Women also engaged in many community activities to help the country. In Tucson, for example, La Asociación Hispano-Americana de Madres y Esposas (The Hispanic-American Association of Mothers and Wives) sold war bonds and stamps, collected clothing for shipment to war-torn countries, gathered scrap metal and other materials useful for industrial purposes, provided child care for women who worked in defense industries, and organized many functions to lift the morale of servicemen. Women from Phoenix also became involved with war-related activities in the barrios. Aside from taking part in bond drives and the like, women organized the Victory Labor Volunteers, whose members sought to meet the labor shortages in the cotton fields around

Phoenix. An estimated five thousand people participated as labor volunteers through this effort. Community organizations and religious groups led by women also encouraged unassimilated Mexicans to learn English and become U.S. citizens, thereby paving the way for involvement in civic affairs.

Another forgotten detail in U.S. military history is Mexico's formal alliance with the United States during World War II and the participation of the 201st Mexican Fighter Squadron in operations in the Pacific. Flyers from the 201st supported the 25th Division (U.S.A.) by flying fifty missions and almost three hundred sorties. Seven Mexican pilots died in action.

Mexican Americans continued the tradition of serving their country unselfishly during the Korean conflict, the Vietnam War, and the Gulf War. Their devotion is dramatically illustrated in a neighborhood in Silvis, Illinois, where a monument on a street popularly known as Hero Street, U.S.A., honors eighty-four soldiers of Mexican descent, including twelve who died in defense of their country, beginning with World War II. Remarkably, Hero Street, U.S.A., is only one and a half blocks long, which means that, at least for World War II and the Korean conflict, "this street reportedly contributed more men to military service . . . than any other place of comparable size in the United States."[18]

While proud of the service rendered by their people, Mexican American leaders continued to express alarm at the disproportionate number of wartime casualties. In 1951, the Peace Committee of the Asociación Nacional México-Americana complained that Korean War casualties among Spanish-surname servicemen from the Southwest far surpassed the percentage of this group in the population. The Peace Committee backed its complaint with the following statistics:[19]

	Colorado	Arizona	Texas	New Mexico
Hispanics in the state population	10%	20%	17%	49%
Hispanic casualties in Korea	28%	44%	30%	56%

During the Vietnam War political scientist Ralph Guzmán compiled similar statistics, revealing that while people with Spanish surnames made up 12 percent of the population in the Southwest, they comprised more than 19 percent of the casualties.

In the 1960s and 1970s the unfair burden placed on Chicanos/as and other minorities in the battlefields of Vietnam fueled the separatist rhetoric heard in many barrios in the Southwest. Angry militants advocated rejection of the military and other European American institutions. Some even called for a complete breakaway from the dominant community. In reality, however, the threatening oratory had little impact outside small circles of a few radical organizations. Mexican Americans continued to enlist in the military in large numbers.

Viewed in a long-term perspective, there is no question that military service and work in the defense industries have transformed the lives of hundreds of thousands of people of Mexican heritage. The military milieu has acted as a powerful agent of socialization, especially for those who previously have had limited opportunities to interact with members of the dominant society. In addition to being drawn into national life, Mexican American servicemen and servicewomen of disadvantaged backgrounds have had opportunities to travel and to receive veterans' benefits. Many have bought homes and attended colleges and universities under different GI Bills of Rights. With the availability of higher education, many members of the working class have been able to enter professional and business occupations. On the home front, defense industries have provided attractive job opportunities for both men and women. Thus, the military has served as a vehicle for entry into the middle class and as a means of establishing closer contact with the mainstream population. Reflecting on the meaning of service to the country, a member of the GI generation of the 1940s and 1950s put it this way: "We developed intense pride in America. Our standard of living . . . improved 100 percent. As veterans, we . . . [became] serious-thinking Americans. We . . . [enlarged] our circle of friends to include not only Mexican Americans like ourselves, but Americans of many other nationalities."[20]

INTERMARRIAGE

The single most revealing indicator of integration of an ethnic group into the U.S. mainstream is intermarriage, for it demonstrates mutual acceptance at the most intimate level of human interaction. In the first few decades of encounters between Mexican-origin people and European Americans, intermarriage took place on a modest scale. That situation remained practically unchanged for generations, reflecting the strained relations that prevailed between the two groups. In the latter twentieth century, however, intermarriage rose sharply, reflecting a significant break from past trends. General conditions had improved for the Mexican-descent population, and the social distance that separated the group from the dominant society diminished appreciably.

Not surprisingly, given the heterogeneity of both the Mexican-origin and European American populations, the rates of intermarriage have differed from place to place. Such variation stems from factors such as the degree of ethnic harmony and the availability of potential spouses within each group. Nineteenth-century San Antonio and Los Angeles exemplify the significance of these variables. In the 1870s, only 4 percent of all marriages in San Antonio involving Spanish-surname persons were exogamous, compared to 12 percent in Los Angeles.[21] Probably the most important factors accounting for the rather low incidence of intermarriage in San Antonio at that time were the highly polarized ethnic climate, the presence of many European American women in the population available to marry European American men, and the strong social connections that local Mexicans/Mexican Americans had with population centers in northeastern Mexico, the source of many brides and grooms. The higher rate of interethnic marital alliances in Los Angeles most likely derived from the town's milder ethnic climate (compared to Texas) and the presence of a Mexican/Mexican American merchant, ranching, and farming class favorably disposed to social merger with European Americans.

Numerous studies of intermarriage during the twentieth century confirm the geographical variations described here. They also show a steady rise over time almost everywhere, with significant acceleration taking place after 1960. The percentage of Mexican/Mexican American exogamous marriages in various communities in the Southwest for select years are as follows:[22]

San Antonio	Albuquerque	Los Angeles	Phoenix
1960: 20%	1953: 23%	1924–33: 17%	1985: 47%
1973: 27%	1971: 39%	1963: 40%	1993: 45%

These figures serve as a powerful reminder that despite the interethnic friction between Mexican-origin people and European Americans that has been present over many generations, individuals from both groups have always been able to find sufficient common ground to make it possible to join their lives. This is especially true of people beyond the first generation of immigrants. At the end of the twentieth century, the overall rate of Chicano/a intermarriage with European Americans actually surpassed that of African Americans and was in the same range as other ethnic groups such as Asians and some white Europeans. Logically the level of intermarriage would be even greater if sustained and continuous large-scale immigration from Mexico and other parts of Latin America had not occurred between 1960 and 2000. That steady influx has strengthened endogamy.

Conclusion

The historical record reveals a long-standing, concerted effort among Mexican-origin people to be recognized and accepted as full-fledged members of American society. While strong ties to Mexico and the presence of large numbers of immigrants in many communities slowed assimilation, the rejection of the group by the dominant society had far greater consequences in promoting marginality. Inevitably, the constant denigration of Hispanics in American literature, movies, television, and the media nurtured self-doubt and even self-hatred among some people of Mexican descent. The denial of Mexican ethnicity became rampant. Tensions between U.S.-born Chicanos/as and immigrants escalated. Attempts to stop such self-destructive behavior began on a large scale in the 1960s with the promotion of ethnic pride and the denunciation of racism. In addition, the recent embracing of multiculturalism and diversity by a host of American institutions has helped to combat feelings of inferiority and nonbelonging. Yet enduring negative attitudes continue to take a toll, and large numbers of people of Mexican extraction remain highly ambivalent about who they are and what they are. Deep uncertainties persist over their place in U.S. society as well as their relationship to Mexico.

Nevertheless, it is important to stress the ability of the human spirit to deal effectively with cultural ambivalence. Such inner tensions are not new in our highly diverse population. Members of other groups have traveled a similar road. While ambiguity over identity remains a matter of concern, it should be understood that Mexicans and Mexican Americans have coped rather well with the problem, just as other ethnic communities in U.S. society have done.

Naturalization, a major indicator of the willingness among immigrants to fully embrace their adopted homeland, seems puzzling in the Mexican case because of the low rates recorded for most of the twentieth century. Is this not evidence that Mexicans rejected Americanization? Not necessarily. Because of extant structural factors, Mexican immigrants in the first half of the twentieth century derived few advantages from U.S. citizenship. As conditions for minorities became more favorable, applications for naturalization picked up considerably. Later, the government threat of elimination of benefits for immigrants prompted more Mexicans to seek U.S. citizenship. Finally, the passage of a law in Mexico in 1998 permitting dual citizenship removed remaining material and psychological disincentives associated with the acquisition of U.S. citizenship. At the end of the twentieth century, then, sufficient propitious conditions finally appeared, and Mexicans rushed en masse to become U.S. citizens.

The pursuit of incorporation into U.S. society has varied among different segments of the Mexican-origin population. Light-skinned and affluent people have had the easiest time with assimilation, and dark-skinned and poor people the hardest. Among the lower middle and working classes, military service has served as a crucial vehicle for demonstrating loyalty and patriotism to a skeptical mainstream population. The military experience also has had enormous impact on Latino/a communities nationwide, speeding up social mobility and promoting greater participation in the life of the country. Finally, the recent tendency toward greater integration and assimilation is most dramatically demonstrated by the rising rates of intermarriage with European Americans.

Evidence presented in this chapter supports the conclusion that although a large percentage of the Mexican-descent population remains on the margins of U.S. society, a significant portion has joined the mainstream. In the future this trend seems likely to continue, especially among those Mexicans/Mexican Americans who have achieved middle-class status and those among the working class who are on the upward mobility track. These themes are taken up in the next section, especially in chapter 6.

PART III

Working and Climbing

❀

Hard work on the northern frontier and deep within Mexico
prepared us for back-breaking labor in the United States.
But we did not anticipate the long and hard struggle
for basic rights, for fair wages, for just treatment.
In the United States of America?
In the land of justice and equality?

By jumping hoops, scaling walls, skirting barriers,
embracing luck, seizing opportunity, and working like devils,
a good number of us penetrated the middle class,
and achieved status and material comfort.

FIVE

Travails of Making a Living

❖

The Mexican-origin labor force in the United States has been overwhelmingly proletarian since the establishment of the border with Mexico. Before 1900 Mexicans and Mexican Americans worked for wages primarily in the agrarian and extractive sectors. Later, as urban centers expanded throughout the Southwest, they began entering industrial and service occupations. Continuous migrations from Mexico assured steady expansion of the workforce, especially in the low-wage, unskilled categories. In the late twentieth century industrial occupations absorbed larger percentages of both U.S.-born and immigrant workers. Members of both cohorts successfully penetrated new and more rewarding sectors of the economy. Yet despite these advances, recent structural changes in the U.S. economy have reduced opportunities for untold numbers of workers, especially those lacking skills and training. At the beginning of the new century the employment situation among Mexican-origin people has become decidedly more complex and challenging. This chapter surveys major developments that have taken place in the world of work over several generations, with an emphasis on the experience of wage laborers, patterns of change in employment, worker-employer relations, and unionization movements.

Agriculture and Ranching

GENERAL CONDITIONS

After the U.S. takeover of the Southwest, the bulk of the Mexican-descent labor force continued working in agriculture and ranching, employed both by Spanish/Mexican landowners and newly arrived European American farmers and growers. Texas serves as an example of patterns duplicated elsewhere. During the 1850s, Tejano and Mexican fieldworkers could be found in many farms throughout the border region and the central part of the state. After the Civil War, the demand for Mexican workers grew in east Texas, giving rise to new migrations. Most farmhands worked for wages, but some engaged in tenant farming, sharing profits with landowners. As cotton cultivation intensified in the 1880s, Mexicans and Mexican Americans became the backbone of the Texas labor force. By the mid-1890s, thousands of migrants from San Antonio, the Lower Rio Grande Valley, and rural communities in Mexico traveled to cotton-producing areas to supply seasonal labor. A newspaper calculated in October 1894 that five thousand workers passed through the town of Beeville on their way to the cotton fields of central and northern Texas. "After the cotton season the majority will work their way back to the border and into Mexico," reported the newspaper.[1] Apart from doing fieldwork, many laborers participated in getting land ready for cultivation by clearing trees and removing brush.

Similar developments, albeit on a smaller scale, characterized agricultural labor activity in New Mexico and Arizona, where crop cultivation grew at a slower pace. In California, Mexicans and Mexican Americans competed with Chinese and Japanese workers in the expanding fruit and vegetable industries. After 1869, when the arrival of the railroads made it possible to ship perishable crops to eastern markets, the demand for labor in the Golden State increased. Mexican-origin fieldworkers assumed added importance along the Pacific Coast when the exclusion of Asian workers occurred through the enactment of the Chinese Exclusion Act in 1882 and the intensification of discrimination against the Japanese.

Cattle- and sheepraising, two other industries that had long-standing antecedents in the Southwest, expanded significantly after 1850 with the infusion of European American capital. The takeover of ranching by European Americans proceeded rapidly in Texas and California and more slowly in Arizona and New Mexico. Throughout the second half of the nineteenth century *vaqueros* (cowboys) and *arrieros* (muleteers) could be found working in ranches from Texas to California, and some obtained employment in the Pacific Northwest as early as the 1850s. Expressing disappointment over the lack of recognition by European American society of the multiple contributions made by vaqueros to the development of the western United

States, Carey McWilliams wrote in the 1940s that "everything that served to characterize the American cowboy as a type was taken over from the Mexican vaquero; utensils and language, methods and equipment." McWilliams also praised the thousands of Mexicans who worked as sheepherders and shearers, characterizing them as "carriers of a great tradition and it has been their skill and knowledge which has sustained the sheep industry in the West." These sheepmen, especially Hispanos from New Mexico, traveled widely within and outside the Southwest. *Pastores* grazed the animals and drove them to markets, while shearers, "the migratory aristocrats of the industry," followed set routes that took them to different places during the fleecing season.[2]

As the twentieth century began, large-scale irrigation projects multiplied throughout the Southwest, making more land available for cultivation. The need for harvest labor skyrocketed, and Mexicans and Mexican Americans heeded the call. Some became sharecroppers and share tenants, but most worked for wages. Agricultural *colonias* mushroomed in areas where migrant workers could spend the winter and await the next round of seasonal employment, rather than returning home. At length Mexican-origin farmworkers became dominant in the agricultural labor force, producing the nation's fruits and vegetables; they also became highly visible in the sugarbeet and cotton industries.

Growers and other employers throughout the United States relied on a recruitment system that had functioned along the border for years. In his classic study of Mexican labor in the early twentieth century, Victor S. Clark reported in 1908 on the activities of companies that had offices in cities like El Paso and Laredo staffed with agents who lured Chicanos/as and Mexican nationals. *Enganchistas*, or contractors, often ignored the Alien Contract Labor Law by going directly into Mexico to secure labor. Sugar-beet companies stand out for the scale of their recruitment activities. In the 1910s, employers hired more than five thousand Mexicans for the beet fields of Michigan and Ohio and, in the two decades between 1910 and 1930, Colorado beet growers imported approximately 30,000 Mexicans.[3] Paul S. Taylor described the year-round experience of countless of these recruits:

In May the sugar beets of the North need thinning—and the Mexicans of the Southwest are called upon to furnish their quota of hand laborers. . . . They are transported by the trainload to the Arkansas and South Platte Valleys and the Western Slope of Colorado, to Wyoming, Idaho, Montana, Nebraska, the Dakotas, Iowa, Minnesota, and Michigan. When they reach the beet fields they are scattered out on the farms, each family under contract to tend its allotted fields at from $23 to $25 an acre. . . . In May and June beets are blocked and thinned. . . . In July and August there is hoeing, and in September comes topping, lasting through October and into November. . . . In the winter the tide of beet workers . . . recedes. But an increasing number stay on, responding to the stimulation of beet farmers or sugar companies who offer houses rent free, or of opportunities to build in colony tracts.[4]

The large-scale recruitment of workers from Texas, especially by northern sugar-beet companies, disrupted that state's labor system and incensed local employers who wanted to keep their labor. Texas growers found ways of intimidating workers to stay put, sometimes resorting to violence against sugar-beet agents, immobilizing their trucks by shooting at the tires. In 1929 employers succeeded in convincing the state legislature to pass the Emigrant Labor Agency Laws, which imposed burdensome and expensive requirements on labor recruiters from outside Texas. These laws slowed down the exodus but did not stop it because northern companies reverted to illegal recruitment procedures and launched successful legal challenges through the courts.

Higher wages outside the Southwest largely explain the motivation for farmworkers to venture far from the border region but, regardless of location, compensation lagged far behind that of workers in other sectors of the national economy. In the early 1910s, for example, factory workers averaged twenty-one cents an hour, while farmworkers earned only fourteen cents an hour. A decade later factory wages increased to fifty-two cents but farm wages rose to only twenty-four cents. Thus farmworkers, who made the lowest wages, lost considerable ground during these years, earning only 47 percent of what factory workers made in the early 1920s, compared to 67 percent a decade earlier.[5]

Farmworkers found themselves at a great disadvantage largely because growers manipulated the market to assure that labor costs would remain low. In California, growers began to construct a system of wage fixing by meeting informally to agree on compensation levels for different crops. The practice became institutionalized with the creation of private labor bureaus that projected labor needs, recruited workers, and dictated wages. To assure the lowest wages possible, bureaus routinely overestimated the number of workers needed in order to intensify the competition among them. According to one estimate, the services performed by the bureaus resulted in savings to the growers of 10 to 30 percent in labor costs.[6]

The migratory lifestyle and lack of legal protections subjected farm-workers to a life of struggle and deprivation. Apart from paying rock-bottom wages, growers and enganchistas abused workers by providing unsafe transportation and substandard housing, doctoring the books, and charging inflated prices for basic commodities sold in the fields and in the camps. Many families annually spent months searching for work and living in many different places. Employers encouraged children to work alongside their parents in violation of compulsory school attendance and child labor laws. Makeshift housing in labor camps and chronic disregard by the authorities created extremely unhealthy conditions in many locations. A minister provided the following description of a wretched camp in California during the mid-1920s:

> Shelters were made of almost every conceivable thing—burlap, canvas, palm branches. Not a single wooden floor was observed in the camp. . . . Chicken yards were mixed in with human shelters, in a perfectly democratic way. Calves and horses wandered at will about the shelters. There was a huge pile of manure close by the houses. . . . This greatly interested a group of children who were having a great time tumbling around in the manure as though it were a hay stack. . . . There were flies everywhere. . . . We found one woman carrying water in large milk pails from the irrigation ditch. The water was brown with mud, but we were assured that after it had been allowed to settle that it would be clear and pure. This is evidently all the water which they have in camp. There were no baths.[7]

Such conditions afflicted the lives of migratory workers for many decades. Deprivation and suffering were especially acute in the 1930s, when the Great Depression uprooted large numbers of people from formerly stable communities and forced them into farm labor. Competition for jobs stiffened, further driving down wages. Dire circumstances frequently forced parents to involve their children in fieldwork in order to boost the family income. A woman from Utah recalled the difficult time she had at age seven trying to do adult work:

We started topping beets in the early season. You were down on your knees, like when you go to church and pray, but this was hour after hour . . . and the sun would be beating on you, and it would rain on you. . . . Lots of times I'd cry. . . . I couldn't understand why I had to be out there. But we were hungry, that's the only thing our parents would tell us. "We have to do it — to feed the younger ones."[8]

From 1942 to 1964 the efforts of U.S. workers to improve their situation were seriously frustrated by the importation of Mexican *braceros* (contracted laborers) and the increased volume of undocumented migration. A Mexican American crew leader from south Texas commented in the 1950s that farmers considered "'wetbacks' . . . the best kind of labor to have around here. You don't have to worry about housing them or taking care of them if they get sick. All you do is work them and then forget about them. . . . The people here [Mexican Americans] don't like them coming because it makes it hard for them. . . . [They] have to go North in the summer to make wages they can live on."[9] A report published by the U.S. Senate Subcommittee on Migratory Labor in the early 1960s referred to braceros as indentured workers, and a grower commented that "we used to own slaves, [but] now we rent them from the government."[10]

Between World War II and the late 1960s an average of about 400,000 domestic workers followed the migrant trails that started in the warm areas of the southern United States and led northward. Along the East Coast, Mexican-descent workers joined African Americans and Puerto Ricans in annual treks through the coastal states as far north as New York. The largest stream of Chicanos/as and Mexican immigrants fanned out from Texas to the deep South, the Midwest, the Great Plains, the Rocky Mountain states, California, and the Northwest. A third migratory movement involved workers from Arizona and Southern California who headed to the mega-agricultural areas of the Golden State and the fields of Oregon, Washington, and Idaho.

Armies of transient men, both U.S.-born and foreign-born, congregated in rundown sections of agricultural towns looking for work. Economist and labor activist Ernesto Galarza provides a graphic description of these depressing places, commonly referred to as skid rows:

These were rows of rundown rooming houses where single wanderers could "flop" for a night or longer, shuffling out in the early morning darkness to make sidewalk deals with the truckers who operated the day haul. Job offers were hawked by foremen and growers who pulled away when a gang was aboard. As daylight came over the dismal scene the crowd on the sidewalks thinned, leaving stragglers who filed out of sight into dingy shops for bad coffee and cheap wine. Occasionally a police patrol car would circle the area, marking the limits within which idle skid-rowers could wander. At night the trucks returned, spilling along the row tired men who disappeared into dank rooms smelling of disinfectant or shuffled to the evening handout of food under the illuminated cross of the Salvation Army which said with persistent compassion: "Jesus Saves."[11]

Throughout the latter twentieth century, migrant workers constituted an essential labor force in agriculture, but mechanization of work brought about a sharp drop in their numbers. By the late 1960s more than half of the overall vegetable crop production and nearly all of the major vegetable crops were mechanized. The shrinkage of jobs caused by mechanization worsened already bad conditions for farmworkers. Countless government reports and academic studies from the 1960s to the 1990s documented the persistence of unemployment and underemployment, low wages, substandard housing, discrimination, lack of educational opportunities, and serious health problems, including illnesses caused by pesticide poisoning. At the end of the twentieth century, farmworkers and their families continued to be the most marginalized sector of the U.S. population.

UNIONIZATION MOVEMENTS

The chronic concern with survival and the constant need to migrate made it exceedingly difficult for farmworkers to collectively press employers for higher wages and better working and living conditions. Yet contrary to popular perceptions regarding the alleged passivity of farmworkers and the impossibility of organizing them, there have been many efforts to build unions in the fields, and some movements have yielded substantial gains for the workers.

Although work stoppages and promotion of unionization among Mexican-descent workers in rural areas of the United States are not unknown prior to 1900,[12] such activity is more associated with the twentieth century. Dissatisfaction with wages and working conditions became widespread by the turn of the century, and fieldworkers responded favorably to calls for action by independent organizers as well as U.S. radical unions such as the Industrial Workers of the World (IWW) and the Mexican labor-oriented movement led by the Partido Liberal Mexicano (Mexican Liberal Party). Between 1900 and 1940 many strikes erupted throughout the Southwest.

In Texas, farmworkers joined independent associations such as La Agrupación Protectora Mexicana (Mexican Protective Association) and La Asociación de Jornaleros (Association of Journeymen Workers) to counter exploitation and abuse. They also became members of the Catholic Workers Union and of leftist groups such as the Land League of America, an affiliate of the Texas Socialist Party. In the years before World War I perhaps up to one thousand Tejanos belonged to labor-oriented socialist organizations. By the late 1930s, large numbers of Tejano field hands and packing-shed workers belonged to the militant United Cannery, Agricultural, Packing, and Allied Workers of America (UCAPAWA), a Congress of Industrial Organizations (CIO) affiliate. Examples of militant activity in Texas launched by workers independently or as part of organized unions include an onion strike in Asherton in 1912, a strike by sheep shearers in west Texas in 1934, a strike of harvesters in Laredo in 1935, and a strike of cotton pickers in Brownsville-McAllen in 1937.[13]

In Arizona, organizing efforts by the State Federation of Labor and the Trade Union Unity League centered on cotton workers. In 1920, about four thousand fieldworkers in the Tempe area braved a harsh antilabor climate and struck cotton growers who predictably used police repression against the workers, including arranging for the deportation of several leaders. In 1933, about 2,500 cotton laborers struck in Yuma, and the following year a like number walked off their jobs in the Phoenix area.

But farmworkers in California engaged in the most militant and prolonged organized labor activity. In 1903, the first strike involving large numbers of Mexicans and Mexican Americans took place in Oxnard, when approximately one thousand workers walked out of the sugar-beet fields under the sponsorship of the Japanese-Mexican Labor Association. Although the workers did not achieve many of their objectives, they managed to reduce the control of a monopolistic contracting company. To the dismay of the strikers, mainstream unions offered little support, a situation that would be repeated frequently in the years ahead. Worse yet, the American Federation of Labor (AFL) turned down the strikers' request for membership as a reorganized union called the Sugar Beet and Farm Laborers' Union of Oxnard. Revealing a streak of racism, AFL president Samuel Gompers agreed to grant the desired charter only if the union guaranteed "that it will under no circumstances accept membership of any Chinese or Japanese." The secretary of the union made it clear that such a condition was unacceptable:

> We [Mexicans] are going to stand by men who stood by us in the long, hard fight which ended in a victory over the enemy. We therefore respectfully petition the AFL to grant us a charter under which we can unite all the sugar beet and field laborers of Oxnard without regard to their color or race. We will refuse any other kind of charter except one which will wipe out race prejudices and recognize our fellow workers as being as good as ourselves.[14]

Another significant labor disturbance of the early twentieth century occurred at the Hurst Ranch in Wheatland, California, in 1913. Hops growers created an explosive situation by recruiting almost twice as many workers as needed in the fields. Close to three thousand workers arrived from throughout the West, including large numbers of non-English-speaking people of many nationalities. The labor surplus encouraged abuses by the growers and created wretched conditions among workers stranded in the camp. As tensions mounted at a mass meeting, deputy sheriffs fired a shot to scare the crowd but instead provoked a riot that left four people dead, including the district attorney and a deputy sheriff. Murder charges against IWW leaders resulted in the conviction and imprisonment of two men.

In the 1920s and 1930s, Mexicans and Mexican Americans in California intensified their participation in unionization movements. In 1927 they established the Confederación de Uniones Obreras Mexicanas (Confederation of Mexican Workers' Unions, or CUOM), a coalition of some twenty locals with a membership of about three thousand. In 1928 CUOM called its first strike in the Imperial Valley, but it was broken up through arrests and deportations. Two years later CUOM struck again but, after some gains early on, the movement fizzled as a result of vicious police intervention. In 1933, some of the largest agricultural disturbances in history took place in the San Gabriel Valley. During the summer about seven thousand workers in the berry, onion, and celery fields struck for higher wages, and in the fall some 12,000 cotton pickers walked off their jobs for the same reason.

Tensions produced by worker militancy, aggressive grower actions, and police intervention caused one newspaper to compare conditions in the fields during the cotton strike to "a smouldering volcano." In 1936, violence erupted again in Los Angeles County when 1,500 police officers began making arrests among 2,000 striking celery workers. In the same year 2,500 citrus workers in Orange County struck for several weeks, but the familiar pattern of violence and arrests was repeated, effectively ending the strike. In all, an estimated 127,000 workers participated in 140 strikes in California during the 1930s, often receiving direct help and inspiration from radical elements in Mexico as well as support from Mexican consuls in the United States.[15]

The period between World War II and the mid-1960s presented unique difficulties for the agricultural unionization movement because of the anti-labor climate created by the Cold War and the existence of the Bracero Program, which supplied growers with large numbers of foreign workers. UCAPAWA, which included thousands of minority women members, flourished during the 1940s but perished by 1951. At its peak, UCAPAWA successfully negotiated contracts that provided benefits such as maternity leave, day care, and vacation pay. Many U.S. and foreign-born Latinas, including veteran labor activist Luisa Moreno, UCAPAWA vice president, participated in the union's activities. Rank and file workers learned valuable leadership and organizational skills as they managed local chapters. Spanish-surname women comprised 21 percent of the top officers of the California locals of this militant union, 46 percent of the executive boards, and 43 percent of the shop stewards. The dream of building a permanent, strong, and democratic food-processing union with significant participation by women eroded rapidly by the late 1940s when the Teamsters Union muscled its way into the industry, aided by the political attacks on UCAPAWA by anti-Communist spokespeople. In the 1950s the U.S. government deported Moreno because of her alleged affiliation with the Communist Party and un-American activities. She eventually settled in Mexico.[16]

In the fields, native workers had to contend with the importation of Mexican nationals who were often used to undercut wages and break up strikes. Thousands of Mexican Americans responded to the challenge posed by the Bracero Program by joining the National Farm Workers Union (NFWU), an AFL union founded in 1947 by Ernesto Galarza. The NFWU and its successor the National Agricultural Workers Union (NAWU) fought tire-lessly to extinguish the Bracero Program and at the same time led strikes against California growers in the San Joaquin and Imperial Valleys. NAWU experienced limited success in winning strikes, and it faded after 1960. Yet its efforts laid the foundation for the creation of the Agricultural Work-ers Organizing Committee (AWOC) and the United Farm Workers Union (UFWU or UFW) by mid-decade. Galarza and other Hispanic and non-Hispanic labor leaders in both rural and urban areas mobilized sufficient public pressure to compel the U.S. Congress to terminate the Bracero Pro-gram in 1964. By then Americans had become more aware and sensitized to the needs of farmworkers and, as a result of the Civil Rights Movement, they had also developed greater understanding of the marginalized condi-tion of minorities such as African Americans and Mexican Americans. The climate was propitious for a new surge in unionization activity.

In 1965, the Filipino-led AWOC followed up a victory for higher wages in the Coachella Valley with a strike in the grape fields of Delano. When the growers put up stiff resistance to the demand for higher wages, AWOC leaders asked the National Farm Workers Association (NFWA), a union founded by César Chávez in 1962, to join the fray. The two unions merged into one in 1966, becoming the UFW. After winning contracts with the Schenley Corporation and the DiGiorgio Company, the new union launched strikes and an international boycott of grapes sold by growers who resisted unionization. This newfound assertiveness allowed the UFW to publicize the exploitation and impoverishment of workers, eliciting ex-traordinary sympathy and support in the United States and Europe. Chávez dramatized his commitment to nonviolence with marches, vigils, and hun-ger strikes. Following years of confrontations and some violence, in 1970 more than two dozen growers in Delano buckled under and signed con-tracts with the union. Farmworkers rightfully celebrated their hard-won victory. In the long and bitter history of agricultural unionization move-ments in the United States, there had never been a comparable accomplish-ment.

Chávez received much of credit for the early successes of the UFW, but many other people contributed significantly to the movement. Countless union leaders, workers, and volunteers played key participant and sup-portive roles in the fields and in cities throughout the United States. Many women successfully juggled family and work obligations and made time for union activism. Families often accompanied men on assignments to faraway places, thereby allowing activists such as Esther Padilla to work alongside her husband in garnering support for the union. The best-known woman in the movement is Dolores Huerta, the UFW vice president who has dedicated her adult life to the union's work. Her leadership abilities and tenacious negotiation style prompted growers to refer to her as the "Dragon Lady." Luis Valdez, the director of the workers' Teatro Campesino who eventually became a Hollywood moviemaker, recalled Huerta's commitment to the cause:

> Dolores was a 35 year old firebrand in 1965, and she was commanding crusty macho campesinos 20 years her senior. What dazzled my radicalized university-trained Chicano mind was that she led through persuasion and personal example, rather than intimidation, and that she was one hell of an organizer. . . . She was . . . a Chicana cutting a swath of revolutionary action across the torpidity of the San Joaquin Valley.[17]

In the 1970s the UFW continued to surmount great obstacles and bring more field hands under its fold. The number of contracts swelled to eighty, covering some 40,000 employees. For the first time large numbers of workers enjoyed decent wages and basic health coverage and other benefits. Feelings of pride, dignity, self-worth, self-respect, and empowerment permeated rural California. Farmworkers reached another milestone in 1975 when, with the prompting of Governor Jerry Brown Jr., the California legislature charged the newly created Agricultural Labor Relations Board (ALRB) with the supervision of union elections to assure that workers had the opportunity to make their choices secretly and without intimidation. In head-to-head competition during 1975–1976, the UFW won 154 elections while the Teamsters won 91; in 1980–1982 the UFW won 53 elections and the Teamsters won only 5. Clearly the ALRB was a godsend for the UFW, but pro-grower forces in the legislature constantly threatened its survival by pressing for termination of its funding. To eliminate its vulnerability in the political arena, Chávez in 1976 led a referendum effort to have the voters approve funding for the ALRB. The growers opposed the measure and it failed. Weakened but still functional, the ALRB continued its work. Then in the mid-1980s conservative Governor George Deukmejian slashed its budget and allowed it to evolve into a pro-grower agency. Farmworkers quickly lost confidence in the ALRB and lobbied for its elimination.

The transformation of the ALRB underscored a precipitous decline in the farmworkers movement. By the mid-1970s membership in the UFW had dropped to about five thousand, and serious internal dissension began to surface. At the 1981 annual UFW convention, 14 percent of the delegates walked out, accusing the leadership of heavy-handed tactics and undemocratic behavior. Firings and resignations of top officials followed that incident. Loss of contracts, power struggles, squabbles over leadership, union involvement in nonlabor matters, court battles with growers, and questions over union finances continued to plague the UFW in the 1980s and 1990s. The union suffered an especially traumatic blow when Chávez died in 1993. That year the UFW membership stood at 21,000, compared to 80,000 in the halcyon days of 1970.[18]

One of the most important legacies of the Chávez-led movement was the blossoming of new unionization activity throughout the country. Yet many workers outside California favored home-grown, independent unions over the UFW. In Texas, former UFW official Antonio Orendáin joined local efforts to establish the United Texas Farm Workers (UTFW or TFW). This union modestly advanced the cause of Tejano/a fieldworkers. Its strikes, however, were largely unsuccessful. In Arizona, the Maricopa County Organizing Project (MCOP) managed to integrate disaffected members of the UFW and other labor activists and formed the Arizona Farm Workers Union (AFWU). In 1977, the Arizona union struck in Maricopa County and at Arrowhead Ranch. Significantly, large numbers of undocumented workers participated in the strike at Arrowhead. Two years later the AFWU forced growers to sign a contract at Goldmar Ranch. In the Midwest, Latinos/as and other workers established the influential Farm Labor Organizing Committee (FLOC) in the late 1960s. FLOC managed to secure dozens of contracts during the 1970s and 1980s. In the mid-1980s, farmworkers in Oregon founded the Pineros y Campesinos Unidos del Noroeste (PCUN), while workers in Washington founded the United Farm Workers of Washington State (UFWWS).

Despite the unionization movements and sustained efforts of supporters to promote the interests of farmworkers over the last several decades, real wages in agriculture plunged by 20 percent or more between the late

1970s and late 1990s. Increasingly workers had to choose between accepting cuts in wages and benefits or losing their jobs. For example, in 1985 1,700 cannery strikers in Watsonville, California, most of them Mexicanas and Chicanas, accepted a cut in wages from $7.07 to $5.85 per hour as well as a reduction in medical benefits. Wages for strawberry workers in Watsonville went down from $6.55 an hour in 1985 to $6.25 in 1997. In Salinas, growers set the minimum wage at $6.00 an hour, compared to the union standard of $7.05 in the early 1980s.

Clearly the decline of the UFW contributed to the erosion of wages, but continuous large-scale immigration of cheap labor from Mexico and elsewhere exacerbated the problem. Yet the UFW continued to press forward to regain lost ground. Led by Arturo Rodríguez, Chávez's son-in-law, the union took on the task of organizing the strawberry workers. In an impressive show of force, 25,000 workers and sympathizers turned out for a solidarity march in Watsonville on April 13, 1997. Representatives from organized labor, civil rights leaders, and movie stars spoke at the rally. In May 1999, however, the UFW suffered a crushing setback when, in a key election, a majority of strawberry workers in Salinas voted to be represented by the Coastal Berry of California Farm Worker Committee, a local union with ties to the growers.

Today the farmworkers movement faces an uphill struggle to overcome the many setbacks experienced in recent years. Employers continue to have the upper hand in shaping policy and conditions in the workplace. And there is the constant threat of government approval of a grower-friendly guest worker program that would allow the importation of large numbers of immigrant workers. Two proposals along these lines surfaced in Congress in 1998. The following year Governor Jane Hull of Arizona escalated her lobbying campaign to create a new Bracero Program.

Railroad Workers

GENERAL CONDITIONS

The construction of railroad lines in the borderlands in the late nineteenth century introduced an important new source of employment for Mexican-origin workers largely concentrated in the agrarian sector. U.S. companies such as the Southern Pacific and Santa Fe tapped labor pools from both sides of the border to build lines across the Southwest and to maintain those already in place. In 1909, an official study revealed that Mexican immigrants dominated railroad construction in New Mexico, Nevada, Arizona, and California. During World War I, railroad companies persuaded the U.S. government to allow recruitment of Mexican nationals for track maintenance. By the 1920s, more than 40,000 Chicanos/as and Mexican nationals worked for railroad companies that had operations throughout the Southwest. Many other *traqueros* (trackmen) found employment far from the borderlands, including Kansas City and Chicago, where they made up 91 percent and 43 percent of all railroad workers, respectively, in 1927–1928.[19]

No doubt reflecting the patronizing and racist views of railroad company officials, the U.S. commissioner-general of immigration explained that Mexicans were ideal railroad workers because of their ability to withstand the heat and other harsh conditions peculiar to the industry. "The peon makes a satisfactory track hand," he added, "for the reasons that he is docile, ignorant, and nonclannish to an extent which makes it possible that one or more men shall quit or be discharged and others remain at work; moreover, he is willing to work for a low wage."[20] Two other observers marveled at the endurance displayed by Mexicans as they performed backbreaking work:

[First observer:] You see that poor devil out there lifting that heavy iron? He is as strong as an ox. . . . Right now he has to have two pairs of gloves so as not to blister his calloused hands. Those are Mexicans. . . . They work when we are sleeping, mush around in the water in big rains. . . . When a wreck occurs, they are the first to get there though it be, as it usually is, at night. . . .

[Second observer:] Yes, and what kind of a chance have they to enjoy their work? They are doing work that the average American would not and cannot think of doing. Last week . . . in the desert the heat killed three Mexicans and prostrated a score more. The temperature was up to 120 degrees.[21]

In order to facilitate the steady flow of laborers from Mexico, the railroad companies engaged the services of employment agencies based at the border, especially in El Paso, where most immigrants entered the United States. Recruiters arranged for transportation for the workers to their destinations, taking care of their basic needs while in transit. Later the companies deducted those and other expenses from the workers' paychecks, often at inflated prices. The border employment agencies processed thousands of Mexicans every year, keeping pace with the ever-rising demand of the companies.

While employers frequently provided housing for the workers, the conditions were far from favorable. Poverty and substandard services predominated in many of the labor camps, making life bleak for the workers and their families. Historian Michael Smith provides a concise description of the hardships that employees in the Kansas City area had to endure in their daily lives during the 1910s:

> Most railroad workers typically lived in boxcar camps. In these crude settlements, situated in the yards or on sidings, workers slept on straw or rough bunks. Even the "improved" housing which the Santa Fe furnished for its workers after 1912 consisted of uncomfortable shacks made from scrap pieces and cheap, secondhand materials including old ties, rails, and sheet metal. The company supplied no furniture, plumbing, or electrical facilities. Workers assigned to the yards often lived packed together in a single large building called a section house; others crammed into small two-room section huts.[22]

Residents of communities that adjoined the railroad camps frequently sought to keep the workers physically segregated. In Cholo Hollow, a barrio in San Bernardino, California, that served as a labor camp for the Santa Fe Railroad Company, Mexicans faced hostility from local residents who resented the company's 1909 plan to move the colony closer to them. Located at the entrance to the city, the camp had become an "eyesore," and company officials wished to shift it to a less conspicuous and more convenient location. European Americans threatened to "give the newcomers a hot reception," but fortunately the move took place without incident.[23]

As in other industries, railroad workers suffered from a variety of employer abuses. Victor S. Clark reported in 1908 that the Southern Pacific Railroad paid Mexican-descent section hands $1.25 per day, while Japanese workers made $1.45 and Greeks $1.60. In 1916, hundreds of workers complained that the Pennsylvania Railroad had reneged on its promise to pay them $1.80 per day, that the company had made excessive deductions on their paychecks, that contract guarantees pertaining to housing and health care had not been carried out, and that mistreatment by offensive foremen had not been curtailed.[24]

UNIONIZATION MOVEMENTS

Low wages and discrimination by the railroads inevitably led to walkouts and work stoppages. Many workers who did not find railroad work to their liking, or who learned of higher-paying job opportunities in urban industries, simply skipped out of their contracts. Others turned to Mexican consuls for assistance in resolving grievances. When all else failed, they went on strike. One of the earliest strikes occurred near Yuma, Arizona, in 1897, when two hundred workers walked off their jobs. In Los Angeles in 1905, seven hundred Mexicans and Mexican Americans employed by the Pacific Electric Railway left their jobs in response to the company's rejection of their wage demands. In subsequent decades Mexican-origin workers frequently joined with other employees to press the railroads for higher wages, better working conditions, and improved benefits. Employer resistance to change made confrontation inevitable, and strikes became a common occurrence.

One of the little-known chapters in the history of railroad workers is the participation in the 1940s of some 100,000 guest workers from Mexico in maintenance work as part of the Bracero Program. Companies such as Southern Pacific; Atchison, Topeka, and Santa Fe; and Western Pacific each contracted thousands of Mexicans to meet emergency needs during World War II. While many of these railroad braceros worked in the Southwest, large numbers wound up in places far from the border such as Utah, Oregon, New York, and Connecticut. In a number of localities braceros made up the bulk of the railroad labor force.

As in other industries during the war, workers and the railroad companies put aside their differences for the good of the country. But after the war tensions resumed. Eventually the climate became less polarized when companies accepted the reality of stronger unions and government protection for workers. Thus unionization increased significantly in the 1940s and 1950s. As discrimination against ethnic minorities subsided, Mexican Americans managed to climb the employment ladder into mechanical, supervisory, and administrative positions. Such a transformation happened in Tucson, where the Southern Pacific, in collaboration with European American–controlled unions, had long kept Mexican-origin workers locked in the lowest-paying jobs. By midcentury, Tucsonense railroad workers were faring much better. Despite advances in Tucson and other places, however, most Latino/a railroad workers nationwide remained concentrated in the menial sector into the 1990s. Moreover, the decline of the industry brought a reduction of employment opportunities.

Los Mineros

GENERAL CONDITIONS

Along with Native Americans and Spaniards, Mexican miners had participated in mining operations in the Southwest for centuries prior to the U.S. conquest of the 1840s. The extraction of precious metals from the earth had been given high priority by both the Spanish and Mexican governments. Not surprisingly, then, *mineros* from the provinces acquired by the United States as well as from prime Mexican mining states such as Sonora and Chihuahua took part in the California gold rush of 1849 and in subsequent gold and silver strikes in Nevada, Arizona, and Colorado.

With the onset of rapid industrialization in the United States during the latter nineteenth century, Mexican-origin workers entered the mining industry in unprecedented numbers. At that time the copper mines, especially in Arizona, expanded their operations to meet demands created by the spread of electricity, and employers eagerly recruited experienced miners from south of the border. But many difficulties beset the workers because of poor conditions and discriminatory practices found throughout the industry. Differential wage scales for European Americans and Mexicans/ Mexican Americans were common. For example, in the late 1870s, Mexican-descent miners made from $0.50 to $1.50 per day, while European Americans doing the same work made $2.00 to $3.00. By 1895, the average wage for unskilled Mexican/Mexican American workers stood at about $2.00 per day, remaining at that level for the next fifteen years. By contrast, the wages paid European American workers rose steadily to about $4.00 during the same period. Copper companies routinely placed Mexican-origin workers in a lower-wage payroll category labeled "Mexican labor," creating a dual wage structure that remained in effect through the 1940s. Unequal treatment on the job also extended to community life, where Mexicans and Mexican Americans lived segregated from European Americans in the mining camps and towns. Certain mining communities became known as Mexican camps, while others were identified as white camps. European Americans often referred to the Mexican sections of mining camps as "frog-towns" and "jim-towns."[25]

In their misguided desire to elevate themselves above the Mexican-origin workers, European American miners seriously undermined unionization efforts. The first strike in the copper mines of Arizona actually centered around the issue of hiring Mexican immigrants. The Western Federation of Miners (WFM) struck the Old Dominion mine in 1896 in an effort to drive out this sector of the labor force. Employers derived significant advantage from the proximity of the border, since they could import low-paid foreign labor, thereby frustrating unionization drives and strengthening antagonistic feelings among European American miners toward Spanish-speaking workers.

Without the help of European American unions, Mexican-origin miners found it difficult to force employers to improve working conditions and grant them higher wages. Nevertheless, they fought for their rights as best as they could. A major confrontation involving thousands of Mexican and Chicano/a miners took place at Clifton-Morenci in 1903 over a decrease in work time in the mines, which in effect reduced the earnings of the workers. Since European American unions had largely written off Clifton-Morenci because of its predominantly "foreign" workforce, the strike caught nearly everyone, including labor leaders, by surprise. In the absence of union assistance, Spanish-surname miners were able to coordinate their protest by other means, particularly through *mutualista* (mutual aid) organizations. Strikers halted production for several days, but a flood and the intervention of Arizona Rangers and federal troops ended the dispute.

Unfavorable publicity given the Clifton-Morenci strike by pro-employer newspapers hurt the image of Mexican-descent workers among the public at large, but their determination caused mainstream unions to take them more seriously. In fact, the WFM temporarily suspended its anti-Mexican strategy during the strike. Once the strike ended, however, the European American unions reverted to their entrenched opposition to "alien" labor. The growing presence of immigrants in the Arizona mines became an increasingly bitter issue for the European American miners.

In 1910, the mainstream unions joined forces with the Democratic Party in a campaign to restrict the hiring of Mexican workers. One successful bill in the Arizona territorial legislature excluded noncitizens from working on public works projects. Another bill that did not pass sought to prevent employers from importing aliens as contract workers. The most controversial proposal during the legislative session required that 80 percent of all workers hired by any individual or firm be U.S. citizens; the same bill also ordered employers not to hire non-English-speaking workers for hazardous jobs. Cognizant of voter support, lawmakers clearly aimed such legislation at the Mexican workers. In effect, the Arizona electorate overwhelmingly approved the 80 percent rule through an initiative in 1914. The following year, however, the U.S. Supreme Court ruled that referendum unconstitutional. Thereafter attempts continued to be made to drive out Mexican workers from Arizona jobs, but the labor-Democratic coalition soon faltered and the movement dissipated.

Despite the unfavorable climate, Mexican workers kept migrating into Arizona and steadfastly demanded justice in the workplace. In 1915, about five thousand Mexicans/Mexican Americans struck the mines at Clifton-Morenci and Metcalf over discriminatory wages and the foremen's custom of selling jobs and forcing workers to buy raffle tickets as a requisite for keeping their employment. The strike lasted almost five months, but the arrest of hundreds of miners by the National Guard finally ended it. Two years later, a strike at Bisbee and at Jerome became infamous because of the inhumane treatment of the strikers. Close to two thousand workers, both European American and Mexican/Mexican American, were rounded up and shipped in railroad boxcars to the desert in New Mexico, where they were dumped and left to fend for themselves.

The hostile environment in Arizona prompted many miners to seek employment elsewhere, although their destinations are unknown. Most likely some workers ventured to mining areas in nearby states, while others left the border region altogether. But they could not escape the unfavorable conditions that permeated the mining industry. For example, in the coalfields of Oklahoma, where Mexicans had worked since the 1890s, miners encountered less repression but not equal treatment. Employers reserved the skilled jobs for white Americans or English-speaking immigrants, relegating Mexicans to the lowest-paying jobs. Coal miners worked under exceedingly risky circumstances, with explosions and cave-ins causing frequent deaths and injuries. Employers added to the misery of the workers by confining them to cheap, dreary, and overcrowded housing that lacked indoor plumbing and sanitary services.

For many years Mexican-origin miners concentrated on surviving the unfavorable climate that prevailed throughout the mining industry, hoping that in the future better conditions for labor organizing would unfold. But they had to wait a long time. The public perception that radical and disloyal elements dominated the labor movement played into the hands of the mining companies, making it easier for them to utilize heavy-handed legal measures and even violence to break the strikes.

In the 1920s Mexican immigrants came under increasing attack by nativists and politicians who blamed foreigners for myriad problems in American society. Then the Great Depression of the 1930s forced a severe cutback in mining operations, and many workers lost their jobs. Pressured by anti-immigrant groups and government officials, thousands left the mining districts and repatriated to Mexico. Others, especially labor leaders, faced forcible expulsion.

Chihuahua native Jesús Pallares, who led the effort to organize La Liga Obrera de Habla Española (The Spanish-Speaking Labor League) in New Mexico, became one such deportee. He played a central role in a raucous mid-1930s strike in Gallup that involved thousands of coal miners. Rioting broke out when the authorities expelled a few hundred workers from land on which they had squatted. Imposition of martial law followed, lasting six months. La Liga succeeded in protecting the strikers from unjust prosecution, but it could not prevent the deportation of Pallares in 1936.

The repression in the mining districts began to ease during World War II, when the United States experienced renewed demand for metals, and the need for labor in basic extractive industries received nationwide priority. The President's Committee on Fair Employment Practices exposed the extant widespread discrimination against Mexican-origin miners and helped establish a foundation for the positive changes that would occur in later years. On the labor union front, the recently created militant International Union of Mine, Mill and Smelter Workers embraced the struggle of miners in Arizona and elsewhere, and a renewed drive ensued to unionize the industry. Veterans from the war returning to their jobs were particularly

adamant about abolishing the dual-wage and dual-job policies still practiced by the mining companies. After years of frustrating negotiations between Mine, Mill and Smelter Workers and such giants as Phelps Dodge
and the American Smelting and Refining Company (ASARCO), the union
called a nationwide strike in 1946. The landmark confrontation lasted four
months, with Mine Mill workers coming out as clear winners. Many of the
exploitative and oppressive conditions that had prevailed for so long were
eliminated, and Spanish-surname copper miners, along with other workers, achieved higher wages, greater job security, and even some political
power.

Stiff opposition to worker demands persisted, however, and bitter con-
flicts broke out during the McCarthy era, when political and corporate
leaders equated militant unionism with anti-American radicalism. For example, a widely publicized strike occurred in Silver City, New Mexico, during a fifteen-month period from 1950 to 1952. Workers from Mine Mill
Local 890, comprised mostly of Mexicans and Mexican Americans, left
their jobs at Empire Zinc when the company failed to negotiate many
grievances, including discriminatory treatment. Predictably, the authorities sided with management, issuing an injunction that forced the workers to end their picketing. To avoid arrest, women took over the picketing,
prompting the authorities to arrest forty-five of them. The steadfast support
of the women's auxiliary for the strikers and their courage on the picket
line, including facing threats of violence, caused great excitement and inspiration for people concerned with workers' rights. In the end the company
managed to suppress the strike, but the strikers succeeded in disseminat-
ing their message far beyond Silver City. Sympathetic moviemakers told
their gripping story in the classic film *Salt of the Earth*. The film itself generated considerable publicity because conservatives in the U.S. Congress
denounced it as Communist propaganda and local mobs attacked the film
crew, warning them at one point to "get out of Grant County or go out
in black boxes." Moreover, the INS arrested Mexican actress Rosaura Re-
vueltas, the star of the movie, accusing her of having entered the country
illegally.

By the 1980s, as demand for metals declined and the antilabor climate
promoted by the Reagan administration took hold, miners suffered significant setbacks. In 1983 in Clifton, Arizona, a strike against Phelps Dodge

broke out over proposed reduction of benefits. Once again women played a prominent role in the strike. Members of the Morenci Miners Women's Auxiliary provided food, fuel, and transportation to strikers and their supporters. They also maintained picket lines, nurtured striking families, and sought help outside of Morenci. But the strike could not overcome the power of the company. With the protection of state troopers and the National Guard, Phelps Dodge kept the mines open by using replacement workers. In 1984 the employees, almost half of them scabs, voted to decertify the United Steel Workers of America as the union that represented the miners. Two years later the National Labor Relations Board confirmed the decertification. Miners in Arizona and elsewhere had lost important gains that they had achieved in previous decades.

Urban Workers

GENERAL CONDITIONS

During the long process of urbanization of the Southwest, both men and women of Mexican descent have filled many different occupations typically found in cities, although most jobs held by these workers have been in the unskilled, low-wage category. Only since World War II have significant numbers held well-paying blue-collar and white-collar jobs. Over the long term, the main sectors in which most ordinary Mexican-origin workers have been concentrated include construction, transportation, manufacturing, cleaning and maintenance, and restaurant work.

Studies in the early twentieth century revealed the presence of Mexicans and Mexican Americans in a variety of occupations. Victor Clark reported in 1908 that Spanish-surname workers in Southern California were amply represented in construction, road work, and public works projects. Two decades later another study indicated that about 28,000 Mexican-origin employees held industrial jobs throughout the state. Almost half of the 695 establishments surveyed reported hiring Mexicans/Mexican Americans. The range of activities included stone, clay, and glass products; metals and machinery; wood manufactures; chemicals, oils, and paints; printing and paper goods; textiles; clothing, millinery, and laundering; and foods, beverage, and tobacco. Much the same pattern of diversified employment could be found in other cities and towns in the Southwest.[26]

Although employed in smaller numbers than men, women also held a variety of urban jobs. A study conducted by Paul S. Taylor in Los Angeles in 1928 documented that Mexicanas and Chicanas worked in offices and in such industries as packinghouses, canneries, textile and apparel plants, shoe factories, laundries, and tortilla plants. Another study that focused on San Diego concluded that half of the Mexican/Mexican American married women in the survey had jobs outside the home and that they contributed significantly to the support of their families. In Detroit, Mexican-origin women held a wide variety of service, clerical, and industrial jobs, working as janitors, laundry workers, domestics, dishwashers, waitresses, cooks, elevator operators, salespersons, cashiers, messengers, needle workers, cigar makers, hairdressers, nurses' and doctors' assistants, inspectors, packers, glass cutters, and solderers.[27] Some women opted for running *casas de asistencia*, or boarding homes, as a way of earning extra income for their families. Such work was frequently all-consuming, as historian Zaragosa Vargas has noted:

> Operating a casa de asistencia was hard work . . . , often as exhausting as the labor the men performed in the factories. In addition to family duties like child rearing, the women likely kept up a hectic pace all day as they fed the men coming and going on the different shifts. They had to reorder cooking schedules, as some men wanted breakfast at dinnertime while others wanted their dinner in the morning. Long hours were spent not only cooking and shopping for food but doing laundry and performing additional housekeeping tasks.[28]

By 1930 most Mexican-origin workers in the industrial centers of the Midwest, both men and women, held jobs in manufacturing. Many of them readily obtained work in major centers such as Kansas City, Chicago, and Detroit and smaller places such as Gary. Historian Richard Santillán writes that Mexicans and Mexican Americans could be found in scores of industries, including "automobile plants, lumber mills, packing houses, tanneries, sugar refineries, oil refineries, nitrate plants, textile mills, farm and construction equipment plants, paint factories, ice houses, and on the docks of the Great Lakes ports."[29] In Chicago, more than six thousand Mexicans/Mexican Americans worked in the steel mills, making up about 14 percent of the labor force. Plants in nearby communities employed thousands more. In Detroit four thousand Mexicans/Mexican Americans worked at the Ford Motor Company, a prime employer in the region.[30]

The fact that Mexican-descent workers obtained employment in so many different industries reveals that they were seen as desirable employees. In California, almost 70 percent of the 312 firms that responded to an official questionnaire in 1928 expressed satisfaction with their Spanish-surname employees. Among comments submitted by different employers are the following:[31]

All Mexicans . . . are good workers.

We find that they are as efficient as any other nationality in the capacities in which they are employed.

We pay Mexicans exactly the [same] scale as other nationalities if they are doing the same work; and it has been our experience that, treated in this manner, they make very loyal and efficient employees. At first we only used them in the common labor manual jobs, but the more intelligent are gradually working up into the better-paid positions with the company.

Interestingly, several employers commented on the advantage of hiring Mexicanas/Chicanas in preference to European American women. One fruit-packing-plant official put it this way: "At the beginning of the season, preference in employment was given to white women. Some of them were so slow and otherwise unsatisfactory that they were let off and replaced by Mexican women who were superior workers. Mexican women are clean and neat workers."[32]

The minority of firms that expressed dissatisfaction with Mexican-descent workers complained mainly of inefficiency, laziness, low productivity, and unreliability. A number of companies stated that they preferred not to hire members of this ethnic group because they were not as good as other nationalities, but the shortage of workers compelled them to do so against their wishes. "Mexican labor is not as reliable as white labor," stated the response from an official of a manufacturing plant, "but they will work in the heat where it is hard to keep other labor."[33] Given prevailing attitudes during the period, it is likely that negative characterizations of Mexican-origin workers stemmed significantly from stereotypes. Undoubtedly some Mexicans/Mexican Americans did not perform well on the job, as would be true for any other group.

World War II marked a major turning point for Spanish-surname workers, as it did for other workers in the United States. Labor shortages in the cities opened new opportunities, and increasing numbers of Mexicans and Mexican Americans entered the industrial labor force. With many of the men serving in the military, women eagerly stepped into occupations previously unavailable to them. The contributions of thousands of women to the economy and the defense of the nation during a time of emergency were indeed considerable, as Richard Santillán has written:

> Mexican American women, in both the Midwest and the Southwest regions, labored as riveters, crane operators, welders, assemblers, railroad section workers, roundhouse mechanics, forklift operators, meatpackers, farmworkers, seamstresses, nurses, secretaries, and shipbuilders. They assisted in the critical production of aircraft, tanks, trucks, jeeps, ships, uniforms, tents, medical supplies, small arms, heavy artillery, ammunition, bombs, and communication equipment. The industrial work which they engaged in was extremely hazardous and physically strenuous, often requiring lengthy hours with few days for rest and relaxation during the entire war.[34]

One of the most dramatic developments since the 1940s has been the growing proportion of Mexican-origin women in the workplace. Before World War II female workers made up less than a fifth of employed Mexicans/Mexican Americans in the Southwest, but by the 1980s they surpassed the 50 percent mark. In 1993, the U.S. Department of Labor reported that the number of female Hispanics (including Chicanas) in the workforce had risen from 2.1 million to 3.7 million over the preceding decade, a climb of 76 percent. Of course, as is true for the men as well, working Hispanic women have been concentrated in unskilled, low-wage jobs.

An encouraging trend is the growing number of workers from both genders who have been able to climb the occupational ladder. That development is the result of rising opportunities in certain sectors of the economy, declining discrimination, and higher levels of education. This has led to the expansion of the Mexican/Mexican American middle class, a subject taken up in chapter 6.

The recent upward mobility, however, does not eliminate the reality that significant portions of the community have remained behind. Poverty, inadequate education, segregation, and discrimination continue to present formidable barriers to advancement for many at the bottom. But perhaps the most significant cause of stagnation, and even regression, is economic restructuring. Since the 1970s the United States has lost millions of manufacturing jobs as a result of automation, the shift to a service economy, and globalization. At the same time, massive relocation of jobs within the country itself has left many cities with much reduced opportunities in the blue-collar sector, an important avenue for social mobility in previous generations. Low-income Hispanics, African Americans, and other people residing in inner-city neighborhoods have been devastated by these trends.

UNIONIZATION MOVEMENTS

Throughout the twentieth century significant numbers of Mexican-origin urban workers sought to improve their condition by forming new unions or joining existing European American unions. Unfortunately for decades mainstream unions such as the AFL practiced discrimination, especially against immigrants, forcing these workers to carry on their struggles independently or to seek affiliation with more inclusive radical unions such as the IWW and the International Union of Mine, Mill, and Smelter Workers. Along with rural workers in the border area, urban workers drew inspiration and often received help from labor leaders in Mexico and from the labor-related efforts of the radical Partido Liberal Mexicano. The AFL did include U.S. citizens of Mexican descent in some craft locals, but the numbers were small because few such workers had skilled jobs. When the racial climate improved in the United States, Mexican Americans in many skilled occupations became members of a wide variety of AFL locals and other mainstream unions. Immigrants, however, continued to struggle for acceptance in organized labor.

The twentieth century witnessed thousands of strikes and other labor confrontations involving urban Mexican-origin workers. Between 1900 and 1930, laborers in such varied sectors as construction, transportation, maritime shipping, smelters, cement plants, steel mills, auto plants, garment factories, laundries, and canneries work fought important battles in southwestern and midwestern cities. Often the workers did not succeed in winning strikes or even building strong unions, but these experiences paved the way for the advances recorded in later generations. For example, during the 1910s and 1920s hundreds of Mexican-descent workers from port cities such as Seattle, Washington; San Pedro, California; and Galveston, Texas, participated in a number of longshoreman strikes. Many of those workers would become activists and leaders in future work stoppages on the docks or would participate in union activity in other industries. In some areas Mexican-origin women played important roles in the early labor movement. In El Paso, hundreds of laundresses formed the Laundry Workers Union and went on strike in 1919 because of substandard wages. Since most were U.S. citizens, the AFL assisted them. Although the laundry workers lost the strike because the employers quickly replaced them with foreign laborers, the dispute raised the consciousness of the workers and community residents. The conflict also allowed women to acquire important leadership and organizational skills.

The Great Depression precipitated unprecedented labor turmoil throughout the United States as American workers responded to massive layoffs and drastic drops in wages and living standards. In the early 1930s strikes involving large numbers of workers broke out in many cities. Violence became a frequent occurrence. Mainstream unions and leftist groups, including the Communist Party, stepped up their organizing efforts in the most marginalized sectors of the labor force, among them the Mexican-descent population.

In that climate of intense labor activism, increasing numbers of urban Mexican Americans and Mexican nationals joined the movement. Steelworkers in Chicago responded enthusiastically to union drives, supported strikes, and rose to leadership positions in the labor movement. Many affiliated with locals of the CIO, a federation that split off from the AFL in 1938. The CIO's efforts in Latino/a communities paid off in a big way. By 1942 it had organized 15,000 Mexican-origin workers in Los Angeles, with many of them filling leadership positions in their locals and acting as official representatives in the CIO council meetings and in regional and national conventions. Bert Corona, a prominent labor and political activist, emerged as a leader during this period. He launched his career by rising to the presidency of Local 26 of the International Longshoremen's and Warehousemen's Union in 1941, and in ensuing years he led many union drives in Los

Angeles. Later Corona would profitably use his extensive labor experience in political organizing.

The revitalized unionization movement of the 1930s reached many types of workers, even those in the lowest wage sectors. In El Paso, domestics organized the Asociación de Trabajadoras Domésticas in 1933. Although the Asociación made only modest gains in its short existence, women in a highly vulnerable occupation learned the power of collective action. A large percentage of Mexicanas/Chicanas worked in the garment industry, where strikes became common when the International Ladies Garment Workers Union (ILGWU) stepped up its organizing efforts. In 1933 and 1936, several thousand women walked off their jobs in Los Angeles, and in 1937 garment workers struck in San Antonio.

One of the best-known labor confrontations in the Southwest involving large numbers of Mexican-origin women is the 1938 pecan shellers strike in San Antonio, in which thousands of workers protested a wage cut and deplorable working conditions. Emma Tenayuca, a native San Antonian and a Communist affiliated with the Workers Alliance, emerged as the firebrand of the strikers. Eventually UCAPAWA assumed the leadership on behalf of the workers and they won some concessions. Within a short time, however, mechanization eliminated most of the pecan cracking and shelling jobs. As noted previously, UCAPAWA also played a significant role in the lives of thousands of women who worked in canneries and food-processing plants in California during the 1940s.

A more recent struggle (1972–1974) in which garment workers again had the spotlight is the strike and boycott against the Farah Manufacturing Company of El Paso. Women activists took action after the company refused to address their grievances, including unfair hiring and firing practices by company officials. The boycott spread nationwide and elicited substantial support from the public at large, forcing owner Willie Farah to recognize the Amalgamated Clothing Workers of America as the bargaining agent of the workers and to sign a contract. Though the terms of the contract were not as favorable as the workers had hoped for, they could justifiably claim a major victory. And they could take much pride and satisfaction from the example they had set for other workers. "When I walked out of that company," commented one of the strikers, "it was like I had taken a weight off my back. And I began to realize, 'Why did I put up with it all these years?

Why didn't I try for something else?' Now I want to stay here and help people help themselves." [35]

By the last quarter of the twentieth century, membership in industrial and service unions had become a fact of life for large numbers of Mexicans/ Mexican Americans. Workers employed in such sectors as assembly plants, steel mills, smelters, refineries, machine shops, garment factories, railroads, construction, transportation, government service, law enforcement, retail stores, warehouses, hotels, restaurants, and many other establishments had much more protection and support than did previous generations. Consequently wages, working conditions, benefits, and the standard of living for many workers improved.

But just as a part of the community began to enjoy the fruits of unionization, organized labor began losing power because of economic restructuring, downsizing, globalization, and the return of political conservatism. People of Mexican extraction, along with other workers, witnessed the disappearance of millions of well-paying unionized jobs and the loss of benefits taken for granted in earlier periods. Membership in unions dropped precipitously, and gains became harder to achieve. Between 1945 and 1985, the percentage of unionized workers in the labor force dropped from 35 to 17. In the early 1980s alone, labor unions lost almost 3 million members. With greater frequency unions failed to translate election victories into favorable contracts. They also often settled for agreements that made unprecedented concessions to management.

Despite the unfavorable climate, workers continued to fight vigorously for decent wages and working conditions. Undocumented immigrants employed in office buildings, hotels, and restaurants in Los Angeles provided one of the most inspirational examples in the labor movement as they courageously put aside fears of deportation and joined unions, went on strike, and lobbied the public for support. Thousands carried on their campaign for a living wage and fair benefits through the Hotel and Restaurant Employees Union and the Service Employees International Union. Using new strategies and multicultural techniques, leaders such as María Elena Durazo, Ana Navarette, Jono Shaffer, Berta Northey, and Rocio Saenz skillfully mobilized workers thought impossible to organize by traditional unionists. By 1995 the movement known as Justice for Janitors succeeded in unionizing large numbers of workers and raising wages from $4.25 to $6.80 an hour.

In the spring of 2000 the janitors' movement remained a force to be reckoned with in Southern California, as it won concessions from employers after conducting a successful strike capped by a massive march.

The labor activism against great odds demonstrated by immigrants has sent a powerful message to American workers in general that new times require renewed energy and militancy. That message has indeed been heard. In the 1990s major unions such as the AFL-CIO embarked on new campaigns to revitalize the movement. Yet in the face of structural changes in the national economy as well as overseas, organized labor in the United States continued to struggle to keep membership from dropping further. The weakened position of unions has seriously diminished opportunities for entry into the middle class for poor Mexicans and Mexican Americans aspiring to get well-paying, stable blue-collar jobs. The reality of the new economy is that achievement of the American dream now requires substantial education and advanced skills. These trends will likely continue as the economy of the United States becomes more technologically and service oriented.

Conclusion

Substantial changes took place in the occupational structure of the Mexican-origin working class in the twentieth century. In 1900, most members of the group worked in low-paying jobs in agriculture, railroad maintenance, mining, construction, light manufacturing, and sundry basic service occupations. Few had blue-collar and white-collar jobs. Beginning in the 1940s, more Mexicans/Mexican Americans began getting skilled jobs with decent pay and benefits. Those workers in large urban areas who joined unions did particularly well. The percentage of well-paid, unionized Mexican-descent labor in the industrial sector rose steadily between 1950 and 1970. As a result more ordinary people enjoyed a middle-class standard of living, reflecting a nationwide trend throughout the population.

But major economic and societal changes applied the brakes on the good times, and working people witnessed devastating setbacks during the last quarter of the twentieth century. Urban workers saw millions of good industrial jobs disappear as the process of economic restructuring set in. Unions lost considerable power. Wages stagnated or declined. In the rural areas, farmworkers lost considerable ground as a result of the following developments: (1) reduced concern for their needs in the government and among Americans in general; (2) a growing anti-union climate; (3) continuous large-scale flows of Mexican nationals into agricultural areas; and (4) dissension within the union movement. Above all, farmworkers found it exceedingly difficult to overcome the immense economic and political might that agribusiness possessed. If these trends continue, powerlessness will remain a fact of life for those who work to keep the nation well fed.

To a significant degree the downturn experienced by both urban and rural workers reflected national trends. Restructuring and globalization have devastated workers of all backgrounds, including European Americans, African Americans, and Mexicans/Mexican Americans. No other part of North America reflects the dilemmas of these trends more than the Mexican border, where nonunion and feebly organized laborers are widely employed by assembly plants run by multinational corporations. Hundreds of thousands of jobs that used to pay high wages in the United States have been shifted to border cities such as Tijuana and Ciudad Juárez, where they now pay bare survival wages to Mexican workers. Among the different components of the Mexican/Mexican American labor force, it is ordinary workers with the least amount of education who face the most daunting challenge in the new global economy.

SIX

Mixed Social Progress

❖

Descriptions of conditions among the Mexican-ancestry population during the twentieth century routinely highlighted impoverishment and isolation from the mainstream society as the most salient problems faced by the group. Observers found substandard housing, poor health, and inadequate schools particularly troubling. In the rural areas, migrant workers often lived under lean-tos or in shabby and dangerous labor camps. Substantial numbers of children dropped out of school at an early age to earn money working in the fields. Mexicans/Mexican Americans fared somewhat better in the cities, but de facto segregation and a lack of concern for the welfare of barrio residents bred deprivation and many social problems.

In the latter half of the century the federal government consistently documented that between one-fifth and one-fourth, and sometimes more, of the Mexican-origin population fell below the poverty line. While community organizations worked hard to bring about improvements, changes came slowly because the political and economic power structure remained largely indifferent and unresponsive to the needs of the proletariat. In addition, the continuous influx of poor immigrants into the barrios enlarged the problem.

Yet despite the persistence of widespread poverty through the end of the century, after 1965 researchers began to notice an encouraging trend: Increasing numbers in the group were significantly improving their economic circumstances. Upward mobility, which had been so restricted in previous generations, became much more attainable because of the profound changes throughout the United States ushered in during the post–World

War II period. This new development would result in a notable transformation of the social and economic profile of the Mexican-descent population.

Conditions among the Masses

For many generations the United States as a society did little to alleviate the
structural problems that kept many people in a perpetual state of material
deprivation. The Mexican-origin population, along with other disadvantaged groups, suffered from that neglect. During the Great Depression of
the early 1930s poverty reached new heights, with Hispanics in the Southwest constituting one of the poorest populations in the country. In New
Mexico, Hispanos/as had the highest death rates, including an infant mor-
tality rate of 144 per thousand. Many rural people could not subsist on mea-
ger earnings from farming activities. Others found themselves heavily in
debt and perilously behind in tax payments. Such scenarios repeated themselves in other parts of the Southwest as well.

The pronounced marginality among most Mexicans and Mexican Americans drew increasing attention from community leaders and academics in
the post–World War II period. Spokespersons seemed particularly appalled
that so little had been done to assist people in improving their standard
of living. In 1949, economist and labor activist Ernesto Galarza published
an article on the conditions of life and work among the Spanish-surname
population, noting continuing serious problems in many areas. Galarza
hoped that policymakers would take action on various social fronts.[1] In the
same year, sociologist Lyle Saunders pointed out to the national convention
of LULAC that Spanish-speaking people lagged far behind other groups in
general well-being:

> Everywhere . . . there is poverty. Not all Spanish-speaking [people] are poor,
> but in general more of them are poor than is true for any other group. . . .
> Everywhere there are slum conditions in both rural and urban areas, and while
> not all Spanish-speaking people live in slums, more of them do than would
> be expected by chance and more of them do proportionately than any other
> population group. Everywhere there is poor sanitation. . . . Everywhere the
> Spanish-speaking are found in the poorest paid, least skilled occupations. . . .
> Everywhere there are problems of education. . . . Everywhere, too, there is seg-
> regation or separation — sometimes voluntary, sometimes enforced — which

TABLE 6.1 Social Indicators of the Mexican-Origin Population, 1989–1994

	U.S. Population	Mexican-Origin Population
Poverty rate (1993)	14%	30%
Unemployment rate (1994)	6%	10%
Median family income (1989)	$34,213	$24,119
Less than high school education (1994)	19%	53%
At least high school education (1994)	81%	47%

Source: Table in Gelbard and Carter, "Mexican Immigration and the U.S. Population," 132, based on U.S. Census Bureau reports.

insures that the Spanish-speaking people will work and play and live largely with other Spanish-speaking people while the Anglos associate mainly with other Anglos.[2]

With the passage of civil rights laws in the 1950s and 1960s, some of these problems diminished, but economic hardship continued to define the general condition of the masses. The statistics in table 6.1 confirm that the gap between Mexicans/Mexican Americans and the dominant society remained persistently large into the 1990s. Poverty and unemployment rates among Mexican-origin people continued to be significantly higher than that of the general population, while income-earning capacity and educational achievement were notably lower.

Several factors need to be taken into account in explaining the disadvantageous circumstances still confronted by large numbers of people of Mexican background. One consideration is the lingering effects of historical discrimination. Granted that racism has declined in recent decades, yet it has not disappeared. Institutional as well as individual prejudice continues to have a deleterious impact on the most vulnerable segments of the group.

The long-standing influx of large numbers of poor immigrants from Mexico must also be weighed in assessing group disadvantage. The newcomers have skewed the statistical socioeconomic profile of the entire Mexican-origin population in a downward direction. Group progress has been obscured by the constant addition of immigrants with low levels of education, limited job skills, and little or no knowledge of the English language.

Finally, recent structural changes in the U.S. economy have resulted in a precipitous decline of the manufacturing sector, seriously reducing opportunities for blue-collar workers to obtain well-paying industrial jobs. Manufacturing supplied 29 percent of all jobs in the country in 1969 but only 19 percent two decades later.[3] As a result, a lower proportion of non-college-educated urban workers have been able to enter the middle class than was the case for earlier generations. Many inner-city Hispanics, along with African Americans and other poor people, have been devastated by plant closures and the flight of factories to the suburbs and to other countries. The Los Angeles area serves as a sobering example of this trend. Major employers that have shut down, reduced their operations, or gone elsewhere in the last quarter century include General Motors, Uniroyal, B.F. Goodrich, Bethlehem Steel, Bemis Company, Oscar Mayer Foods, Alcoa Aluminum, Aluminum Forge, and International Metals. With the disappearance of well-paying jobs such as those provided by these companies, working-class Chicanos/as have been forced to take low-paying jobs in the service sector. Across the nation the gap between rich and poor widened after 1980, and achieving the American dream became much more difficult for families supported by uneducated, unskilled workers.

Upward Mobility for the Fortunate

While acknowledging that the level of deprivation among Mexican-origin people has indeed been exceedingly high over the years, it is important to recognize that in recent times segments of the population have been able to better their circumstances, some considerably. This is particularly true for the generations beyond the immigrant cohort. Comparing conditions among the foreign-born and fourth-generation natives, a national study conducted in 1989–1990 confirmed "substantial socioeconomic gains across the generations. For example, the percentage holding managerial and professional jobs increases from 4.7 to 11.6 [foreign-born compared to fourth-generation natives]; the percentage of household incomes above $30,000 increases from 27.3 to 35.2; and the percentage of high school and college graduates increases from 24.7 to 49.4 and 5.4 to 9.6 respectively."[4] Data for Los Angeles (table 6.2) corroborate these findings. Between 1960 and 1990, native-born Mexican American Angelenos/as improved their educational and occupational status relative to European Americans. Women in par-

TABLE 6.2 Educational and Occupational Status of Mexican-Origin Men and Women Relative to European Americans, Los Angeles, 1960 and 1990

Educational Attainment Ratios (percentage of non-Hispanic white completion rates) [a]

| | High-School Graduates | | | |
| | Men | | Women | |
	1960	1990	1960	1990
Native-born	53	76	50	67
Immigrants	22	27	18	32

| | College Graduates (Four-Year Degrees) | | | |
| | Men | | Women | |
	1960	1990	1960	1990
Native-born	25	28	25	31
Immigrants	11	8	9	10

High-Status Occupational Ratios (percentage of non-Hispanic white rates) [a]

| | Men | | Women | |
	1960	1990	1960	1990
Native-born	30	39	32	53
Immigrants	19	13	20	18

Source: Extracted from tables 6.1 and 6.2 in Allen and Turner, *The Ethnic Quilt*, 170, 172, based on U.S. Bureau of the Census, *Census of Population* reports, 1960, 1990.

[a] These ratios measure the distance that separates Mexican-origin people from European Americans. For example, by 1990 native-born Mexican American women had improved their high-school graduation rates to slightly more than two-thirds the rate of whites and their representation in high-status occupations to slightly more than half the rate of whites.

ticular made significant strides in climbing to higher levels in the ranks of professional workers. More recent official statistics for the country as a whole confirm continuing gains recorded by U.S.-born Chicanos/as. In 1997, third-generation households had higher incomes than both second- and first-generation households, while second-generation households had higher incomes than first-generation households.[5]

The degree of progress experienced by Mexican-origin people as a whole has been a matter of debate, but no one denies that significant socioeconomic advances have taken place, especially in recent times. Decades ago very few workers of Mexican extraction held jobs outside the low-wage, unskilled sector. A significant portion was concentrated in agricultural labor. That dismal situation has changed appreciably. Since midcentury, the number of Mexicans and Mexican Americans in well-paying, skilled blue-collar and professional and technical occupations has increased significantly, while the proportion engaged in such dead-end occupations as farm labor has declined drastically.

These changes occurred as a result of powerful forces that affected Mexican-origin people and other groups in the U.S. population beginning in the 1940s. First, changes in the economy spurred a massive movement from rural areas to urban centers. In 1930 less than 60 percent of the Hispanic population in the Southwest resided in cities, but by 1970 the figure had risen to more than 85 percent. Thus the rapidly expanding, better-paying jobs produced by a booming urban economy became more accessible to greater numbers of Mexicans and Mexican Americans. Simultaneously the Civil Rights Movement resulted in the passage of laws that made discrimination illegal. Occupations previously closed to members of the group opened up. The trend toward greater employment opportunities received another boost with the implementation of affirmative action programs from the 1960s to the 1990s.

Recent improvements in occupational status have been accompanied by significant advances in education as well. At the time of World War I, only one in ten Mexicans/Mexican Americans of secondary school completion age actually finished high school, and only a handful went to college. By the World War II period the high school graduation ratio had improved to about one in five, and the number of students going to college had also risen, although at a much lower rate.

Rapid change for the better ensued when the GI Bill of Rights made educational benefits available to veterans, and thousands of Mexican-ancestry former servicemen and servicewomen pursued college educations. As the Chicano/a middle class expanded after midcentury, so did educational achievement. By 1970 about half of all Mexican-descent individuals in the 20–24-year age group had completed high school, a significant improvement over previous generations.[6] More of these students pursued higher education, and soon colleges and universities witnessed a dramatic rise in Hispanic enrollments. Between 1982 and 1993, the number of Hispanics attending institutions of higher learning increased from 519,000 to 989,000, a 91 percent leap. Significantly, by the early 1980s Hispanic women began to surpass Hispanic men in the number of undergraduate degrees earned, and that trend widened in the 1990s. For example, women received 51 percent of the 22,000 bachelor's degrees awarded to Hispanics in 1981 and 56 percent of the 41,000 bachelor's degrees awarded in 1992.[7]

The most significant development of all during the last generation has been the impressive growth of the middle class. Statistics on income distribution among Hispanics in general reflect trends in the Mexican-origin community, since the group constitutes the largest cohort of that population. In 1972, 191,000 Hispanic households had an income of $50,000 (in 1988 dollars). By 1988 that number had risen 234 percent, to 638,000. In 1988 nearly 11 percent of all Hispanic households were classified as affluent, compared to 7 percent in 1972. The proportion of affluent Hispanics still lagged far behind that of European Americans (23 percent in 1988) but surpassed the proportion for African Americans (10 percent).[8]

In 1990, the U.S. Census Bureau reported that 32 percent of Hispanic households had incomes above $35,000. Further breakdown of the data revealed small but notable increases in the number of Hispanic households that now had high incomes. Two percent had incomes of $100,000 and above, 3 percent from $75,000 to $99,999, 11 percent from $50,000 to $74,999, and 16 percent from $35,000 to $49,999. California and Texas, where people of Mexican ancestry are heavily concentrated, reported the largest numbers of Hispanic households that had incomes above $35,000.[9] In Los Angeles, Hispanic households with incomes of more than $50,000 grew "an incredible 112 percent" from 1992 to 1995.[10] Increased affluence swelled the buying power of the Hispanic population to unprecedented levels nationwide. Calculated at $111 billion in 1980, Hispanic buying power was projected to rise impressively to $276 billion in 2000.[11]

Most Mexican-origin people who have moved into the middle class since the 1950s have been native-born, long-time residents of the United States. First-generation, working-class Mexican immigrants have found it much more difficult to make such a transition. Yet exceptions to this rule can be found in almost any community. Following are examples of individuals from different immigrant generations who have experienced social mobility in recent years.

Anna Macías Aguayo, a reporter, is a third-generation Mexican American who pioneered her family's entry into the middle class. In 1994 Ms. Macías Aguayo provided *Hispanic Business* some revealing details about her life:

> Sixty-eight years ago my undocumented immigrant grandfather worked as a gardener at the *Dallas Morning News*. Today I am a news reporter at this same company, only I came seeking employment with a university education. When I joined the newspaper I was the first in my immediate family to begin earning what could be called a middle-class income. . . . This summer we [she and her husband] purchased a custom-built home with a lush, landscaped lawn. We boast two late-model cars and every conceivable kitchen gadget and appliance. And we enjoy our season tickets to the Dallas Opera. . . . After three generations my family finds itself a part of the American middle class. I'm not sure what drove our ascent. Perhaps it was the dream my father, Arnulfo Dávila Macías, had for his children. "I did not have the opportunity to get an education, daughters, but you shall," he would say in Spanish. "Continue, with the help of God." [12]

Raoul Lowery Contreras, a U.S.-born journalist and radio/TV commentator, is another example of a new member of the middle class. His parents were immigrants. He remembers growing up in poverty in Southern California during the 1950s, but a change in family circumstances and his drive to get an education paved the way to a better life. He wrote the following in 1994:

> My family came to Southern California from Mexico with $50. I guess you could say we were poor. Things changed when my mother married my step-father, the policeman. What a leap that was, from $50-a-week to $100-a-week. I didn't have to shine shoes anymore and my grandmother and I could go to the movies. . . . Getting an education was the key for me. No one in my family had ever graduated from high school or attended college. I had no role models, except perhaps the Navy and Marine officers in my tract neighborhood, most of whom had attended the Naval Academy and most of whom were jet flyers. There were a few Mexican Americans in the neighborhood who worked in aerospace as engineers, and had attended college thanks to the GI Bill. [13]

One of the most celebrated recent success stories is the case of María Guadalupe Vásquez, a young immigrant from a homeless, migrant-worker family who received two degrees from Stanford University and became an engineer in the computer industry in Silicon Valley. Her story appeared in the *Los Angeles Times* in 1996:

> [Vásquez's story] is an American success story, an immigrant tale pointing up the value of education and hard work. It's a story about the rise from a [homeless] shelter to Stanford, and about the drive to overcome long odds. . . . She came to the United States illegally when she was 2 and did not become a legal resident until 1988. . . . [Her family] drifted across the Southwest before bottoming out in an Oxnard homeless shelter nearly a decade ago. Vásquez spent her high school years dreaming of a life beyond the poverty that plagued her family. So when it became apparent that there was little hope of escape if she stayed put, she decided to chase those dreams just as far as her straight-A grades would allow. . . . [When] she graduated second in her class in 1989 . . . she won widespread acclaim. She was named ABC's newsmaker of the week on a national broadcast. Actor Edward James Olmos put her under contract to do a movie about her life. . . . But most important, Vásquez assembled a collection of state, federal, and university grants, scholarships and fellowships that paid the bulk of her nearly $30,000-a-year education. . . . That is how she landed at Stanford University, the first in her family to attend high school or college and perhaps the first homeless person ever admitted to the prestigious private school.[14]

Progress in the Professions

The drive to advance to the top of the economic ladder has always been a strong cultural characteristic among Mexican-origin workers. This trait has been underappreciated by many scholars and writers. Whether in Mexico or in the United States, Mexicans/Mexican Americans have diligently sought to achieve status, recognition, and material rewards. The key variable has been opportunity. Favorable circumstances have spawned success for many, while unfavorable conditions have nurtured frustration and stagnation.

In the nineteenth century the Southwest offered acutely limited opportunities for social mobility for working-class people of Mexican ancestry. Moreover, individuals already at the top of the occupational structure often found it difficult to hold on to their positions because of the disadvantageous climate created by European Americans who dominated the social order established after 1836 in Texas and 1848 in the rest of the Southwest. The decline of the Spanish/Mexican elite in the context of this encroachment has been documented by numerous authors.[15] Yet cadres of Spanish-speaking professionals continued to function in many communities, for the most part serving the needs of their own people. Mexican American elected officials, law enforcement officers, bureaucrats, newspaper editors, physicians, pharmacists, priests, teachers, and attorneys could be found throughout the Southwest even in the worst of times. Interestingly, many of these professionals were immigrants lured by opportunity in Mexican barrios routinely neglected by the European American business establishment.

As the economy of the United States grew in complexity in the twentieth century, the need for more specialized professionals rose, and Mexican-origin people sought such positions whenever the opportunity existed. Things changed slowly, however, and the number of Mexicans and Mexican Americans holding high-status, well-paying jobs remained small for decades. In the 1910s and 1920s the ranks of professionals expanded somewhat as a result of the great influx of Mexican immigrants who left Mexico during the years of revolutionary upheaval. A small proportion of the newcomers had white-collar credentials and, as in earlier generations, they often found opportunities to exercise their professions in predominantly working-class Spanish-speaking communities. Most of these middle-class Mexicans settled in the Southwest, but some ventured deep into the interior of the United States.

Historian Juan R. García notes the presence of Mexican professionals in diverse fields in the Midwest during the 1920s. Their occupations, appearance, and lifestyles are probably similar to those of elite Mexicans who lived in the Southwest:

> The larger cities . . . attracted Mexican physicians, lawyers, dentists, engineers, teachers, ministers, musicians, journalists, publishers, scholars, and government officials. Many of them found employment with American firms in need of highly trained professionals with Spanish-language skills. Companies in Chicago with overseas interests employed more than 400 young Mexicans in white-collar jobs, including two cartoonists on a major newspaper and several clerks in the export divisions of large corporations. Young, single, and marketable, many of these professionals earned better wages and enjoyed a higher standard of living than other Mexican workers. Emanating from the

upper and middle classes in Mexico, they were well educated, fluent in English, and well schooled in the social graces. They also tended to be more noticeably White than other Mexicans, which served them well in their search for employment. Living apart from the rest of the colonia and adhering strictly to their own class, they tended to acculturate quickly. Their style of dress, speech, mannerisms, and tastes reflected those of the "hip" generation.[16]

Unfortunately the opportunities that had been available for Mexican-descent professionals in the 1920s became more restricted in the 1930s as jobs disappeared from one end of the occupational spectrum to the other during the Great Depression. Then as repatriations and forced deportations thinned the populations of barrios throughout the United States, the need for Spanish-speaking professionals shrank further. Soon lawyers, accountants, managers, and the like departed en masse to Mexico, diminishing the size of the Mexican/Mexican American middle class in the United States. In the case of El Paso, by 1940 only 1.8 percent of all Spanish-surname workers occupied high-white-collar positions, compared to 3.8 percent in 1920. Similarly, in Tucson, 3.5 percent of Mexican-origin workers held high-white-collar jobs in 1940, a drop from the 5.2 percent who had had such employment in 1920.[17]

Recovery from the Great Depression began to be felt among Mexican-origin people during the World War II period, reflecting national trends. As the economy expanded, as discrimination eased, and as more Mexicans and Mexican Americans graduated from college, the size of the professional class began to grow again. Change proceeded slowly, however, and the gap between people of Mexican extraction and the larger society remained quite large. The presence of Mexican-origin professionals varied significantly from place to place. New Mexico serves as a good example of the overall situation in 1966. In Albuquerque, Spanish-surname individuals made up about 22 percent of the general population, but only 14 percent of the lawyers, 11 percent of the dentists, and 3 percent of the physicians. In Santa Fe, Spanish-surname persons constituted approximately 51 percent of the city's population, but only 17 percent of the lawyers, 31 percent of the dentists, and 4 percent of the physicians. While the level of representation in these professions in these two cities lagged far behind the Hispano/a proportion of the population, each community nonetheless had a cluster of professionals. By contrast, in towns and villages elsewhere in the

TABLE 6.3 Select Hispanic Professional Associations

Organization	Year Founded	Membership (1997)
American Association of Hispanic CPAS	1972	800
Society of Hispanic Professional Engineers	1974	8,000
Interamerican College of Physicians and Surgeons	1979	4,500
National Association of Hispanic Nurses	1976	800
National Hispanic Medical Association	1995	500
Hispanic National Bar Association	1972	22,000
National Hispanic Employee Association	1991	10,000
National Society of Hispanic MBAS	1988	1,000
National Association of Hispanic Federal Executives	1984	500
National Association of Hispanic Journalists	1984	1,800
National Hispanic Academy of Media Arts and Sciences	1984	3,000

Source: *Hispanic Business*, February 1997, 14–18.

state almost no Spanish-surname lawyers, dentists, and physicians could be found.[18]

The big push toward greater representation in the professions began in the 1970s. Both genders in the Mexican/Mexican American population increased their numbers impressively, but women more so than men. Between 1980 and 1990, the number of male Hispanic executives, administrators, and managers grew from 224,874 to 362,858. Among women that number climbed from 110,178 to 290,938. By 1990 women outnumbered men in the following occupations: accountants and auditors, financial managers, other financial officers, personnel and labor relations managers, education administrators, and medicine/health administrators.[19] In 1997, *Hispanic Business* identified twelve Hispanic women among the sixty-two Hispanic boardroom directors serving in Fortune 1000 corporations, and forty Hispanic women executives among the 249 Hispanic executives working for such companies.[20] Expanded numbers of professionals gave rise to new Hispanic organizations in many different fields. Table 6.3 provides a sampling of such recently established associations and their membership as of 1997.

Progress in Business

One of the least-known facets of the experience of people of Mexican descent is their participation in business enterprises. Stereotyped thinking and limited research have led many observers to assume that business know-how and drive have simply been absent among members of the group. This perception is absolutely false. Mexicans inherited a strong tradition of entrepreneurship from their Spanish and Indian ancestors, and early explorers and colonizers on the northern frontier of New Spain carried on trade and commerce with each other as well as with indigenous peoples. By the early seventeenth century, sizable wagon trains traveled regularly from Mexico City to the far north of the Spanish Empire to supply distant towns and missions. Increased contact between Spanish/Mexican frontier settlements and the outside world led to extensive trade with French, English, and American colonists from Louisiana and the areas that adjoined Florida. On the California coast, ranchers regularly traded with Yankee merchant ships. Entrepreneurs from New Mexico and Chihuahua played a central role in building a transnational commercial network that reached all the way to the eastern United States and to Europe. The business highway developed by these merchants and later also utilized by U.S. caravans is known as the Santa Fe–Chihuahua Trail.[21]

After the Southwest became a part of the United States, Mexican merchants throughout the borderlands faced greater competition from newly arrived European American entrepreneurs. At the same time, new market opportunities opened up, and local as well as immigrant *empresarios* (entrepreneurs) took advantage of them. Records in Carson County, Nevada, reveal the active involvement of numerous Spanish-surname individuals in business transactions, especially in the real estate sector, during the mining boom at the Comstock Lode during the 1850s and early 1860s. In New Mexico, 154 Hispanic merchants had a net worth of $2.4 million dollars in 1860.[22]

Even in the face of the tough competition posed by the arrival of American corporations, many Spanish-speaking businesspersons found ways of staying afloat, keeping alive the long tradition of entrepreneurship on the frontier. Some held on to their status as leading citizens in their communities for decades after the U.S. takeover. Tucson is a good example of the continuity of a Mexican/Mexican American business elite throughout the latter nineteenth and early twentieth centuries, as table 6.4 illustrates. Interestingly, the majority of the Tucson entrepreneurs of that era hailed from Mexico. One individual who stood out in the group is Federico Ronstadt, a native of Sonora. Ronstadt achieved prominence by building an empire

TABLE 6.4 Prominent Businesspeople, Tucson, Circa 1850 to Early 1900s

Entrepreneur	Birthplace	Businesses
Aguirre brothers	Chihuahua	Freight, ranching, stage line
Amado Family	unknown	Cattle, real estate, bottling
Rosario Brena	Sonora	Saddle shop, soap factory, grocery store
Leopoldo Carrillo	Sonora	Freight, ranching, ice-cream parlor, saloon, bowling alley, feed stable, real estate
Perfecto Elías	unknown	Jewelry/watch repair shop
Carlos Jacome	Sonora	Department store
Fernando Laos	Sonora	Barber shop, tobacco shop, billiard parlor
Estevan Ochoa	Chihuahua	Freight, retail, dry goods, smelting, mining
Sabino Otero	Arizona	Ranching, freight, real estate
Bernabe Robles	Sonora	Ranching, real estate, saloon, grocery store, dairy, stage line
Federico Ronstadt	Sonora	Carriage shop, hardware, car sales, car repair, ranching
Mariano Samaniego	Sonora	Freight, ranching, saddle/harness shop
Ramón Soto	unknown	Ranching, dairy
Hilario Urquides	Arizona	Saloon, hotel
Carlos Velasco	Sonora	Newspaper
Felipe Villaescusa	unknown	Saddle shop, wagon shop

Source: Torres and Amado, "The Quest for Power," 80; Sheridan, Los Tucsonenses, chapters 3, 6.

in transportation and merchandising. He took particular pride in making wagons and custom carriages. When automobiles came along, Ronstadt established a dealership and repair shop. Finally, he sold farm implements and supplies through his hardware business. His clientele extended south of the border deep into the state of Sonora. Ronstadt's prominence in Tucson is reflected in his selection as a director of the Arizona National Bank and as head of the local Chamber of Commerce.[23]

Businessmen of Mexican descent with status similar to or higher than that of Ronstadt lived in other places as well. In El Paso, New Mexican native Felix Martínez owned or had interests in a variety of enterprises, including publishing, transportation, construction, cement, utility, real estate, and brokerage firms. He sat on several important boards and wielded considerable political power. In 1915 President Woodrow Wilson appointed Martínez to head two U.S. commissions whose work related to Latin America. When he died, wealthy mourners "in their top silk hats and fine suits" filed past his coffin, which "lay in state in the chamber of commerce for two days under police guard."[24]

Exceptionally prosperous empresarios continued to maintain a presence in several communities after 1900, but small business owners far outnumbered them. Women ran some of these businesses. María and Clotilde Amador, for example, took over family farming operations in the Mesilla Valley after the death of their parents, producing cash crops and marketing poultry. They also managed properties in Las Cruces. María "Chata" Sada owned and operated a hotel, café, trading post, and general store in the Big Bend area of Texas. She also raised animals and kept a garden. Faustina Porras Martínez made the transition from field hand to businesswoman when she opened an eatery in Dallas in 1918. In time her business would grow into a chain of restaurants throughout central Texas and Oklahoma.[25]

In cities such as Los Angeles, Tucson, El Paso, and San Antonio, Mexicans and Mexican Americans ran modest-sized restaurants, grocery stores, drugstores, meat markets, bakeries, laundries, saloons, hotels, gas stations, mechanic shops, movie theaters, newspapers, print shops, and furniture stores. European Americans owned similar establishments, but they were usually larger and more upscale because they served the needs of affluent consumers. The better-financed and better-connected European Americans also dominated the manufacturing concerns and large retail establishments such as department stores and auto dealerships.

Expansion of Hispanic businesses accompanied the growth of communities swelled by immigration during the second and third decades of the twentieth century. In 1928, for example, 228 Mexican/Mexican American business concerns operated in the Chicago, Illinois–Gary, Indiana, area, including 76 pool halls, 52 restaurants, 27 barbershops, 20 grocery stores, and 11 tailor shops.[26] In El Paso, the *City Directory* for the same year listed hundreds of individuals associated with Mexican/Mexican American businesses, including 347 grocers, 61 bakers, 52 restaurant workers, 32 shoemakers and shoe repairers, 30 operators of tortilla mills, 24 butchers, 21 fruit and vegetable stands, 14 druggists, and 13 brokers. The majority of these individuals were probably employees, but many undoubtedly owned or managed those businesses.[27]

During the Great Depression the number of businesses owned by people of Mexican descent declined as bankruptcies proliferated and as businesspeople returned to Mexico during the repatriation period. Merchants, shopkeepers, theater owners, restaurant owners, grocers, printers, and many other entrepreneurs joined the exodus across the border to escape

TABLE 6.5 Mexican American Businesses Started in the Northwest, 1940s—1960s

Family Name	Type of Business	Location	Year Founded
Rodríguez	Barber shop	Nampa, Idaho	1949
Gonzáles	Tortilla factory	Ontario, Oregon	1952
Espinoza	Restaurant	Seattle, Washington	1954
Rodríguez	Restaurant	Nampa, Idaho	1954
Martínez	Food distribution	Seattle, Washington	1955
Mendez	Restaurant	Sunnyside, Washington	1955
Benavidez	Restaurant	Othello, Washington	1964
Medina	General store	Woodburn, Oregon	1965
Rodríguez	Bakery	Nyssa, Oregon	1965
Zavala	Restaurant	Othello, Washington	1965

Source: Adapted from Maldonado, "An Overview of the Mexicano/Chicano Presence in the Pacific Northwest," 11—12.

the hostility and unfavorable conditions in the United States. The mass departure of that population had a devastating effect on many communities with a great need for the stability, leadership, and resources provided by economically well-off elements. It would take time to start the process of building up this vital segment of the Mexican/Mexican American middle class all over again.

After 1940 business growth returned as demographic expansion and new waves of immigrants provided a sizable market for a new generation of entrepreneurs. Corner groceries, fruit and vegetable stores, restaurants, barbershops, laundries, and the like mushroomed. According to one study, by 1946 Mexican-descent people in Tucson owned 119 businesses, including 20 grocery stores, 10 restaurants, 8 barbershops, 8 shoe repair shops, 7 service stations, 6 garages, and 5 beauty shops.[28] These types of establishments appeared for the first time in many communities far from the Southwest as they were settled by new immigrants or native migrants from places like south Texas who sought agricultural work in far-off places. The Pacific Northwest is a case in point. Examples of new small businesses that blossomed in Idaho, Washington, and Oregon from 1949 to 1965 are listed in table 6.5.

By the late 1960s conditions had become much more favorable than in any previous era for business development in minority communities in the United States. Markets had grown significantly. Discrimination had declined as attitudes changed and civil rights laws took effect. Loans had become easier to get because of expanding capital. The Small Business Administration reached out to ethnic entrepreneurs more aggressively than ever before. Businesspersons of Mexican ancestry eagerly took advantage of the new opportunities.

Between 1969 and 1987 the number of Hispanic-owned businesses in the United States grew by 321 percent, from 100,212 to 422,373. Revenues increased by 586 percent, from $3.6 billion to $24.7 billion.[29] Mexican-origin individuals owned slightly more than half of all the Hispanic businesses in 1987, and their establishments appeared in all fifty states. Table 6.6 lists the ten states and metropolitan areas that had the most firms owned by people of Mexican origin. Not surprisingly, the southwestern states had the largest concentration of these businesses, with the biggest numbers by far in California and Texas. Illinois, Florida, Washington, Michigan, and New York became significant centers as well. Among the metropolitan areas, Los Angeles–Long Beach, San Antonio, and Houston dominated the firm count. Chicago, in tenth place, constituted the only non-southwestern city on the list.

By the 1990s, the Hispanic business sector included an impressive number of corporations worth millions of dollars. A new generation of powerful entrepreneurs emerged as heads of firms doing business in the mainstream domestic market as well as in the international arena. One of the striking characteristics of these companies is their great diversity. For example, top Mexican/Mexican American–owned enterprises featured in a recent issue of *Hispanic Business* carried on transactions in the following sectors: food processing, food distribution, food sales, real estate, banking, media and publishing, agriculture, ranching, oil and gas, car dealerships, restaurant chains, high-tech engineering, and lumbering. The personal wealth attributed to the owners of these businesses ranged from $50 million to $85 million.[30]

Reflecting the economic boom of the 1990s in the United States, by 1998 the number of Hispanic-owned businesses had climbed to about 1.7 million, more than triple the figure recorded eleven years earlier. Significantly, Hispanic women owned nearly 537,000 firms, providing an unprecedented level of female competition in a historically male-dominated arena. Most of the Hispana-owned establishments are small and centered in sectors such as food service, but some are multi-million-dollar operations in traditionally

TABLE 6.6 Hispanic and Mexican-Owned Firms, Ten Leading States and
Metropolitan Areas, 1987

	Total		Mexican Firms with Paid Employees	
	Hispanic Firms	*% Mexican Firms*	*Number of Firms*	*Number of Employees*
States				
California	94,548	71.5	19,654	66,832
Texas	83,380	88.0	18,552	44,563
New Mexico	8,656	60.5	2,249	6,366
Arizona	8,246	83.8	1,941	8,016
Colorado	6,394	67.2	1,229	3,400
Illinois	5,637	58.5	1,006	3,120
Florida	2,821	4.4	431	1,729
Washington	1,792	66.7	393	1,465
Michigan	1,704	64.2	296	1,031
New York	1,244	4.4	207	514
Metropolitan Areas				
Los Angeles/ Long Beach	38,505	67.9	7,030	24,788
San Antonio	13,575	89.1	3,219	8,338
Houston	12,793	80.1	2,530	3,281
San Diego	8,397	81.0	1,671	5,550
Riverside/ San Bernardino	8,079	79.2	2,004	4,823
El Paso	7,589	92.4	1,970	6,367
McAllen/ Edinburgh/ Mission	7,191	91.6	1,838	5,098
Dallas	5,651	83.8	1,122	2,691
San Jose	4,487	72.5	961	2,323
Chicago	4,413	56.2	925	2,619

Source: U.S. Bureau of the Census, *Economic Censuses, 1987: Survey of Minority-Owned Business Enterprises, Hispanic*, tables 5, 7.

male-dominated fields. Elizabeth Pohl of Albuquerque is the chief executive officer of one of these pioneering firms, Trinity Construction Enterprises, Inc., which in 1997 ranked forty-third among the one hundred fastest-growing Hispanic businesses. The company recorded an annual revenue growth of 163 percent between 1992 and 1996. In 1997 Trinity Construction employed ninety-six people and reported revenues of $4.45 million. For Elizabeth Pohl the construction industry was a natural fit, since both her father and husband worked in the field. Yet running such a company has at times created uncomfortable moments for her because of the stereotypical expectations of others, especially men. "Ms. Pohl once attended a trade conference where a man stopped her at the door and directed her to the 'spouse bus' headed for a shopping mall. When she insisted she came to participate in the conference, he was incredulous. Likewise, she has attended client meetings where everyone assumed she was a secretary."[31]

A little-known recent development is the remarkable success of Mexican immigrants in a variety of enterprises and the role that these entrepreneurs have played in revitalizing formerly depressed areas and industries. As the immigrant population has spread nationwide, businesses have followed them, even in faraway places like the East Coast that lack a historic Mexican American presence. New York City is a prime example. By the 1980s, tens of thousands of Mexican nationals had settled there, and their need for goods and services presented unique opportunities for alert entrepreneurs. Fernando Sánchez, formerly an undocumented laborer who worked for years in low-paying jobs in factories and restaurants, is a case in point. In 1986 "El Gordo" Sánchez, as he is affectionately known, opened the Tortillería Piaxtla in Brooklyn with $10,000 in hard-earned savings. (Piaxtla is the name of his hometown in Puebla.) The investment paid off in a big way. Within a decade he employed around fifty workers, mostly immigrants from Puebla, acquired several properties and six trucks, and sold tortillas as far away as Philadelphia and Montreal. He expanded his operations to include a grocery store, several bakeries, and another *tortillería* in Rhode Island. Annual sales hovered around four million dollars. "El Gordo" Sánchez has also helped several former employees to start their own tortilla businesses, figuring that the expanding market could handle added competition. His neighborhood in Brooklyn is now called the Tortilla Triangle, in reference to three tortillerías in close proximity to one another.[32]

Immigrant entrepreneurship also extends to rural areas of the United States, where Mexicans and others have been part of a quiet revolution in agriculture. A significant number of former farmworkers have become farmowners, infusing a declining institution, the American family farm, with new vitality and energy. During the 1980s and 1990s, the number of Hispanic-owned farms increased substantially in many states, but especially in the states bordering Mexico. As growing numbers of disillusioned European American farmers sold their properties, Mexicans and other Hispanic immigrants entered the industry with a fresh outlook and optimism. In Texas and California the number of Hispanic family farms grew by 694 and 412, respectively, between 1987 and 1992, while in each of the following non-southwestern states Hispanic farms increased by an average of twelve farms annually: Florida, Idaho, Iowa, Kentucky, Missouri, Montana, New Jersey, North Carolina, North Dakota, Oklahoma, Oregon, South Carolina, South Dakota, and Virginia.[33]

Alberto and María Solís, former undocumented immigrants from Zacatecas, are good examples of this new breed of rural entrepreneurs. In 1978, despite their illegal status, they purchased a farm with a down payment of $2,000 and continued working as migrants, saving money to buy more land. Their big break came in 1986 with the amnesty program that formed part of the Immigration Reform and Control Act. That made it possible for them to legalize their status. Alberto Solís recalls: "[Before legalization] I walked around with a fear that at any moment I could be deported and lose everything. I was afraid to do anything, to buy anything, to plan. With papers I felt better. I was able to work better. I could buy what I wanted: machinery, a new pickup, anything I wanted. And without fear. So we bought two more ranches." Alberto also brought in two of his brothers from Zacatecas, allowing him to grow more squash and eggplant. By 1997 the Solís estate was worth more than $150,000.[34]

A Persistent and Growing Gap

Individual successes as well as general gains made in employment, education, the professions, business, and growth of the middle class underline in a powerful way the emergence of affluence on a large scale in the Mexican/Mexican American community. As impressive as these advances have been, however, Mexican-descent people and other Latinos/as still lag far behind the European American population, and the separation is getting larger. Education is a case in point. After narrowing the education gap during the post–World War II generation, Hispanics have witnessed a widening once again in recent years. The proportions of students graduating from high school and those going to college have been rising at higher rates for European Americans than for Latinos/as. During the 1980s, the percentage of Hispanic students from low- and middle-income families who entered college after graduation from high school fell from 50 percent to 35 percent, prompting the American Council on Education to label the trend "an educational failure . . . of intolerable magnitude."[35]

Other statistics confirm the pattern of deterioration. Between 1985 and 1996, the percentage of European American 25–29-year-olds with high school diplomas went up by 3 points (from 90 to 93), but that of Hispanics remained the same (at 61). With respect to college attendance, between 1972 and 1995 the percentage of white students aged 18–24 increased by 10 points (from 32 to 42), while that of Hispanics rose by 7 points (from 26 to 35). Additionally, Hispanics enrolled in community colleges in much higher proportions than did European American students.[36] The meaning of these statistics is that much higher percentages of Hispanics have been pursuing vocational careers rather than better-paying professional occupations.

Equally disturbing is the growing elimination of affirmative action programs by institutions of higher learning, leading to some crushing setbacks. In 1995 and 1996 respectively, both the University of California system, via a board decision, and the University of Texas Law School, via a court order, abolished the use of race and ethnicity in admissions decisions. Devastating enrollment drops among students of Mexican descent ensued. Between 1996 and 1997, Hispanic admissions at the University of Texas fell by 15 percent among undergraduates and by a whopping 74 percent among aspiring law students. At the University of California, Hispanic admissions dropped by 7 percent between 1996 and 1997, and Hispanic applications to the state's medical schools declined by a third between 1995 and 1997. U.C. Berkeley, the flagship university in the system, accepted only 264 Hispanic freshmen for the fall of 1998, compared to 492 the year before.[37]

Mexican American politicians and activists in Texas and California responded to these depressing developments by pressuring their legislatures to mandate automatic acceptance of the highest-ranked high school graduates, regardless of school location, into the top public universities in each state. Both states recognized the problem and took action on that relatively simple but highly significant proposal. In Texas all students, regardless of ethnicity, who graduated in the top 10 percent of their classes became eligible for admittance into the University of Texas at Austin; similarly, in

California the top 4 percent of graduating seniors qualified for spots at the elite campuses of the University of California. These legislative initiatives began to pay off as the percentage of Latinos/as eligible to enter top educational institutions in both states gradually increased. At the University of Texas, freshman Hispanic enrollment rebounded to 14 percent in 1999, only slightly lower than what it had been in 1996, the last year of affirmative action in the Texas higher education system. At the University of California at Berkeley, the admission of Latino/a freshmen increased by 18 percent between 1999 and 2000.[38]

The lessons learned recently in the public universities of Texas and California provide institutions of higher learning throughout the United States with significant guideposts for handling diversity issues in the post-affirmative-action age. Clearly, there is no shortage of Chicano/a and Latino/a students who are qualified to do the academic work required at the postsecondary level. Colleges and universities must now do a better job of identifying able minority students, admitting them, and providing them with sufficient financial support. All along, the fundamental problem has been the traditional system that favors students from the affluent and privileged sectors of society who, because of social and cultural advantages, score higher on entrance exams. In reality these tests have little predictive value for academic success. Nevertheless, they have been used in precisely that way by admissions committees — to the great detriment of disadvantaged minority students, whose scores tend to be lower. One positive development arising from the disasters in California and Texas following the elimination of affirmative action is that more and more educators have realized the need to place less weight on standardized exams and to assign more weight to other, more tangible measures such as grades and rankings in graduating classes. Cognizant of the implications of economic and social marginality, admissions committees have also been taking into greater consideration income levels of applicants and neighborhood and high school environments. If higher education institutions across the land henceforth modify their selection procedures to systematically utilize variables such as these, then perhaps the deleterious effect of the termination of affirmative action based on race and ethnicity will be appreciably diminished.

Conclusion

For more than a century following the U.S. conquest of the Southwest, upward mobility eluded the preponderant majority of Mexican-origin people. Formidable barriers blocked their path to material improvement. After the 1960s, however, opportunities for advancement rose sharply for most disadvantaged groups in the United States. Significant numbers of Mexicans/Mexican Americans and other Hispanics took full advantage of the more favorable climate, especially in the all-important field of education. They attended universities and earned degrees that opened the door to a multitude of professional occupations and executive positions in both the private and public sectors. Simultaneously, the number of businesses owned and operated by Mexicans/Mexican Americans expanded in an extraordinary fashion. All these developments led to improvements in the standard of living among those who advanced into the middle class and those privileged few who made it into the top echelons of society.

The masses, however, continued to live below, directly at, or slightly above the poverty line. European American racism and unabated immigration of poor immigrants from Mexico and Central America have undeniably had a detrimental impact on overall conditions. As well, since the 1970s, economic restructuring, corporate streamlining, merging, deindustrialization, and globalization have taken a heavy toll on the working-class sector of the Mexican/Mexican American population, especially those concentrated in depressed barrios in the large cities. Traditional avenues of upward mobility such as well-paying, unionized factory work have shrunk dramatically. More and more workers have had to settle for low-paying service jobs that offer few benefits. Other recent major blows to poor people include the growing lack of commitment in government circles and society as a whole to reduce poverty, as well as swelling opposition to affirmative action in education and employment. Increasingly a stigmatized and marginalized Mexican immigrant proletariat finds itself isolated from the native-born Chicano/a population, whose circumstances in general are much better.

Not surprisingly, the socioeconomic gap that separates Mexican-origin people from European Americans has widened in recent years. The forces that have spawned improvements in society as a whole have simply been much more powerful in the mainstream population, and the forces that have produced deterioration have fallen disproportionately on disadvantaged minority groups. Put differently, European Americans have been in a better position than Hispanics to benefit during times of progress and to be shielded from the effects of bad economic currents. At the end of the twentieth century Mexicans/Mexican Americans continued to be one of the most vulnerable groups in the United States to disruptive and injurious economic cycles.

PART IV

Politics and Challenges for a New Century

We knew the power of unity
and the importance of the vote.
And here and there, where we could,
we had victories, now and then.
But it was hard, and it took so long,
to begin breaking the colossal chains
that locked us out, collectively.

Many generations have come and gone,
and much struggle waged and pain endured.
But not for a moment did we stand still.
We labored, we mobilized, we organized,
and we fought with all our might,
to secure our rights and our rightful place
under the northern eagle's sun.

SEVEN

Community and Political Power

✦

Despite grinding socioeconomic disadvantages and myriad obstacles, Mexican Americans have been deeply involved in the nation's political process, serving in a wide array of local, state, and national offices and exercising their right to organize, lobby, and agitate for change. In every historical period and everywhere they have lived, working-class, middle-class, and elite Mexican Americans have been political actors, capitalizing on opportunities for achieving power where these have been available while steadfastly fighting barriers that have inhibited participation and representation. The subgroup with by far the most impressive record is the Hispanos/as of New Mexico, whose substantive involvement in electoral politics spans many generations.

Yet the political achievements of Mexican Americans have not been proportionate to the numbers the group has represented in the overall population. Historically, underrepresentation in elected offices has been a serious, chronic problem, and the response of elected officials and the government bureaucracy to many community needs has left much to be desired. In reality politics has had little meaning for large segments of the Mexican-origin population. Disenfranchisement and powerlessness have prevailed in many communities over many generations. The result of these conditions has been a long history of political struggle. In the late twentieth century, however, new and promising trends emerged. Cumulative positive change became a salient tendency, and the political landscape improved significantly. That led to unprecedented advances.

Historical Structural Considerations

The existence of formidable structural disadvantages goes a long way in explaining the limited participation in electoral politics among the majority of Mexican Americans for most of the time they have been a part of U.S. society. Economic underdevelopment has long been a part of their reality, with large percentages of the population living in poverty. Since voting is an activity associated predominantly with people of middle-class standing or above, masses of working-class Mexican Americans have lacked the resources, education, and know-how to be effective political participants. Before World War II, limited opportunity for social mobility reinforced the marginal background of huge sectors of the Mexican-origin people. The economy of the Southwest, where most Mexican Americans lived, relied heavily on agriculture, transportation, and the extractive industries. These sectors greatly exploited and marginalized their workers. Since Mexican Americans were heavily concentrated in low-wage occupations, they tended to occupy the bottom levels of the labor force hierarchy. Additionally, underdevelopment has been continuously reinforced by the streams of impoverished immigrants from Mexico. Noncitizen immigrants, of course, cannot vote. The effects of endemic poverty and incessant immigration, then, partially explain the historical pattern of political underrepresentation among Mexican Americans.

But the group has also been seriously disadvantaged by external circumstances deeply rooted in history, namely racism in American society and exclusiveness inherent in the political system itself. Following are a few of the most harmful policies and practices created or sanctioned by the government or political parties. The effects of these instruments of discrimination have been strongly felt by Mexican Americans even until recent decades.

CITIZENSHIP RESTRICTIONS

Throughout the nineteenth and early twentieth centuries, European Americans illegally restricted the political participation of many Mexican Americans through the denial of citizenship rights. Usually only those Mexicans who had a white-appearing complexion could expect to be accorded the privilege of citizenship. The Naturalization Law of 1790, which barred nonwhite immigrants from becoming U.S. citizens and from voting and seeking public office, technically applied to Mexicans of Indian, Chinese, and African origin. The law reinforced the common view that since Mexicans, including those born in the United States, were essentially of the Indian race, they could not be recognized as U.S. citizens. That interpretation allowed many local officials to classify Mexican Americans as nonwhite and to exclude them from voting or running for office. The law also helped to legitimize segregation and dispossession of property. All these practices violated the Treaty of Guadalupe Hidalgo, which implicitly recognized Mexicans as whites and explicitly granted them citizenship rights and protection under the U.S. Constitution. The Walter-McCarren Act of 1952 finally eliminated the discrimination against dark-skinned immigrants embodied in the law of 1790.

DENIAL OF THE VOTE TO WOMEN

Women did not receive full voting rights until the passage of the Nineteenth Amendment in 1920, although some states that had significant Mexican American populations, including California (1912) and Arizona (1912), did adopt women's suffrage a few years earlier. Even when they received the vote, however, few Chicanas exercised it because of their subordinated condition. Decades passed before Mexican American women were substantively incorporated into the political process.

"ENGLISH ONLY" LAWS AND PRACTICES

In the post-1848 period, state, territorial, and local governments in the Southwest did little to translate laws, documents, and proceedings of official meetings for the benefit of non-English-speaking people. For example, a California law in 1855 explicitly prohibited the translation of statutes and regulations into Spanish, reversing the 1849 state constitutional provision, which had mandated such translation. Language assistance declined over time. Among the southwestern states, only New Mexico retained language safeguards for the Spanish-speaking population. Not until the 1970s, when the U.S. Congress extended the Voting Rights Act to cover Hispanic communities, did bilingual voting materials and ballots become widely available.

LITERACY TESTS

Prior to the 1960s and 1970s, many states required proficiency in the English language as a part of the voter registration process. Biased registrars often rejected applicants deemed to be deficient in this area. This practice obviously placed Spanish-speaking people with little or no training in U.S. schools at great disadvantage.

THE POLL TAX

In concert with the custom in southern states of discouraging African Americans and other poor people from political participation, between 1902 and 1966 Texas required payment of a poll tax ($1.50 to $1.75) as a prerequisite for voting. Consequently large numbers of Tejanos/as did not become voters, and thousands were subjected to control and manipulation by political bosses who eagerly paid the tax for them. The United States declared the poll tax unconstitutional in 1966.

SINGLE LOCATIONS FOR VOTER REGISTRATION

For many years Texas and other states limited voter registration to one location, usually the courthouse, a site often distant from Mexican American barrios. The courthouse also served as the center of power for hostile European American judges, law officers, bureaucrats, and politicians. By the 1960s registration was permitted at different locations, and the number of Mexican American voters increased.

WHITE MAN'S PRIMARIES

Designed originally to exclude African Americans from the political process in the South, this system limited voting in the Democratic primaries to whites only. Since the Democratic Party dominated the South, including Texas, candidates elected in the Democratic primaries automatically won the general elections. This system effectively disenfranchised not only blacks but many Hispanics in Texas who could not pass as whites. In 1944, the U.S. Supreme Court struck down the white-only primary system.

ANNUAL VOTER REGISTRATION

Following the 1966 U.S. Supreme Court ruling on the unconstitutionality of the poll tax, Texas instituted a system of annual voter registration confined to a period of a few weeks, which meant that voters had to register with frequency and far in advance of elections. Many voters, including legions of Mexican Americans, disappeared from the rolls for failure to register within the whimsical and unreasonable specified period. In 1971 the U.S. Supreme Court declared this procedure unconstitutional.

CONGRESSIONAL AND STATE LEGISLATIVE DISTRICTING

Until the early 1960s, when the U.S. Supreme Court handed down highly significant rulings on apportionment and redistricting, rural areas had vastly disproportionate representation in Congress and the state legislatures while cities were seriously underrepresented. Thus urban residents in general suffered from the concentration of power among legislators who advocated rural interests and values. Mexican Americans, who by the 1930s lived largely in cities, acutely felt the impact of this system when dominant rural conservative representatives opposed progressive legislation on social and civil rights issues. Consequently Chicanos/as welcomed the institutionalization of the "one man, one vote" principle following the historic Supreme Court decisions of 1962, 1963, and 1964.

AT-LARGE ELECTIONS

Originally instituted to provide communitywide representation and to avoid political fragmentation and pressures from interest groups, this system allows for the election of representatives to such bodies as city councils and school boards on a citywide rather than district basis. Although well intentioned, at-large elections over the years have tended to be European American dominated, resulting in systematic dilution of the voting strength of minorities, leaving them with little or no representation. The voting rights legislation enacted in 1965 and afterward made legal challenges to the at-large system possible. Lawsuits and threats of lawsuits starting in the 1970s forced cities throughout the Southwest to switch to the district system.

GERRYMANDERING

An old practice in U.S. politics, *gerrymandering* refers to the drawing of electoral district boundaries to favor one group over another. European American–controlled legislative bodies frequently gerrymandered the

Mexican American electorate, resulting in the absence of districts with sufficient Chicano/a voters to elect their own representatives. In the early 1970s
the U.S. Commission on Civil Rights identified gerrymandering in California as one of the chief causes of political underrepresentation of Mexican
Americans in the state.

These barriers and obstacles wrought devastation among the Mexican
American electorate. Of course, political discrimination varied according to
time and place. Texas, reflecting its southern ties, practiced the worst forms
of exclusion, whereas New Mexico, mirroring the influence and power of
its large Hispano/a population, proved to be the most democratic and inclusive. Following is a historical survey of the political experience of the
Mexican-origin population, with an emphasis on changes that have promoted incorporation of this group into the political process.

Before 1900: Marginality Institutionalized

After the U.S. takeover of the Southwest, with some exceptions Mexican-
origin people functioned on the margins of the new political process. Members of the group recognized as white and granted citizenship rights by the
power structure participated in politics to the extent the system permitted.
On the other hand, the disadvantaged, dark-skinned masses had little or no
role in selecting their representatives and in shaping legislation. This became the general pattern. Yet marginality took different forms across an
expansive and heterogeneous landscape.

In some areas exclusion did not set in right away because Spanish-
speaking people retained numerical strength and managed to hold on to
substantial wealth. Elites in such communities temporarily withstood the
economic competition posed by European American newcomers who set
up trading posts, farms, and ranches that did not differ much from what
already existed in the region. By voting as a block, Mexican Americans
wielded influence and controlled a variety of elected offices. That pattern
lasted until such time as new waves of European American settlers caused
a further power shift away from the native population.

In the case of Texas at the time the rebellion from Mexico erupted in 1836,
two Mexicans signed the Declaration for Independence and three (out of
fifty-nine delegates) signed the new constitution. These foundational documents conferred citizenship on Mexicans who resided in Texas on March 2,

the day of independence. Juan Seguín served in the Texas senate from 1838 to 1840 and as mayor of San Antonio from 1840 to 1842. As more European Americans arrived in Texas, Tejano/a political power diminished, and by 1845, when the Texans wrote another constitution on the occasion of annexation to the United States, only one Mexican served as a delegate to the convention. Yet Tejanos/as managed to hold on to some power at the local level. In San Antonio, fifty-seven Spanish-surname individuals served as aldermen between 1837 and 1847, seventeen between 1848 and 1857, and eleven between 1858 and 1866; thereafter their numbers declined drastically as the swelling European American population established hegemony. In communities along the Rio Grande such as Brownsville, Laredo, and El Paso, during those years numerous Mexican Americans served regularly in offices ranging from justice of the peace and city assessor to mayor and county judge.

In California, eight Mexicans (out of the forty-eight delegates) participated in the convention that produced the 1849 state constitution, a document that restricted voting rights to white males only, including Mexican white males. The new political order thus disenfranchised dark-skinned Mexicans. To its credit, the assembly agreed to have state laws translated into Spanish. In 1855, however, the legislature stopped this practice. That action signaled the decline of Californio/a influence at the state level. Yet even under increasingly unfavorable circumstances a few persons of Mexican extraction managed to become politically prominent. For example, Lieutenant Governor Romualdo Pacheco became governor in 1875 when Newton Booth resigned to run for the senate. Californios/as also retained political strength at the community level. In Los Angeles, Mexican-descent individuals consistently held elected state, county, and city offices between 1850 and 1879. Antonio Coronel and Cristóbal Aguilar served as mayors in the 1850s and 1870s respectively. The most impressive representation of Mexican Americans manifested itself at the county level, where twenty-seven Spanish-surname officeholders served in the 1850s, seventeen in the 1860s, and sixteen in the 1870s.[1]

Until they achieved statehood in 1912, New Mexico and Arizona functioned differently than Texas because of their territorial status. They comprised one territory from 1850 to 1863 (under the rubric Territory of New Mexico) and two separate ones from 1863 to 1912. On the question of citizenship, the U.S. Congress specified in 1850 that Mexicans in the territories formed from land acquired from Mexico qualified for this privilege based on the provisions of the Treaty of Guadalupe Hidalgo. Hispanics in New Mexico found themselves in a favorable position to exercise influence because they retained significant wealth and enjoyed numerical superiority over European Americans into the early twentieth century. Thus they made their political presence felt more strongly than did Mexicans elsewhere in the Southwest. Apart from serving in many local offices, between 1853 and 1901 nine Hispanos represented the Territory of New Mexico in Congress. Miguel A. Otero also served as territorial governor from 1897 to 1906. In Arizona, Mexican-origin people managed to wield some power at the local level. For example, Hispanic elites in Tucson thrived in the new political order established after the Gadsden Purchase (1853), serving in city, county, and select territorial offices. Estevan Ochoa, a prominent businessman, became Tucson's mayor in 1875.

The real political exclusion in most of the Southwest started in the 1880s with major economic and population restructuring. Powerful American companies established a new capitalist economy that destroyed many local businesses. In the case of railroad and mining corporations, for example, independent Mexican-descent entrepreneurs such as freighters could not compete with the cheaper, faster, and safer service offered by the iron horse, and small-scale miners could not compete with the modern technology, processing plants, and markets at the disposal of mining syndicates. The same pattern repeated itself when large-scale agricultural concerns wiped out local farmers and ranchers. In short, by 1900, outside of New Mexico, Mexicans/Mexican Americans controlled only a limited amount of the wealth in the Southwest, and that had a profoundly negative impact on their political participation. The number of Spanish-surname officeholders declined substantially in many communities.

Demographics played a crucial role as well. As European Americans arrived in the Southwest in greater numbers, the percentage of Mexican-origin people became smaller and smaller. This is particularly true for Texas and California, where European Americans overwhelmed the local population almost immediately following the separation of those provinces from Mexico. By 1900, Spanish-surname persons comprised less than 10 percent of the estimated 5.4 million people living in the Southwest. In California, they made up only 1 or 2 percent of the population.

At the community level, Mexican-descent people often had to contend with a European American population dominated by young and middle-aged men with significant resources at their disposal. In Tucson, for example, between 1860 and 1900 the age structures of these two groups differed dramatically. The Spanish-speaking population had far fewer economically active individuals, especially men in their prime, than the European American population. In 1860 the percentage of Spanish-surname adults in Tucson aged fifteen through sixty-four stood at 57, growing to 64 percent by 1900. By contrast, among newly arrived European Americans in 1860, nearly 100 percent were men in that age group, and that percentage dropped only slightly to 90 by 1880. As a result of these gender, age, and economic disparities, European Americans as a group enjoyed basic advantages such as much greater involvement in lucrative economic activity and fewer family responsibilities. They could more easily concentrate on expanding their wealth. Not surprisingly many of them could start up businesses, purchase ranches and farms, and acquire mines.

The political implications of the contrasting demographic profiles are clear. Even in communities like Tucson, where Mexican-origin people predominated, the advantage quickly shifted to the European Americans as a result of their greater wealth and higher concentration of politically active and influential individuals. In short, European Americans had the critical ingredients necessary to dominate politics, and the Hispanic Tucsonenses did not. The increasing power of European American Arizonans is reflected in their successful efforts to separate Arizona from the New Mexico Territory in 1863 and to move the capital from Tucson to Prescott in 1864 and then to Phoenix in 1887. The major motivation for creating the Arizona Territory derived from the European American fear of political domination by the mass of Hispanics in New Mexico, and shifting the capital away from Tucson represented similar uneasiness over the high concentrations of Spanish-speaking people in southern Arizona.

1900–1940: Nascent Mobilization

As the twentieth century began, the patterns of marginality developed in the preceding two generations were firmly established. At the state and territorial levels, only Hispanic New Mexicans held on to a significant share of the regional and local political power. Elsewhere European Americans overwhelmingly dominated the major executive offices, state legislatures, and congressional seats. Only in some select areas where the Mexican-origin population constituted the majority and/or had a significant afflu-ent class could Mexican Americans match the representation found in the New Mexican communities. In south Texas, for example, Hispanics occu-pied more political offices in those counties where they owned most of the land.

One of the most significant manifestations of the role of ethnicity, num-bers, and economic power in politics is found in the efforts of Arizona and New Mexico to gain statehood. As these two territories struggled to convince Congress to admit them as full-fledged members of the Union, anti-Hispanic sentiment rose to the fore. When a congressional committee proposed in 1906 that Arizona and New Mexico be admitted as one state, European American Arizonans became alarmed with the prospect of being a minority in a Hispanic-majority state. A senator from South Carolina stated that Arizona's opposition to the plan was "a cry of a pure blooded white community against the domination of a mixed breed aggregation of citizens of New Mexico, who are Spaniards, Indians, Greasers, Mexicans, and everything else."[2] Not surprisingly, Arizona voters, most of them Euro-pean Americans, overwhelmingly rejected the proposal, 84 percent to 16 percent, while New Mexicans strongly supported it, 64 percent to 36 per-cent. Arizona not only got its wish to be free from the control of Hispanics in New Mexico, it also disenfranchised large numbers of Arizonenses by passing a literacy law in 1909. Application of literacy laws notoriously dis-criminated against minorities. The following year Arizonans wrote a consti-tution in anticipation of statehood, which Congress finally granted in 1912. Given that only one of the fifty-two delegates at the Arizona state conven-tion had a Spanish surname, it is not surprising that the convention seri-ously debated (but did not pass) a number of anti-Mexican measures related to labor issues, and that the new constitution failed to extend any specific rights to the local Spanish-speaking people.[3]

New Mexico also became a state in 1912, but its constitution explicitly safeguarded the rights of the Hispano/a population, including prohibit-ing disenfranchisement on the basis of race or language. The document also mandated publication of all state laws in Spanish, outlawed school segregation, and required training of bilingual teachers. To make the sections of the constitution containing these guarantees practically unamendable, the delegates included the following protective language: "This section shall never be amended except upon a vote of the people of this state, in an election at which at least three-fourths of the electors voting in the whole state and at least two-thirds of those voting in each county in the state shall vote for such amendment." What made possible the inclusion of these remarkable safeguards? The answer lies in the fact that Hispanics comprised one-third of the convention delegates and that New Mexico had a Spanish-speaking population of considerable size and economic clout. The Hispanic delegates well recognized the decline in power experienced by Mexican-descent people in other parts of the Southwest and, having the means to do so, they determined to prevent it in New Mexico. Spanish-speaking New Mexicans also reacted out of great frustration and resentment that had been accumulating since the 1850s over repeated rejections by the U.S. Congress to petitions for statehood. Many European American congressmen had alleged that most of New Mexico's population was unfit for self-government, calling attention to their supposedly high levels of illiteracy, superstitious nature, loose morals, ignorance, and blind submission to the Catholic Church. One lawmaker referred to the Nuevo Mexicanos/as as "a race speaking an alien language" and not possessing the "best blood on the American continent."[4]

Outside New Mexico, the institutionalized political subordination established by the European American community in the nineteenth century generally grew worse after 1900, and disenfranchisement among Mexican Americans increased. Instruments of exclusion developed in the South during the Jim Crow period for the purpose of rendering the African American population powerless spread to the borderlands and were used against Chicanos/as. For example, Texas enacted the poll tax in 1902. Two years later the Texas Democratic Party allowed county committees to require voters in the primaries to affirm, "I am a white person and a Democrat," before allowing them to cast ballots. Polling officials rejected those persons deemed to be nonwhite. In Wharton County the constitution of the White Man's Union Association specifically stated that "the term White Citizen . . . shall not include any Mexican who is not a full Spanish blood. . . . Only persons who are white citizens, as that term is used herein . . . shall be permitted to vote at any primary or other election held by this association." Thus began Texas' White Man's Primary system. Further disenfranchisement occurred when a Texas state law in 1918 prohibited the presence of interpreters at the polls and mandated that only voters who had been U.S. citizens for at least twenty-one years could receive assistance from election judges.[5]

Difficult registration procedures, along with property and literacy requirements, likewise discouraged potential Mexican American voters. Most insidious of all, intimidation by officials, law officers, and racist organizations diminished the voting lists and undermined ethnic minority candidates. An example of bullying and coercion occurred in Corpus Christi in 1919, when Texas Rangers warned Mexican American voters that they would wind up in the penitentiary if, lacking proficiency in the English language, they went ahead and voted. Given the reputation of the Rangers as brutal and racist, many people understandably stayed away from the polls. In El Paso in 1922, the Ku Klux Klan harassed Mexican American voters they suspected of voting illegally.[6]

Apart from the preceding impediments to participation, many Mexican Americans had long avoided politics because of their dependence on European American employers. Involvement in partisan campaigns, or even simply casting ballots, carried risks of alienating bosses, who often retaliated by firing or demoting workers or cutting wages. Given the restricted employment opportunities that had predominated since the mid-nineteenth century in many parts of the Southwest, few Mexican Americans could afford to ignore the negative consequences that frequently accompanied political activity.

At the same time, economic dependence enmeshed many Mexican-descent people in machine politics. For decades, areas with large numbers of poor, uneducated people, especially non-English-speaking immigrants, constituted fertile grounds for political manipulation and control by power brokers who dispensed patronage and favors in exchange for votes. In essence, political bosses served as protectors and benefactors for impoverished individuals in need of jobs, shelter, food, or welfare services.

Along the Texas border, the machines routinely paid the poll tax for thousands of poor voters and herded them to the polls on election day. Few Mexican Americans could afford the $1.50 charge for the privilege of voting at a time when ordinary workers barely earned that amount for a whole

TABLE 7.1 Hispanic Elected Representation in New Mexico, 1918–1938, as Percent of All Representatives

	State Senate	State House	County Offices
1918	29	53	37
1928	21	43	31
1938	25	39	31

Source: Fincher, Spanish-Americans, 251–59.

day's work. Commonly the machines won elections by fraudulently padding the voting lists with fictitious people, foreigners, and deceased individuals. Often bosses paid voters to cast ballots for specified candidates. Understandably, reformers fought against the corruption embodied in the machine system, championing the poll tax and the White Man's Primary to counter illegal voting. In their zealousness to rid the system of bossism, however, the reformers disenfranchised large numbers of Chicanos/as. Regardless, clever machine operatives found ways to circumvent the restrictions and continued their nefarious activities.

Such degrading conditions pervaded electoral politics among the Mexican-heritage population in many communities largely because of the small size of the middle class. The number of genuinely independent voters remained small and Latino/a advocacy organizations lacked the strength to effectively challenge the European American–dominated power structure.

The bright spot in the political arena during the first few decades of the twentieth century remained New Mexico where, from 1919 to 1923 and 1931 to 1935, Hispanos/as continued to elect their own to the U.S. Congress.[7] They also maintained a high profile in state and county politics by electing many Spanish-surname representatives (table 7.1). Though state representation dropped in the 1920s and 1930s, it still remained at a respectable level. Such representation derived from high voter turnout in Hispanic counties: 82 percent in 1932, 83 percent in 1936, and 80 percent in 1940. These rates exceeded those for New Mexico as a whole.[8]

Wherever underrepresentation and marginality prevailed in the Southwest, activists sought to bring about improvements to the extent that their circumstances permitted. Dissatisfaction with the status quo drove increasing numbers to join labor unions (see chapter 5) and other militant organizations. The Partido Liberal Mexicano (PLM), which originated in Mexico as an opposition movement against the dictator Porfirio Díaz, was influential in the United States. Exiled PLM leaders embraced both labor and political concerns of Mexicans living in the United States, offering inspiration, advice, and support in a number of causes. Newspapers such as *La Opinión* in Los Angeles, *El Fronterizo* in Tucson, and *El Imparcial de Texas* in San Antonio kept the community informed and constantly editorialized against discrimination and abuse.

Mexicans and Mexican Americans also became members of mutual aid societies, civic groups, protective leagues, fraternal lodges, social clubs, and ethnic heritage associations. In 1911 in the border city of Laredo, delegates from such organizations throughout Texas held El Primer Congreso Mexicanista for the purpose of forging a collective response to a variety of political, economic, and social grievances, among them judicial abuse, police brutality, and school segregation. Responding to the call for institutionalized unity, the participants created the Gran Liga Mexicanista de Beneficiencia y Protección, encouraging individual communities to form local chapters. The *congresistas*' ambitious dream of achieving national unity failed to materialize, however, as the Gran Liga quickly faded because of lack of resources and opposition from European Americans. Nevertheless, the experience gained by the highly diverse participants in this endeavor would contribute mightily to the establishment of a foundation necessary for the more successful coalition building that would occur in later years.

Mutual aid societies, long present in many barrios, became an essential part of the effort to mobilize the community. These organizations emerged from the need to address basic problems faced by individuals and families, especially during hard times. *Mutualistas* collected dues and in turn provided low-interest loans and insurance benefits, assisted members who got in trouble with the law, helped with the financing of special occasions such as weddings and baptisms, and sponsored holiday celebrations and dances. In addition, mutualistas promoted ethnic pride and encouraged unity among Mexican-heritage people. By the 1920s, hundreds, if not thousands, of mutualistas had been established in communities throughout the United States, bearing names that reflected the interests of the sponsoring groups. Examples from the Chicago area include the Club Atlético Y Social Cuauhtémoc, Sociedad Obreros Libres, and Sociedad Caballeros de Nuestra Señora de Guadalupe; women's associations include the Sociedad Femenil Mexicana, Sociedad Recreativa Femenil Guadalupana, Sociedad Josefa Ortíz Domínguez, Hijas de María, and Cruz Azul. Cruz Azul became one of the most important women-led organizations in the Midwest and elsewhere. During the 1920s, for example, the Cruz Azul chapter in Cleveland worked closely with the Mexican consul to deliver badly needed social services and to establish youth-oriented programs. In Los Angeles, Elena de la Ilata led Cruz Azul in holding fundraisers, assisting people left homeless by natural calamities, helping the unemployed, and meeting many health and medical needs in the community.

Some mutualistas originated in response to destitution and privation, but many community organizations had their roots in Mexican nationalism. They promoted respect and reverence for the motherland by extolling Mexico's heritage and paying tribute to national heroes. Much of their activity focused on celebrating patriotic holidays (*fiestas patrias*) such as El Día de la Independencia (Mexico's independence day). Middle-class and elite Mexicans, especially exiles who planned to return to Mexico, tended to be the force behind these associations. Examples include, from Chicago, the Sociedad Miguel Hidalgo y Costilla and the Sociedad Benito Juárez; from Los Angeles, the Club Independencia and the Comisión Honorífica; and from El Paso, La Junta Patriótica Mexicana.

The Alianza Hispano-Americana, founded in Tucson in 1894, became the most successful and most politically active mutual aid society. Within a generation after its birth, the Alianza had spread throughout the country, although most of its chapters functioned in the Southwest. By 1929 it had 13,459 members, and ten years later that number had risen to 17,366. Thereafter the membership dropped gradually as conditions changed, but the Alianza managed to survive into the 1960s. From the beginning, the Alianza fought against discrimination and promoted candidates for office in local and state races in Arizona. In the 1890s and early 1900s several *aliancistas* held elected positions in Tucson, prompting one observer to characterize this period as a "golden age" for local Hispanic politicians.[9]

The Liga Protectora Latina stands out as another activist association whose agenda included considerable political activity. Organized in Phoenix in 1914, the Liga vigorously condemned discriminatory bills in the Arizona legislature and openly backed and opposed political candidates.

In 1916 and 1918 Liga activists campaigned against two European American gubernatorial candidates because of their support for legislation that would hurt Mexican-origin workers. Most of all, the Liga fought tirelessly against the blatantly discriminatory treatment of Mexican-origin inmates, who found themselves framed, unjustly convicted, tortured, and executed at much higher rates than European American prisoners.[10]

Mexican Americans took a major step forward in their quest for justice and equality when they organized the League of United Latin American Citizens (LULAC) in 1929. Leaders of many different community groups in Texas succeeded in forming a confederation that over time would spread nationwide and have lasting power, going strong even in the late twentieth century. Organizers of LULAC sought to promote and protect the interests of Hispanics and to encourage and facilitate assimilation into mainstream society. LULAC encouraged immigrants to learn English, acquire a formal education, become U.S. citizens, be civic-minded, and become involved in community affairs. Women made their presence felt in LULAC by taking charge of many activities, including registration drives and fundraisers for scholarships and charities. For example, Mrs. J. C. Machuca led the movement to create ladies' councils, while Alice Dickerson Montemayor served in several leadership positions and agitated for women's rights within male-dominated LULAC.

Although explicitly a nonpolitical organization, from the beginning LULAC pursued political agendas. One founder explained that "with our vote and our influence we shall endeavor to place in public office men who show by their deeds respect for our people."[11] LULAC members actively supported and campaigned for candidates through an offshoot organization known as the League of Loyal Americans. LULAC also became heavily involved in the struggle to desegregate education. In 1930, LULAC joined the legal challenge to the segregation of children by the Del Rio (Texas) School District. In this case LULAC and the other plaintiffs won a battle but lost the war. The court ruled unconstitutional the segregation of students based solely on their national origin but let stand segregation based on academic or linguistic considerations. LULAC and other community organizations became discouraged with the position of the courts and pursued change directly in the community, pointing out to school officials the unfairness of separating Hispanic students. As time passed LULAC broadened its agenda to include a wide variety of civil rights issues. By 1940 approximately two thousand LULAC members in the Southwest carried on the organization's work through 150 councils.[12]

In the 1930s new forms of activism appeared as a result of economic distress associated with the Great Depression and the accompanying restructuring of the Mexican-origin population in the United States. Organizations created primarily to address economic issues also tackled political questions, especially in the cities. Participation in the U.S. electoral process assumed greater importance for many groups and individuals who had previously confined their attention to immediate needs of the community and to religious, ethnic, and cultural activities. The repatriation and deportation to Mexico of 500,000 to 1,000,000 Mexican-origin persons played a major role in the reorientation toward greater political activity in the United States among the U.S.-born Mexican Americans. In 1930, an estimated 43 percent of the Mexican-heritage population had been born south of the border but, as a result of repatriations, by 1940 that figure had declined to approximately 35 percent. It is apparent that as the proportion of the immigrant population dropped, the great majority of the remaining, predominantly U.S.-born Mexican Americans, adopted an overwhelming American orientation. Mastering and using the American system to advance the interests of the group became all-consuming for larger numbers of individuals, many of whom received inspiration from New Deal initiatives promoted by the federal government and by progressive groups that fought hard to improve conditions among working people. Community organizations led by second-, third-, and fourth-generation Mexican Americans began to relegate Mexico-oriented activities to secondary consideration, placing much greater emphasis on becoming full-fledged members of American society. They stepped up the promotion of the English language and urged non–U.S. citizens to become naturalized without delay. Above all they encouraged people to vote.

The most powerful impetus toward increased political activity during the 1930s derived from the struggles on behalf of workers led by militant labor unions (see chapter 5). In major cities such as Los Angeles, for example, an array of unions functioned in the community, often overshadowing the efforts of other organizations. For the first time, significant numbers of Mexican Americans fought for economic justice side by side with other

American unionists in the new environment created by the New Deal politics. Inevitably the ideology of labor rights fused with that of citizens' rights, and many Mexican Americans extended their activism into the political arena. In the process, their identities as Americans grew stronger.

1940–1965: Drive toward Inclusiveness

After the Great Depression conditions changed dramatically in the United States, and Mexican Americans, along with the rest of society, confronted the new reality of warfare abroad and profound social transformation at home. Economic activity related to World War II and the Korean conflict stimulated migration from the countryside into the cities, opening up new opportunities for marginal sectors of the labor force. During a time of emergency and great labor shortages, many working-class Mexican Americans found employment in the defense industries that proliferated throughout the Southwest, earning higher incomes and realizing gains in their standard of living.

Hundreds of thousands of young Mexican Americans entered all branches of the military and came in direct contact with European Americans from all walks of life and from different parts of the country. Such interaction provided a powerful, eye-opening experience for individuals who had previously known only the communities where they lived. They learned more about American society and, just as importantly, they experienced far less discrimination in the military than what they had left behind in civilian life. For the most part the military treated them as soldiers, not as despised Mexicans. Different branches of the service recognized many Americans of Mexican descent for their valor and decorated them with the highest awards that the nation could bestow on its heroes, including the Congressional Medal of Honor. Service in the military also qualified Hispanic veterans for the GI Bill, which provided valuable housing and educational benefits. The number of Mexican Americans enrolled in college increased significantly.

On the home front during the war years, many women of Mexican heritage gained valuable experience as community organizers and leaders through involvement in a variety of patriotic causes. In Tucson, Chicanas organized La Asociación Hispano-Americana de Madres y Esposas to facilitate the selling of war bonds, assisting the Red Cross, promoting the conservation of resources, raising funds for community projects, and organizing activities to sustain the morale of servicemen.[13] After the war many of these women became stalwarts in civil rights organizations.

Experiences in the military likewise helped to prepare many veterans for political activism on behalf of their communities. After risking their lives for their country they determined to eliminate discrimination at home. Military service had made them more self-confident and had given them new tools to fight for justice. Not surprisingly, many joined the struggle to uplift the condition of Mexican-origin people who remained impoverished, exploited, and manipulated by the political system. Veterans organized the American GI Forum following the refusal in 1948 by a European American-run funeral parlor in Three Rivers, Texas, to allow a wake to be held for Félix Longoria, a soldier who had been killed in the Philippines. The outraged veterans enlisted the aid of Senator Lyndon Johnson, who secured the soldier's burial in Arlington National Cemetery. The Three Rivers incident launched the GI Forum as one of the most successful organizations in the pursuit of veterans' rights and the struggle for social justice. Politically, the GI Forum engaged in activities common to other groups, training candidates to run for office, holding fundraisers to help voters pay their poll tax, organizing voter registration drives, and helping to get out the vote on election day. In addition, its leadership, especially principal founder Dr. Héctor P. García, became deeply involved in Texas Democratic politics. Eventually the GI Forum established chapters throughout the country and increased its membership into the tens of thousands.

Veterans, as members of organizations or as individuals, also took part in the effort to end machine politics in their communities. In McAllen, Texas, for example, in the late 1940s a group of veterans founded a newspaper and challenged the local ring that sustained the traditional *patrón-peón* relationship. Appalled that despite comprising well more than half of the population in McAllen, very few Mexican Americans held elected or appointed offices, the veterans blasted the *jefes* (bosses) in the community for selling out to the European American power structure. Editorials encouraged the people to break off their ties with the machine.

It is time that our Latin American element, as the Anglo-Saxons are accustomed to calling us, make use of their rights as citizens, and if tomorrow we wish to vote for a cooper, may it be our conscience that tells us to do so without the intervention of the dirty lunch of barbecue and beer with which the inferior politicians are accustomed to buying our vote. Let us vote as our conscience dictates, then, and not as our friends, who are paid by the political machine, tell us.[14]

The political situation in McAllen reflected general conditions throughout Texas at midcentury. In San Antonio, where Mexican-origin people made up about 40 percent of the population, Spanish-surname elected officials in the city and the county amounted to a mere school board member and a justice of the peace. A machine controlled by a powerful, well-connected, patronage-wielding European American sheriff held dominion over a substantial portion of the Mexican American vote. Other European American bosses ruled over blocs of voters such as city employees with the help of Hispanic *jefecitos* or *coyotes* who served as intermediaries. In El Paso, where people of Mexican extraction comprised half of the population, only one Spanish-surnamed individual, a school board member, held political office. No Mexican Americans appeared among the state representatives or on the lists of elected and appointed city and county officials. Bossism, patronage, and fraud characterized El Paso politics, prompting liberal writer Carey McWilliams to suggest the need for a congressional inquiry. "It comes as something of a shock to be told," wrote McWilliams in *The Nation*, "that the secrecy of the ballot in western Texas is a myth. El Pasoans with whom I discussed local politics are convinced that ballots are customarily checked to see how certain individuals voted and that afterward people often lose their jobs."[15]

The well-known activist, lawyer, and university professor José Angel Gutiérrez has characterized the experience of casting a ballot during the 1950s as a "nightmare" for large numbers of Tejanos/as who attempted to exercise this right:

Mexican Americans presenting themselves to vote either absentee or in person at the polling place were subjected to intimidation by the clerks and precinct judges. The first questions out of a clerk or election judge usually were framed in a loud, angry tone of voice, in English: "What is your name?" "Are you a citizen?" "Can you speak English?" "Where do you live?" Rather than being helpful, hospitable and supportive of the voter, their demeanor was one of contempt and suspicion that the voter was up to no good. Usually, the clerk or election judge would fire off several more questions in the same ugly tone: "Where is your voter registration card?" "Where is your poll tax receipt?" "What proof of eligibility do you have?" "Where do you work?" This last question was the most ominous, as your job could be on the line if the clerks spoke to your employer about you.[16]

In California, the post–World War II period spawned Unity Leagues that attacked discrimination and fought for greater political representation. Unity Leaguers in Chino conducted a successful voter registration drive that led to the election of Andrew Morales to the city council in 1946. Three years later another new group, the Community Service Organization (cso), led the effort to elect World War II veteran Edward Roybal to the Los Angeles City Council, the first Mexican American to sit in that body since 1881. In 1962 Roybal won a congressional seat and held it for decades. In the same year voters elected John Moreno and Philip Soto to the California state legislature, the first Mexican Americans to sit in that body since the nineteenth century. The cso grew in influence, registering tens of thousands of new voters and helping Mexican Americans from small communities to win elected office. It also attacked discrimination in housing and education and fought vigorously against police brutality. In 1962, at its peak, the cso claimed twenty-two chapters in California and Arizona. cso, the Alianza Hispano Americana, and other groups became instrumental in the election of several Mexican Americans to the Arizona state house during the 1950s. Underrepresentation in Arizona's state government prevailed, however, as exemplified by the appointment of very few Mexican Americans to gubernatorial boards and commissions. In 1953, only eleven of 452 members of such bodies had Spanish surnames; in 1965 the number was eight out of 449.[17]

Back in Texas, in the 1950s machine politics began to wane as the Mexican American middle class expanded and as more veterans exerted leadership, making it possible for the group to wield its political muscle in an independent manner as never before. Thus in 1951 Henry B. González, an advocate of civil rights, won a seat on the San Antonio City Council. That marked the beginning of his long and distinguished political career. In 1956 González became the first Mexican-descent member of the Texas state senate, and in 1961 he won election to the U.S. Congress, also a first for a Tejano/a. Interestingly, González won his congressional seat with the help of Mexico's hugely popular comic and movie star Cantínflas, who made appearances at campaign rallies in San Antonio. González served in Congress for nearly four decades.

In west Texas, Raymond Telles overcame great odds to become the mayor of El Paso in 1957, the first Latino/a in the twentieth century elected chief executive of a large southwestern urban center. Victory in the Telles campaigns of 1957 and 1959 required extraordinary mobilization of the Mexican American community, including large-scale involvement of volunteers from organizations such as LULAC and the Veterans of Foreign Wars, and major fundraising drives to pay poll taxes for large numbers of poor voters. Telles, a decorated air force ex-major, downplayed his ethnicity in order to minimize European American opposition and, to survive two terms in office, he pursued moderate reforms rather than attempting to make structural changes. European Americans watched his running of the city closely, and many became supporters after witnessing his honest and efficient performance in office. Yet some European American influentials revealed their deep-seated prejudice by asking repeatedly, "How can we hold our heads up in the state of Texas when we have a Mexican mayor?" [18] European American Texans hostile to the election of Mexican American candidates had no choice but to accept the new reality of greater Hispanic representation in the state by the mid-1960s, as exemplified by a dozen Spanish-surname incumbent mayors, twenty-eight county commissioners, and seven state legislators.[19]

The political gains in Texas and California in the post–World War II period had great significance, of course, but these new levels of representation still lagged far behind those achieved by the Hispanos/as of New Mexico, who had long enjoyed much more favorable conditions that made possible greater success at the polls. At the time that Mexican Americans in Texas and California acquired some tools to begin prying open the political system in the late 1940s, Hispanos/as in New Mexico already comprised 34 percent of all county officeholders in their state, 41 percent of the members of the state house of representatives, 38 percent of the state senate, and 46 percent of elected state executives and judges. Many Hispanic New

Mexicans had served in Congress since the 1870s. For the period under discussion, Antonio Fernández held a congressional seat from 1943 to 1956, and Joseph Montoya from 1957 to 1964. More impressively, Dennis Chávez served in the U.S. Senate from 1935 to 1962, and in 1964 Joseph Montoya became a U.S. Senator as well, remaining in that office until 1977.[20] That level of representation would be maintained in New Mexico throughout the latter twentieth century.

The emergence of explicitly political organizations among Mexican Americans marks one of the most important developments in the Southwest during the period. A new level of energy could be detected in the 1960 presidential campaign, when many communities formed Viva Kennedy clubs in order to mobilize voters on behalf of Senator John F. Kennedy. Encouraged by the enthusiastic response to political activity both before and during the Kennedy campaign, political activists formed two political organizations: the Texas-based Political Association of Spanish-Speaking Organizations (PASSO), and the California-based Mexican American Political Association (MAPA). Both groups had nonpartisan agendas designed to promote the interests of Mexican Americans within the established political parties and to directly assist Chicano/a candidates for office. MAPA became instrumental in getting several Mexican Americans elected to office in California during the early 1960s, while PASSO's greatest triumph took place in 1963 in Crystal City, Texas, where it joined a coalition that ousted European Americans from city government and replaced them with Mexican Americans. Although the influence of MAPA and PASSO declined in the ensuing years, they left a lasting impact on the community by inspiring greater political action. For example, in Arizona in 1962, a PASSO-type organization known as the American Coordinating Council on Political Organization helped to elect five Mexican Americans to the city council in the town of Miami.

The proliferation of organizations with labor, civil rights, and political agendas stimulated the creation of confederations that would make it possible for the Mexican American community to speak forcefully and in unison on issues where broad agreement existed. On the left, El Congreso del Pueblo de Habla Española, or The Congress of Spanish-Speaking Peoples, which functioned from 1939 to 1942, brought together many unions and activist organizations. In addition to its emphasis on workers' rights, El

Congreso adopted a strong civil rights agenda, encouraging Latinos/as to register to vote and exercise their rights as citizens. The affiliation of some of its leaders with the Communist Party subjected El Congreso to red-baiting and weakened its support in the community. When the United States entered World War II, many of its members joined the military and the organization faded. Luisa Moreno, Josefina Fierro de Bright, Emma Tenayuca, Eduardo Quevedo, and Bert Corona provided much of El Congreso's leadership between its founding in 1939 and its demise in 1942.

Another radical coalition, the Asociación Nacional México-Americana (ANMA), emerged in 1949 when leaders from the International Union of Mine, Mill and Smelter Workers joined supporters of former presidential candidate Henry Wallace and other community organizers to form "a permanent national organization to defend the rights of the Mexican American people." For about five years ANMA pursued a pro-worker, pacifist agenda that invited red-baiting and harassment by the FBI. Like El Congreso, AMNA effectively incorporated women in leadership positions. For example, Isabel Gonzáles and Celia Rodríguez served as vice presidents (at different times), Xochitl Ruiz as secretary-general, and Florencia Luna as secretary-treasurer. At its peak in the early 1950s ANMA had chapters throughout the Southwest and a membership of between two and four thousand.[21]

Moderate, middle-class organizations also sought to form alliances to strengthen the voice of the Mexican American community. Thus in 1951 representatives from the Unity Leagues, the Alianza Hispano-Americana, LULAC, CSO, and the GI Forum established the American Council of Spanish-Speaking Organizations for the purpose of increasing political participation among Latinos/as and ending discrimination in employment, housing, and education. Headed by Dr. George I. Sánchez, a professor at the University of New Mexico, the council emphasized educational issues. As with other coalitions, the council's life lasted but a few years as member organizations gradually diminished their involvement and support.

Since 1965: New Breakthroughs and Accelerated Participation

In the 1960s, powerful social forces precipitated profound changes in the United States, significantly altering the lives of Americans, including Mexican Americans and other minorities. The African American–led Civil Rights Movement reached its apogee as it prodded the U.S. Congress to pass legislation designed to strengthen and expand the tools used to elevate the status of subordinated groups. On the all-important issue of school desegregation, the Civil Rights Act of 1964 fortified the Brown decision issued by the U.S. Supreme Court ten years earlier. The Act mandated nondiscrimination in employment and in the use of public facilities and accommodations. In 1968 Congress passed another Civil Rights Act that prohibited discrimination in housing. The elimination of barriers to political participation, first attempted in the Voting Rights Acts of 1957 and 1960, received a powerful boost with the passage of the Voting Rights Act of 1965 and adoption of subsequent amendments and extensions. Social justice emerged as a national imperative as Americans became more aware of the civil rights problem and the incidence of extreme poverty among such groups as whites in Appalachia, blacks in the Deep South, and Mexican-descent farmworkers in the Southwest. The Lyndon B. Johnson administration responded to the growing sentiment to help the downtrodden by launching the War on Poverty, the centerpiece of an ambitious initiative to build the Great Society. Federally funded projects intended to improve the lives of the poor sprouted throughout the country.

Meanwhile, activists mobilized against the war in Vietnam, which they saw as immoral and a drain on the nation's resources. Demonstrations frequently occurred on college campuses and in the streets of large cities. As the war dragged on, public opposition surged among the mainstream population and in minority communities. Vietnam brought to light the disproportionate share of the burden placed on the poor to fight an unpopular war.

By the mid-1960s many young Chicanos/as had become activists in the Civil Rights Movement and the Anti-War Movement. As militancy rose in the barrios, members of traditional organizations such as LULAC and the GI Forum looked on with apprehension. Veterans of World War II and the Korean conflict became apprehensive at the boldness with which the young challenged the political establishment. Not surprisingly, a split emerged along generational lines over participation in public demonstrations and open repudiation of the draft and the Vietnam War. Despite these differences, however, the old and the young agreed strongly on the need for improving social and economic conditions in the community and empowering Mexican Americans in the political arena. As a result, increased activism ensued on both ends of the age spectrum. That ushered in the Chicano Movement, a transformational development unprecedented in the history of Hispanics in the United States.

Dramatic events during the mid-1960s marked the beginning of the Movement. The turbulence that followed stunned a country accustomed to thinking of Mexicans and Mexican Americans as a passive people. In 1965, César Chávez led militant agricultural strikes and boycotts that attracted extraordinary publicity. Volunteers descended on Delano, California, to help the strikers. The spectacular victories scored by the farmworkers and civil rights activism in the cities encouraged greater assertiveness among Mexican American leaders long frustrated by the slow response of the federal bureaucracy to a host of problems in their communities. In 1966 and 1967 walkouts from government-sponsored conferences occurred in Albuquerque and El Paso respectively. Impatient Chicanos/as no longer played along with government officials who conducted studies and held hearings but took little direct action to solve pressing problems. In northern New Mexico, Reis López Tijerina and his Alianza de Pueblos Libres (Alliance of Free Communities) captured the nation's attention in the summer of 1967 with daring actions that dramatized efforts to regain land lost by Hispanos/as in the nineteenth century. Invasions of federal land and a shooting incident in a courthouse prompted New Mexican officials to call out the National Guard as the hunt for aliancistas intensified. Tijerina was arrested and convicted of destruction of federal property, and served time in prison. But the land movement continued as the Alianza kept the spotlight on the plight of Hispanos/as who had been stripped of their birthright.

College students, especially in California and Texas, played key roles in the unfolding rebellions in their communities. The Civil Rights Movement, antiwar demonstrations, farmworkers' struggles, and the Tijerina uprising captivated their interest. Many also drew inspiration from the Crusade for Justice, a youth-focused organization located in Denver and headed by the charismatic Rodolfo "Corky" González, a former boxer and Democratic Party activist. González' epic poem "I am Joaquín" extolled the Chicano/a heritage, and his sponsorship of a conference in 1969 produced El Plan Espiritual de Aztlán, which promoted Chicano/a nationalism. Beginning in

1966, students across the Southwest formed organizations such as UMAS (United Mexican American Students), MECHA (Movimiento Estudiantil Chicano de Aztlán), and MAYO (Mexican American Youth Organization). Concentrating on change in colleges and universities, activists pressured officials to recruit more Mexican American students, to offer more scholarships and grants, to hire more Mexican American faculty, and to establish courses and programs that related to the Mexican/Mexican American experience. Young militants also got involved in community issues, joining grassroots groups engaged in bringing about improvements for the masses. In particular, restless youth participated in the organizing of demonstrations against educational institutions deemed indifferent to the needs of the community. The massive public school walkouts and boycotts that occurred in California, Texas, Arizona, Colorado, Michigan, and other places in 1968 and 1969 played a decisive role in escalating the activism seen in many communities. In Los Angeles, veterans of the school walkouts later used their experience to organize the Chicano Moratorium, an antiwar crusade that culminated in a massive demonstration in 1970. Tragically, the event erupted in violence that led to the death of popular journalist Rubén Salazar at the hands of the police.

Chicano/a activists who felt alienated from the mainstream political process frequently discussed the need for political mobilization of the masses. Thus leaders of the Chicano Movement proposed the creation of an independent, leftist party dedicated to addressing the needs of La Raza. The idea caught on quickly, and in 1970 some three hundred Tejanos/as launched La Raza Unida Party in Texas. Boasting chapters and affiliates in seventeen states by 1972, the party held its first national convention in El Paso, where José Angel Gutiérrez, who had participated in the successful political takeover of Crystal City, Texas, in the 1960s, emerged as spokesman. Throughout the 1970s La Raza Unida scored impressive victories in Tejano/a communities, especially small towns in the border region. Moreover, Ramsey Muñiz, the Raza Unida candidate for the Texas governorship, garnered 214,000 and 190,000 votes respectively in 1972 and 1974. Outside the Lone Star State the party enjoyed less success but still managed to elect some of its members to local offices.

It is clear that the early 1970s constituted the golden age of La Raza Unida. The second half of the decade brought rapid decline as internal dissension, criminal convictions of key leaders, external attacks, and a drop in membership took their toll. Perhaps the biggest cause of the decline was the unwillingness of most Mexican Americans to embrace a party perceived to have a radical ideology and narrow ethnic interests. Though defunct by the end of the decade, La Raza Unida left a legacy of progressive political ideas and activism, and a record of history-making electoral victories.

The bold and aggressive initiatives pursued by La Raza Unida and other groups that formed the core of the Chicano Movement had the effect of spurring greater political activism among established community organizations. The feeling grew that Mexican Americans in the past had been too deferential and polite in dealing with the power structure. Members of the new generation pressed for novel approaches and quicker results. Thus traditional leaders who had previously accepted the system on its own terms began to step up their own exhortations for rapid and meaningful change. LULAC presidents in particular assumed a more vocal and assertive stance in demanding greater representation in public appointive offices and increased allocation of government resources. As new funding opportunities opened up in the public and private sectors, LULAC and other organizations, including local groups, established outreach and service centers in Mexican American communities throughout the United States. Invariably political activity swirled around many of these projects.

The Chicano Movement spawned new organizations whose level of sophistication and effectiveness elevated advocacy on behalf of the Spanish-speaking population to new levels. Former activists who successfully made the transition from fighting the system from the outside to working to change it from within founded or staffed many of these groups. The National Council for La Raza, established in 1968 with the help of the Ford Foundation, evolved from a small, regional coalition to a nationwide confederation based in Washington, D.C. In the late 1990s its long-time leader, Raúl Yzaguirre, could look back at three decades of highly visible advocacy in the political arena, the government bureaucracy, and the private sector. Another important organization, the Mexican American Legal Defense and Educational Fund (MALDEF), also began in 1968 with the assistance of the Ford Foundation. Patterned after the Legal Defense Fund (LDF) of the National Association for the Advancement of Colored People (NAACP), MALDEF functioned mostly as a legal aid society for the first five years.

Subsequently, however, it aggressively litigated many cases pertaining to issues of great significance like immigrant rights, educational segregation and financing, employment discrimination, and political representation. In one of its most important initiatives, MALDEF persuaded Congress in the 1970s to extend the Voting Rights Act to Hispanics. That obligated the federal government to scrutinize local electoral practices and eliminate barriers and irregularities that diminished Latino/a participation in the political process. Additionally, non-English-speaking voters received language assistance, including bilingual materials and ballots.

Using the Voting Rights Act and other legal weapons, for several decades MALDEF has assisted many communities in their quest for empowerment. Texas represents the best example of MALDEF-led political change. As a result of countless voting rights lawsuits in the 1970s and 1980s, many Texas cities and towns had to abandon the at-large voting system, which gave the advantage to European American candidates, in favor of election by district, which made it possible to elect more Mexican Americans. Meanwhile, the Southwest Voter Education Project (SVEP), founded in 1974, collaborated closely with MALDEF to expand the ranks of registered voters in the barrios, particularly in Texas. Predictably, the number of Tejano/a elected officials went up significantly at the local level and in the state legislature.

Other organizations that have also made enormous contributions toward improving social conditions and increasing political representation in recent decades are locally based, grassroots federations supported by the Catholic Church and other religious denominations. Mexican American women have been heavily involved in these groups. Their modus operandi derives from the Saul Alinsky school of community organizing, which advocates galvanizing support in poor neighborhoods for basic projects such as infrastructure improvements and using strength in numbers to elect responsive candidates and to hold accountable those already in office. Perhaps the most successful of these groups is the San Antonio–based Communities Organized for Public Service (COPS). Following its birth in 1974 COPS compiled an impressive list of accomplishments, quickly evolving into a major player in the local political process. Activism and pressure promulgated through the COPS network, along with the involvement of MALDEF and SVEP, largely explain the dramatic transformation in the late 1970s and early 1980s of the traditional European American elite–dominated political system in San Antonio to a new one characterized by power sharing with Mexican Americans and other formerly marginalized groups. During that period of rapid change San Antonio witnessed several notable breakthroughs, including a dramatic rise in the number of Mexican Americans on the city council and the election of Henry Cisneros as mayor in 1981. Cisneros became the first Mexican-descent chief executive of the city in almost a century and a half. COPS-like organizations in other cities include the El Paso Interfaith Sponsoring Organization (EPISO), Pima County Interfaith Council (PCIC) in Tucson, and United Neighborhoods Organization (UNO) in Los Angeles.

One of the most interesting recent examples of grassroots activism is the work of the Mothers of East Los Angeles (MELA), an impressive network founded in 1985 by ordinary Chicanas concerned with quality-of-life issues. MELA surfaced as a movement when California announced its intent to build a prison in the community. Rallies and demonstrations forced the authorities to drop the proposal. MELA achieved another victory when it blocked a plan to build a toxic waste incinerator. As the organization became institutionalized, it took on a variety of projects, including water conservation, job promotion, environmental awareness, community cleanup, and fundraising for scholarships. In short, the women of MELA "transformed the everyday problems they confronted in their neighborhoods into political concerns."[22] Their success has served as an inspiration to community activists throughout the Southwest.

Another type of institution that has made a significant difference for Mexicans/Mexican Americans is the Community Development Corporation (CDC), a unique public/private, quasi-political organization. The CDC concept unfolded during the 1960s when the federal government promoted local efforts to bring about economic development and community rehabilitation. Between 1964 and 1973 six major Latino/a-run CDCs sprouted in California, Arizona, New Mexico, Colorado, and Texas. The East Los Angeles Community Union, or TELACU, evolved into the largest CDC. Boasting three hundred million dollars in assets in 1993, TELACU could look back at twenty-five years of intense involvement in physical and economic improvements in Latino/a neighborhoods, including housing rehabilitation, revitalization of public places, founding of industrial parks, and creation of new businesses. Leaders of TELACU worked closely with elected officials to secure public funds for projects. Frequently they also acted as power brokers in the selection of candidates for office. That kind of political activism raised eyebrows, as did the salaries and perks enjoyed by high-living TELACU executives. In the 1980s the organization's reputation suffered from media and government investigations of alleged corruption, but TELACU survived the storm by making timely reforms. Thus it continued to play a major role in the economic development arena.[23]

Clearly organizational activity has been a significant factor in the political advancements recorded by Mexican Americans since the 1960s. With the support and involvement of the vast array of new community groups, more Chicanos/as have become public figures and have represented Latino/a interests. In particular, impressive results have been achieved by aggressively using the Voting Rights Act to stimulate increased electoral participation and to bring about replacement of the system of at-large elections with district representation. Between 1984 and 1997, the number of Latino/a elected officials increased by 73 percent, from 3,128 to 5,400. At the state level, by 1996 Mexican Americans in Texas made up nearly one-fifth of the 150 house members and nearly one-fourth of the thirty-one state senators; in California they increased their share of seats in the state assembly by thirteen. Hispanos/as in New Mexico, ever the trendsetters in political representation, expanded the number of mayoralties under their control from 24 percent in 1985 to 37 percent in 1992. In San Antonio in 1992, Latinos/as made up almost half of all elected officials, compared to only 26 percent in 1970. Among women, electoral successes have been impressive as well. Between 1984 and 1993 Latinas nationwide experienced a 179 percent growth in the number of offices won at the polls. In Arizona, Latinas made up 27 percent of all Hispanic elected officials in 1993, 29 percent in California, 19 percent in Colorado, 22 percent in New Mexico, and 20 percent in Texas.[24]

Outside the Southwest, Mexican Americans made similar progress, especially in cities where they had substantial numbers. Chicago is a case in point. In the 1980s Chicano/a activists joined Puerto Ricans and other Latinos/as in a successful challenge to the machine politics long practiced by those in power. A court decision led to the redrawing of aldermanic districts, including the creation of four Hispanic wards. As a result, by 1992

Chicago had four Latino/a alderpersons, four state representatives, two state senators, and one congressperson. In Illinois as a whole in 1993 Latinas made up a whopping 65 percent of all Hispanic elected officials.[25]

The political breakthroughs extended into executive and judicial offices at the state and national levels as well as the U.S. Congress. In the 1970s and 1980s three Mexican Americans served as governors of southwestern states: Raúl Castro in Arizona and Jerry Apodaca and Toney Anaya in New Mexico. In Texas, Raúl A. González held a seat on the State Supreme Court from 1984 to 1998, and Dan Morales held the post of attorney general from 1990 to 1998. Whereas only seven Hispanics served in the U.S. House of Representatives in 1977, nineteen held seats in 1997. With respect to the executive branch of the federal government, five Mexican Americans served in the president's Cabinet during the 1980s and 1990s: Lauro Cavazos as Secretary of Education, Manuel Luján as Secretary of the Interior, Henry Cisneros as Secretary of Housing and Urban Development, Federico Peña as Secretary of Energy and Secretary of Transportation, and Bill Richardson as Ambassador to the United Nations and Secretary of Energy.

In 1996, Latinos/as could justifiably take pride in the 6.6 million registered voters in their communities and the 5 million turnout in the general election, both records for the group. The 56 percent Latino/a voter turnout—the percentage of eligible voters who actually voted (5 million out of 8.9 million)—surpassed the 49 percent recorded for the general population. One of the notable breakthroughs that year included the election of Cruz Bustamante as the speaker of the California Assembly, the first Latino to hold this powerful position since 1871. Loretta Sánchez achieved another milestone in the 46th Congressional district in Orange County, California, when she defeated ultraconservative incumbent Bob Dornan. High naturalization rates among immigrants and a concerted voter registration drive in Hispanic neighborhoods proved decisive in piling up votes for Sánchez, prompting a jolted Dornan to charge that thousands of illegal immigrants had voted in the election. Subsequent investigations proved Dornan wrong, allowing Sánchez and the Mexican American community to take control of one more congressional district. Meanwhile another Latina, Lucille Roybal-Allard, savored reelection to her third term in Congress as representative of the nearby 33rd district. Along with Los Angeles County Supervisor Gloria Molina, a veteran politician who had previously held seats in the Los Ange-

les City Council and the California Assembly, these three women constituted a powerful force in Latino/a politics. Other recently elected Latinas
in Southern California include state assembly persons Marta Escutia, Grace
Napolitano, Diana Martínez, and Hilda Solís, and Los Angeles Board of
Education members Vicky Castro and Leticia Quesada.[26]

The dramatic trend toward greater electoral representation continued in
1998, when Latino/a candidates won significant victories across the country.
In California, Cruz Bustamante captured the office of lieutenant governor,
becoming the first Spanish-surname individual to hold a statewide post in
more than a century. California's Latinos/as also picked up an additional
six seats in the legislature (for a total of twenty-four), won the mayoralty
in San Jose, and claimed the office of sheriff of Los Angeles County. Elsewhere, Latinos/as won more seats in the legislatures of Arizona (two), New
Mexico (two), and Colorado (one). They also swept the following statewide
offices:

Texas: secretary of state and railroad commissioner
Colorado: attorney general
New Mexico: attorney general, secretary of state, state auditor, and state
    treasurer.[27]

These developments clearly show that the political status of Mexican
Americans has improved substantially and dramatically. Yet it is just as clear
that an immense gap still remains between the group and the dominant society. In many places Spanish-surname persons continue to have little or no
representation. For example, in the San Diego area in 1996, only three Lati-
nos/as sat on city councils of nine different cities, although in most of these
communities they comprised sizable portions of the population. Only four
Latinos/as claimed seats on the school boards of sixteen different districts;
in half of those districts the proportion of Latinos/as in the population
ranged from 27 to 43 percent, yet no Latinos/as served on their respective
school boards. Arizona is cited as a state where Hispanics, who make up 22
percent of the population, have made significant progress. While true, the
following statistics for 1998 are sobering: Mexican Americans did not hold
a statewide office, did not sit on the University Board of Regents, did not
occupy a seat on the Phoenix City Council, and held only one of the state's
eight congressional seats.[28]

Conclusion

The road to self-determination for Mexican Americans in the political arena has been long and difficult. Subordination, including exclusion from public office and lack of proportional representation in decision-making bodies, can be traced as far back as 1836, when Texas began functioning as a political entity separate from Mexico. Marginality continued as the predominant tendency until the post–World War II period, when change driven by new economic opportunities and a fledgling Civil Rights Movement became apparent. During the 1960s, the Chicano Movement spurred a dramatic increase in involvement in public affairs and representation in public office. By the end of the twentieth century, marginality had been reduced to the point that Latinos/as constituted powerful voting blocks in local, state, and national elections.

The interplay between economic forces and population numbers, in combination with racial practices in the dominant society largely explain the political experience of the group. In broad terms, the European American takeover of the Southwest in the nineteenth century imposed a new economic order that pushed Mexican-origin people to the periphery and a demographic structure that relegated them to minority status. These new conditions triggered a political decline particularly evident after 1880. Efforts to reverse the downward slide yielded limited results through the first half of the twentieth century but, following World War II, demographic expansion and social mobility in the Mexican American community set the stage for rapid advancements.

The recent breakthroughs at the polls would not have been possible without the extraordinary growth of the national economy since the 1940s, which engendered a steady expansion of the Mexican American middle class. Greater affluence assured increased independence from both the European American power structure and machine politics in the barrios. Another enormously important factor is the decline in discrimination brought about through civil rights legislation and affirmative action programs, at least through the early 1990s. Finally, the explosive expansion of the Hispanic voting-eligible population has yielded a larger electorate than ever before. A part of that growth derives from the hundreds of thousands of undocumented immigrants who received amnesty in 1986, subsequently became U.S. citizens, and are now voters. Other immigrants who are not yet citizens but are on the waiting lists to undergo naturalization will become a part of the electorate as well in the near future. In sum, the foundation for continued growth in Mexican American political power is in place, and the group can expect greater visibility and influence in the new century.

EIGHT

Reflections

❖

This concluding chapter summarizes major findings in the book and ponders the meaning of historical change for Mexicans and Mexican Americans in the United States at the turn of the new millennium. Specific topics addressed include demographic change, social and economic advances, upward mobility among Mexican immigrants, the effect of lingering stereotypes in the mainstream population, the growing significance of transnational connections and globalization, and the implications of contemporary public debates regarding highly divisive issues.

Numbers and Diversification

In the last 150 years, Mexican-heritage people have evolved from a small, regionally based group into a large, nationally significant population. Numbering about 87,000 in 1850, the group grew to approximately 500,000 in 1900, to at least 2.3 million in 1950, and largely as a result of large-scale immigration from Mexico after midcentury, to some 20 million by 2000. In 1910, Mexicans and Mexican Americans made up only 2 percent of the total population in California, but by 1990 that figure had risen to 21 percent; in Texas the corresponding percentage jumped from 6 to 23.[1] Nearly the entire Mexican-descent population lived in the Southwest in the early 1900s, but at the start of the twenty-first century, significant numbers can be found far beyond this region. Mexicans and Mexican Americans now live and work in every state in the union, including Alaska and Hawaii.

Notwithstanding strong common elements such as language, culture, religion, humble origins, and identification with Mexico, from the start people of Mexican extraction have been characterized by heterogeneity. Diversity among individuals and groups derives from distinct historical backgrounds, connections with different parts of the United States or Mexico, and singular local economic, social, and cultural environments. The Hispanos/as of New Mexico are perhaps the most distinct subgroup. They have stood apart from the rest of the Mexican/Mexican American population largely because of their strong link with the Spanish colonial period. Many of them actually trace their ancestry to migrations from central Mexico between the sixteenth and nineteenth centuries. The fact that a large percentage of Nuevo Mexicanos/as have lived in isolated mountain villages shaped by pastoralism and self-sufficient agriculture also underlines their distinctiveness. New Mexico differs dramatically from states like California and Texas in having limited appeal for immigrants from Mexico; this is explained by New Mexico's historical isolation, its largely localized agrarian economy, and the lack of heavy industry. Over time remoteness and limited immigration reinforced the feeling among substantial numbers of Nuevo Mexicanos/as that their way of life reflected so-called Spanish, rather than Mexican, norms.

In contrast to New Mexico, Hispanics of Mexican heritage in other parts of the country have experienced less isolation and have maintained stronger connections with Mexico. But ongoing links with the homeland do not negate diversity. Regional and cultural heterogeneity remains a constant because of the inherent, long-standing, internal variation of the overall Mexican-origin population. Immigrants have come from many states in Mexico, each with its own cultural characteristics. And in the United States itself, life for Chicanos/as has varied considerably from coast to coast.

In California, the state with the largest immigrant cohort, most people of Mexican ancestry have lived in large and small industrial cities along the coast and in interior communities sustained by commercial agriculture. Although some native Californios/as have maintained a Spanish orientation, the continuous heavy influx of immigrants from many parts of Mexico has assured strong identification with many strands of Mexican culture. Mexican-descent Arizonans are also mostly derived from recent immigration flows. In both the large cities of Phoenix and Tucson and in

the small towns and mining camps scattered throughout the state, Arizonenses have exhibited a predominance of Sonoran cultural influences as a
result of the steady (albeit modest) influx of people from the neighboring
Mexican state. Native as well as immigrant Tejanos/as have clustered primarily in cities, ranching areas, and agricultural communities situated near
or adjacent to the international boundary with Mexico. In south Texas and
especially the Lower Rio Grande Valley, a Tex-Mex identity that mirrors
the cultural patterns and folkways of northeastern Mexico set in long ago.
Tejanos/as who live along the border with Mexico, portrayed as a people
from "a distinctive borderland subregion" by geographer Daniel D. Arreola,
are a good example of regional particularism. Arreola documents the singular Mexico origins of Tejanos/as in this area, along with the area's unique
"place personality," "townscape," "peculiarity of Spanish-language habit,"
and the "popularity of [Mexican] cultural celebrations." [2] Applying the kind
of criteria employed by Arreola and other cultural scholars, many Mexican/
Mexican American subregions can be identified, not only in the Southwest
but also in the Pacific Northwest, the Great Plains, the Midwest, and other
areas of the United States distant from the border region.

Since incorporation into the United States the Mexican-origin population has always been divided into two major subgroups: native-born people
and foreign-born people, who at times have acted in opposition to each
other. These two categories can be subdivided further. Within the native-
born designation are people whose roots in the United States go back only a
few years, several generations, or several centuries. Within the foreign-born
category are found legal residents versus undocumented residents, and
long-term residents versus short-term residents. Between 1900 and 1930
foreign-born people constituted well more than half of the Mexican-origin
population, but after that the percentage dropped. The massive exodus of
Mexican immigrants back to their homeland during the Depression era led
to a significant rise in the percentage of U.S.-born persons in the overall
Chicano/a population, and that trend has continued to the present. In the
1980s, however, immigration increased substantially, and by 2000 almost
two-fifths of the Mexican-origin population claimed foreign birth. If the
foreign-born are combined with the native-born of foreign parentage, it
becomes clear that Mexican-origin people of "foreign stock" have become
(once again) a majority in the Chicano/a community.

Race and class are significant distinguishing variables as well. All gradations of skin color are found among people of Mexican extraction, ranging from very dark to very fair. Intermarriage with European Americans over many generations has resulted in the "whitening" of a portion of the Mexican-origin population. Most members of the group, however, continue to manifest physical characteristics associated with the mestizo population of Mexico. Similarly, all social classes have been present in this community. Nevertheless, over time most Latinos/as of Mexican descent have occupied the lower rungs of the socioeconomic ladder, both in their home and in the United States. Only since the mid-twentieth century has the Chicano/a middle class expanded sufficiently to become a significant cohort in U.S. society.

Finally, the degree of assimilation has varied substantially among the different sectors that comprise the Mexican-origin population. Affluent people in urban settings, especially fair-skinned ones, have attained the highest rates of assimilation. At the opposite end, poor people in isolated rural communities and in marginalized urban barrios have experienced the least assimilation. Individuals situated economically and socially between these two poles have functioned in mixed, fluid environments where movement toward assimilation has, depending on time, place, and circumstances, happened fairly slowly or fairly quickly.

Figure 8.1 summarizes the influence of several of the preceding variables on the changing composition of the Mexican-origin population. The data reveal that during the twentieth century the following occurred: (1) an extraordinary increase in the size of the population, from 1.5 million in 1930 to 20 million in 2000; (2) a decline by 1960, and then a dramatic increase at century's end, in the percentage of the foreign-born; (3) a significant rise in upward mobility—and consequent expansion of the middle class—during the latter twentieth century; and (4) further substantive internal diversification caused by continuous large-scale immigration from Mexico and growing intermarriage with other groups.

Mixed Progress

Demographic and other social changes imply significant economic transformations. This is certainly the case with respect to employment patterns.

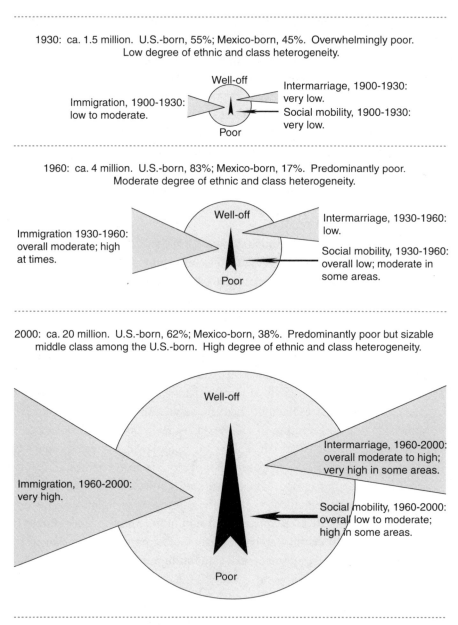

1930: ca. 1.5 million. U.S.-born, 55%; Mexico-born, 45%. Overwhelmingly poor.
Low degree of ethnic and class heterogeneity.

Well-off

Immigration, 1900-1930:
low to moderate.

Intermarriage, 1900-1930:
very low.
Social mobility, 1900-1930:
very low.

Poor

1960: ca. 4 million. U.S.-born, 83%; Mexico-born, 17%. Predominantly poor.
Moderate degree of ethnic and class heterogeneity.

Well-off

Immigration 1930-1960:
overall moderate; high
at times.

Intermarriage, 1930-1960:
low.

Social mobility, 1930-1960:
overall low; moderate in
some areas.

Poor

2000: ca. 20 million. U.S.-born, 62%; Mexico-born, 38%. Predominantly poor but sizable
middle class among the U.S.-born. High degree of ethnic and class heterogeneity.

Well-off

Immigration, 1960-2000:
very high.

Intermarriage, 1960-2000:
overall moderate to high;
very high in some areas.

Social mobility, 1960-2000:
overall low to moderate;
high in some areas.

Poor

FIGURE 8.1. Changes in the natural growth, immigration, intermarriage,
and social mobility of Mexican-origin population, 1930–2000.
(From data in chapters 1, 2, and 6)

Once the vast majority of Mexican-origin people had low-paying jobs in rural areas. After decades of continuous migration to the cities, however, most of them settled into urban occupations, meaning jobs in industry and the service sector. In reality Mexicans and Mexican Americans have been a predominantly city people since the 1930s, but most decidedly so after the 1960s. The group increased its numbers particularly in those large urban centers that offered good employment possibilities. For example, between 1930 and 1990 the percentage of Mexican-origin people in Denver grew from 2 to 16, in Houston from 5 to 22, and in Los Angeles from 8 to 27.[3]

Unfortunately, the extraordinary gains in numbers and the transformation from a rural people to an urban population have not been matched by proportional social advances. The group ascendance that unfolded in the last third of the twentieth century, admittedly impressive, touched only a minority of Latinos/as. Today large segments of the Mexican/Mexican American population remain disadvantaged and marginalized. Since the 1980s the social gap that has long separated the group from the mainstream society has actually widened. For many at the bottom of the occupational ladder, wages have declined and the struggle to survive has become more difficult. The plain truth is that the American dream of a middle-class standard of living is still unattainable for legions of Mexicans/Mexican Americans trapped in chronic poverty. Educational achievement remains far below the levels of the non-Hispanic white population. Only small portions of the Mexican-extraction population have managed to attain college degrees and professional occupations.

The bleak circumstances faced by the majority of yesterday's and today's Mexican-origin masses, however, should not obscure the fact that economic success has also been an important part of the story, even if confined to a minority of the group, select geographic locations, or specific time periods. Viewing the issue from a national perspective and dividing the twentieth century into three separate generations, the evidence suggests that the first cohort (1900–1930s) witnessed painfully limited social mobility; the second cohort (1930s–1960s) experienced only modest gains; but members of the third cohort (1960s–2000s), who found themselves better situated than previous generations to take advantage of newly created opportunities, recorded advances in the moderate to impressive range (see figure 8.1).

Beginning in the 1960s, a great social restructuring took place among

Mexicans/Mexican Americans, leading to a weighty expansion of the middle class and the emergence of a small but increasingly influential elite. More people of Mexican ancestry obtained well-paying jobs and bought homes in the better neighborhoods of countless cities. An increasing number of students graduated from colleges and universities, including elite private and public institutions. Entrepreneurs founded many new businesses. The number of Mexican Americans serving in public office went up dramatically. By the 1990s Chicano/a elected officials controlled or had significant influence in countless towns and cities where Mexican Americans comprised a majority or a substantial portion of the electorate. The transformation can be seen in cities such as San Antonio and El Paso, where Spanish-surname persons now occupy elected and appointed positions at all levels, including the very top ones.

Such progress reveals much about the will, energy, grit, steadfastness, determination, and perseverance of Mexican-origin people who have broken through many barriers that have stood in their way. These are qualities that have always been present among members of the group but have often been ignored or downplayed by researchers because of the traditional emphasis on underdevelopment and the condition of the oppressed masses. The fact is that in every generation over the last century and a half there have been Mexicans/Mexican Americans of humble origins who have overcome great impediments and realized the American dream. The difference in the late twentieth century, as compared to previous eras, is that the number of obstacles declined and the number of opportunities rose, at least for those advantageously situated to capitalize on them.

Group improvement, whether recorded in the recent or distant past, could not have happened without mass mobilization and persistent pressure applied to public and private institutions long characterized by discriminatory and exclusive policies and practices. Contrary to the views of some, Mexican-descent people have always understood the causes of underdevelopment in their communities. They have always known what hurdles blocked their path to a better life, and they have fought courageously and continuously to bring about change. Whether of working-class, middle-class, or elite status, all sectors have taken part in social movements of varied kinds. There has never been a time when Mexican-origin people have been passive in the face of oppression and discrimination. Each succeeding generation has built upon the efforts of the preceding ones, and by the latter twentieth century the accumulated hard work over many decades yielded many meaningful and impressive results.

Apart from the internal energy expended by Mexicans and Mexican Americans to better their conditions, the effects of broader structural changes in U.S. society on that process cannot be underestimated. In 1900 the United States had a predominantly agricultural economy. Few opportunities existed for working people to improve their circumstances appreciably. As the century progressed industrialization and urbanization came to dominate American life, and the possibilities for upward mobility increased. By 2000, decades of technological innovations and accelerated integration with other countries had produced extraordinary transformations whose effects rippled with great force across ethnic, racial, and class lines.

The post-1960s economic expansion in the United States opened many new opportunities for minorities in high-wage sectors, but at the same time brought structural changes that deeply hurt ordinary workers. In contrast to middle-class and upwardly mobile working-class individuals able to capitalize on the best economic and racial climate of the century and who enjoyed many successes, unfavorably placed persons, in particular farmworkers and people residing in inner cities, encountered formidable roadblocks amidst the climate of prosperity. In effect, over the last several decades, industrial restructuring and the onset of globalization have eliminated many factory and other blue-collar jobs previously within the reach of workers with low levels of education. Minimum-wage and sub-minimum-wage employment in service occupations, along with massive unemployment, have become the norm in barrios throughout the country. Escape from poverty has been made more difficult by crumbling public education, cutbacks in government programs, and increasingly complex social problems that have wreaked havoc on the structure of families.

One of the factors that has had a substantial effect on the condition of the Mexican-origin population is the unabated influx of impoverished immigrants over many decades. Great concentrations of unskilled foreign workers in urban centers such as Los Angeles have driven down wages and made unionization more difficult. The unfavorable economic impact, coupled with heightened social problems, have resulted in more intense apprehension and hostility among various sectors of society, including European Americans, African Americans, and even residents of Latino/a communities. Finding the right formula to lessen the enmity of Americans toward Hispanic immigrants and diminishing the injurious effects the issue carries into communities populated by Mexican-origin people remain formidable problems.

Mexican Immigrants and Social Mobility

One common, determining element is shared by the preponderant majority of Mexican immigrants whether of recent or earlier generations: prevalent humble origins and a life of protracted struggle in the United States. Relatively few of these newcomers have possessed the kind of personal attributes that serve to facilitate rapid integration into American society, including fair skin, behavioral traits that blend in easily with those in the mainstream culture, English-language skills, sufficient formal education, past residence in large urban centers, and work experience in an advanced industrial, technologically driven economy. The tiny minority of Mexican immigrants who have possessed such traits have indeed been a favored lot, especially those who have settled in dynamic regions of the United States where economic, educational, and cultural opportunities have been accessible to foreigners. Fair-skinned, educated, English-speaking immigrants with business or professional backgrounds who have made their homes in major cities such as Los Angeles or San Antonio have been able to prosper in their adopted homeland at similar levels as other immigrants with like characteristics, including Europeans and Asians.

But historically most Mexican immigrants have not enjoyed such advantages. The overwhelming majority of the largely dark-skinned Mexican campesinos and urban proletarians who have entered the United States, both in the distant past and recently, have had little or no formal education and have had no choice but to take unskilled, low-paying, and typically dead-end jobs. Because of their low-income status they have been forced to reside in severely disadvantaged communities. In the early decades of the twentieth century, large numbers settled out of necessity in racially intolerant rural areas in underdeveloped regions of the United States, while most recent immigrants have established their residence in problem-ridden cities overcrowded with struggling poor people, including immigrants from other lands and marginalized African Americans. Under these circumstances, it is not hard to understand the perennially formidable odds the newcomers from Mexico have faced in their quest to achieve the American dream. For the bulk of the Mexican-immigrant population, then, slow and limited progress has been the norm.

The experience of Mexican immigrants contrasts sharply with that of other foreign groups whose ranks have included sizable numbers of skilled, well-educated, professional, and affluent people. Large percentages of European Jews who settled in the United States in the early twentieth century, for instance, had predominantly urban antecedents and strong commercial and manufacturing backgrounds that served them exceedingly well in their adopted land. Two-thirds of all Jews of working age who arrived at Ellis Island between 1899 and 1910 qualified as skilled workers. The favorable employment experience of that cohort of Jewish immigrants allowed them to take ready advantage of opportunities in the rapidly expanding economy of the northeastern United States.[4] Mexican immigrants during that period, on the other hand, mostly hailed from peon or campesino backgrounds. American employers recruited them to work in the fields, mines, and railroads of the Southwest, an area that functioned as an extractive and cheap-labor colony of the northeastern United States.

More recently, the waves of Cuban refugees who arrived after 1959 included significant numbers of elite and middle-class families well prepared to make a successful economic transition in their new American environment. Generous aid provided by the U.S. government made their resettlement and integration easier still. At the time the Eisenhower and Kennedy administrations placed high priority on the incorporation of refugees from Communism in order to score propaganda points against the Castro regime in Havana as well as the Soviet Union.[5] By contrast, Mexicans who entered the United States concurrently with the early Cuban migration included very few non-working-class individuals. And rather than receiving help from the U.S. government to facilitate integration, Mexicans continued to be the main target of an increasingly restrictionist Congress and an aggressive Immigration and Naturalization Service bent on expelling as many improperly documented immigrants as possible.

In the case of Asians, large numbers of people from several nationalities have arrived recently in the United States with occupational antecedents that have been among the most impressive in the history of immigration. For example, for the years 1969–1971, 70 percent of Koreans, 70 percent of Filipinos, 47 percent of Chinese, and 45 percent of Japanese had professional backgrounds. In 1996, nearly half of all Korean, mainland Chinese, and Filipino adult immigrants with labor force experience declared their occupation as professional, executive, administrative, or managerial. For the Taiwanese and Japanese, the percentages were 69 and 66 respectively. Again, the profile of Mexican immigrants differed drastically. In 1996, only 4 percent of entering Mexican immigrants had such occupational backgrounds. Not surprisingly, those starkly divergent employment portraits are replicated in educational statistics as well. Asian immigrants have extremely high levels of education, while Mexican immigrants have among the lowest.[6]

The implications of such data are obvious. Because of their humble origins, for generations Mexicans have started the journey toward economic success in the United States far behind other groups. That explains why the rate and speed of integration has been lower and slower. Yet, under the right circumstances, even the most disadvantaged of these Mexican immigrants have penetrated the U.S. middle class. That many of them have been able to rise above both their unfavorable social antecedents and harsh obstacles in their adopted land is a testament to their fiber and determination. Seldom have Mexican immigrants received credit for this accomplishment.

Lingering Stereotypes

Several historical factors have made the relationship between the dominant society and Mexicans/Mexican Americans stand out from the interaction with other immigrant/ethnic groups. First, the United States absorbed half of Mexico by force, converting the people north of the Rio Grande into conquered subjects. That meant that after 1836 in Texas, and after 1848 elsewhere in the Southwest, Mexican immigrants encountered a climate of colonialism in the land of their forebears. Second, the history of U.S.-Mexico relations since the mid-nineteenth century is replete with conflict, much of it centered in the border region. That friction has inevitably spawned anti-Mexicanism in the United States. Third, Americans have traditionally disparaged Mexico and its people. And fourth, Mexican immigrants have been very vulnerable to stereotyping because of their predominant mestizo appearance and humble origins. Further, they have frequently become scapegoats during downturns in the U.S. economy. These realities incited xenophobia, ultra-nationalism, and disdain toward Mexicans/ Mexican Americans at various times during the twentieth century.

One of the erroneous notions held by many members of the dominant society is that Mexican-descent people are an immigrant population relatively new to the United States. This idea stems from the nonstop coverage by the media of massive immigration from Mexico. Decade by decade the problems faced by new cohorts of unassimilated newcomers have received considerable attention, contributing to a persistent impression that Mexican-origin people are unable or unwilling to join the mainstream. Americans with little or no knowledge of Mexican/Mexican American history have had trouble separating U.S. Latinos/as who have lived here for decades, generations, or even centuries, from brand-new arrivals. As a result, the majority population has internalized incorrect and damaging impressions of Mexican-origin people as perpetually downtrodden immigrants. By focusing constantly on the newcomer cohort, many Americans have consistently failed to see the successful integration of large numbers of Mexicans and Mexican Americans. Coupled with extant racist attitudes, that explains why people of Mexican extraction are often unfairly viewed as less able than Europeans, Asians, or Cubans when it comes to achieving the American dream.

The perception Americans have had of people of Mexican extraction has been strongly influenced by negative views toward Mexico. All along Mexico has been seen as a seriously troubled country that exports its problems abroad. The vilification of our neighboring republic began early in the relationship between the two countries. Fictional and nonfictional literature, the news media, movies, and television have painted Mexico as a lawless, corrupt, and undemocratic country. In the 1990s, Mexico's image suffered yet another catastrophic blow as a result of widespread publicity given to political assassinations, bungled legal investigations, drug corruption scandals in high government circles, drug-related killing fields, ubiquitous street crime, peasant rebellions, and rampant suffering brought on by economic collapse.

While the causes of Mexico's political instability are internal, in truth other disasters such as the drug scandals/violence and the devastating economic downturns are closely linked to Mexico's substantial interdependence with the United States. Yet most Americans, inclined toward simplification and stereotyping, have seen that country's troubles as completely homegrown, as nothing more than the fruits of a corrupt society. Many have even blamed Mexico as fundamentally responsible for the drug problem in the United States, failing to see or admit that the ever-growing American appetite for narcotics is the engine that drives international drug trafficking.

The relevance to Chicanos/as of Mexico's degradation by Americans is that the neighboring country's population has been viewed as a tainted people. Such disparagement has been transferred as well to Mexican-origin people in the United States. Unlike other groups who are seen as "model" populations partly because they originate in regions of the world considered enlightened or progressive (e.g., much of Europe and portions of Asia), Mexicans are stigmatized as a highly problematic minority, partly or perhaps largely because they are seen as products of a decadent country.

Transnational Connections

If many of the perceptions of Americans toward Mexico lack legitimacy, resting as they do on prejudice and shallow understanding of the root causes of that country's problems, it is indeed the case that large numbers of Mexican-origin people in the United States have maintained close links with Mexico. And that reality surely constitutes an important dimension in the Chicano/a experience. For generations, border cities such as Tijuana, Mexicali, Nogales, Ciudad Juárez, Nuevo Laredo, Matamoros, and interior centers in the border states, such as Hermosillo, Chihuahua City, and Monterrey, have been integral parts of the binational living and working space for people from many communities in the U.S. border region. Intense cross-border interaction has evolved in many forms, including job commuting, family visits, shopping, and tourism. Sustained contact with Mexico has kept Mexican culture vibrant in the United States and given impetus to a binational identity.

The decision of the Mexican government in 1996 to allow Mexicans abroad to retain their citizenship even if they become naturalized U.S. citizens has further strengthened extant transnational bonds. Previous apprehensions among immigrants about losing basic rights and privileges in Mexico, especially with respect to property ownership in coastal and border areas, have been eliminated.

But Mexico's role in the lives of millions of U.S. Mexicans and Mexican Americans goes far beyond the influences occasioned by frequent border crossings and dual citizenship. Long-standing economic ties between the U.S. Southwest and Mexico's northern states have had other profound impacts. Mexico's border cities have served as extraordinary cheap labor pools for U.S. employers, in particular agricultural growers. The availability of abundant fieldworkers so close to home has kept wages pathetically low and made unionization exceedingly difficult throughout the U.S. borderlands. While many employers have enriched themselves from the resultant high profits, farmworkers in the United States, both natives and foreigners, have struggled to survive. Increased marginalization in turn has slowed down Mexican/Mexican American entry into mainstream society.

Since the mid-1960s, a generation before the advent of the North American Free Trade Agreement (NAFTA), Mexico's border cities have acted as offshore assembly centers for U.S. industries, siphoning off hundreds of thousands of jobs from American communities in the Southwest and elsewhere. The disappearance of such jobs has forced many displaced U.S. Mexican and Mexican American workers into the low-wage service sector and others into the ranks of the unemployed. By the late 1990s, more than two thousand *maquiladoras* (substantially foreign-owned assembly plants) employed more than a million people in Mexico's border region and in the interior of the country. The maquiladora sector grew dramatically in the 1980s and 1990s, when wages in Mexico dropped precipitously as a result of massive currency devaluations associated with two separate national economic depressions.

The rapidly expanding U.S-Mexico integration linked to NAFTA poses fundamental questions for the future of Mexican-origin people in the United States. It seems certain that in the twenty-first century the transfer of manufacturing and assembly jobs to Mexico and other cheap-labor countries will continue. The bifurcation of the U.S. economy into a technology-driven, high-wage sector requiring technical expertise and advanced education versus an extremely low-wage, basic services sector will intensify. Given the current climate of U.S. government cutbacks and grossly inadequate support for the education of the poor, the vast majority of future

Mexican and Mexican American workers seem destined to wind up in the second sector. It is likely that Chicano/a communities throughout the country will see a growth of the gap that now separates the middle class from the underprivileged masses. In short, if current trends continue, fewer poor people will have a chance to significantly improve their circumstances than has been the case in the past. Class bifurcation among Mexican-origin people — meaning a minority within the group who has achieved success coexisting with a majority who has not — may become institutionalized, replicating the situation in the African American community.

Contemporary Public Debates and the Chicano/a Agenda

Immigration and bilingual education are two high-profile policy matters that are closely tied to accelerated growth of transnational interdependence and integration between Mexico and the United States. Both issues have raised considerable apprehensions among Americans. Deciphering the bombastic rhetoric is no easy matter because ignorance, confusion, and misunderstanding have been rampant among ordinary citizens, public officials, and the media.

To be sure racism and xenophobia are partly to blame for the strident anti-immigrant, anti–bilingual education postures assumed by Californians during the 1990s. Yet prodigious gray areas surround these controversies. It is important to recognize that economic concerns and fear of higher taxes, rather than racism or xenophobia, have driven many people to favor such punitive measures. Large numbers of Chicanos/as voted for the notorious California Propositions 187 (calling for denial of services to undocumented immigrants) and 227 (calling for an end to bilingual education). Across the country many Latinos/as have joined members of the dominant population in pressing for greater enforcement to reduce undocumented immigration. A dramatic illustration of such support comes from El Paso, where more than 70 percent of the population is Chicano/a. In this border city, former Border Patrol Chief Silvestre Reyes, the architect of Operation Hold the Line, the anti-immigrant blockade of 1993, emerged as a hero. The voters rewarded him by electing him to Congress in 1996. And in California, a group of Latino/a parents started the latest anti–bilingual education movement.

On the highly convoluted issue of affirmative action, the split with the dominant society has been much more pronounced. Many Latinos/as demand continuation of affirmative action to make up for generations of discrimination, but a majority of European Americans feel that such programs have gone on long enough. Affirmative action, involving as it does preferential treatment based on race, ethnicity, and gender, is a concept difficult or impossible for European American males, who feel victimized by that policy, to accept. Given the probability that the brand of affirmative action in place since the 1960s will soon fade away, perhaps the time has come for Chicano/a activists to switch to a class-based affirmative action strategy. Some form of affirmative action is still necessary to allow people from the bottom of society to get on the track that will lead them to success. Related initiatives such as state mandates to require state public institutions of higher learning to admit the top 4 percent and 10 percent of all high school graduates in that state, as California and Texas have implemented respectively, are certainly part of the remedy. Another important strategy is to hold both public and private colleges and universities accountable for having diverse student populations.

Because of their complexity and potential for polarization, issues such as immigration, bilingual education, and affirmative action will continue to cause internal divisions among the Mexican-origin population and between the group and the dominant majority. In the larger scheme of things, however, globalization dwarfs all other contemporary concerns. For Mexicans/Mexican Americans as a group, the new economy remains the biggest challenge because of the continuing shrinkage of good jobs for the poorly educated and low skilled. Unfortunately most Mexican and Chicano/a workers are situated in that disadvantaged sector. To qualify for the well-paying jobs of the high-technology age requires increased access to higher education for greater numbers of people. That will require much better preparation for Latino/a pupils at the primary and secondary school levels, much lower dropout rates, and sufficient financial support for disadvantaged students at the university level. To enhance the chances of getting ahead for all marginalized Americans in the twenty-first century, the politics of good education and good jobs must continue to head the Chicano/a agenda and must remain at the top of the nation's blueprint for the successful integration of all groups into society.

NOTES

Introduction

1. Blauner, "Colonized and Immigrant Minorities."

2. The importance of social origins in helping to determine material success in U.S. society is highlighted to some extent in selections in Pedraza and Rumbaut, eds., *Origins and Destinies*.

3. Steinberg, *The Ethnic Myth*, chapter 3; Blauner, "Colonized and Immigrant Minorities."

4. Takaki, *Strangers from a Different Shore*, 43–46, 53, 216, 420–32, 459; U.S. Immigration and Naturalization Service, *Statistical Yearbooks* (recent years).

5. The following works provide general overviews of Chicano/a history or significant analyses of broad topics pertaining to the twentieth century: Acuña, *Occupied America*; Barrera, *Race and Class in the Southwest*; Juan García, *Mexicans in the Midwest*; M. García, *Mexican Americans*; Gómez-Quiñones, *Chicano Politics, Mexican American Labor*, and *Roots of Chicano Politics*; M. Gonzáles, *Mexicanos*; Griswold del Castillo and De León, *North to Aztlán*; McWilliams, *North from Mexico* (1990 edition updated by Meier); Meier and Ribera, *Mexican Americans/American Mexicans*; Rendon, *Chicano Manifesto*; Rosales, *Chicano!*; Ruiz, *From out of the Shadows*; and Samora and Vandel Simon, *A History of the Mexican-American People*.

6. The following presses have significant lists of humanities-oriented publications in Chicano/a Studies: Arte Público Press, Bilingual Review/Press, and the presses from the major universities in Arizona, California, New Mexico, and Texas.

CHAPTER 1. From Regional to National Minority

1. Kerr, "The Chicano Experience in Chicago," 20.

2. Cárdenas, "Los Desarraigados," 153–86; Juan García, *Mexicans in the Midwest*, 26.

3. Quoted in Santillán, "Midwestern Mexican American Women," 85.

4. Taylor, "Mexicans North of the Rio Grande," 135.

5. U.S. Bureau of the Census, *1930 Census of Population*, 3:1, 7; Taylor, *Mexican Labor in the United States*, vol. 1 (Report #3 on Migratory Statistics), 26–29.

6. Hoffman, *Unwanted Mexican Americans*; Balderrama and Rodríguez, *Decade of Betrayal*.

7. Acuña, *Anything but Mexican*, 3; Rothstein, "In Search of the American Dream," in Lowenthal and Burgess, eds., *The California-Mexico Connection*, 177.

8. Carlson, *The Spanish-American Homeland*, 103–6; Griego and Merkx, "Crisis in New Mexico," 386.

CHAPTER 2. Contours of Mexican Immigration

1. The U.S. government has kept track of legal immigration from Mexico since 1820 but has provided official estimates on the number of undocumented immigrants only in recent years. The Immigration and Naturalization Service calculated that 3.4 million people were living illegally in the United States in 1992, with 1.3 million identified as Mexicans; the overall estimate for 1996 was 5 million, with 2.7 million identified as Mexicans. U.S. Bureau of the Census, *Statistical Abstract of the United States, 1995*, 12; U.S. Immigration and Naturalization Service, *Statistical Yearbook, 1996*, table P.

2. The full text of the corrido appears in Cardoso, *Mexican Emigration to the United States*, 80–82.

3. Bryan, "Mexican Immigrants in the United States," 730.

4. Quoted in Reisler, "Always the Laborer," 243.

5. Quoted in Kiser and Silverman, "Mexican Repatriation during the Great Depression," 49.

6. Hoffman, *Unwanted Mexican Americans*, ix; Balderrama and Rodríguez, *Decade of Betrayal*, 120–22.

7. McKay, "Texas Mexican Repatriation," 100, 148, 337–44; Camarillo, *Chicanos in California*, 49–50; Balderrama and Rodríguez, *Decade of Betrayal*, 99.

8. Quoted in Balderrama and Rodríguez, *Decade of Betrayal*, 47.

9. Betten and Mohl, "From Discrimination to Repatriation," 385.

10. Quoted in Hoffman, *Unwanted Mexican Americans*, 128.

11. Bogardus, *The Mexican in the United States*, 91.

12. Quoted in Sánchez, *Becoming Mexican American*, 219.

13. *Bracero* derives from *brazo*, or "arm." Thus a bracero, typically a farmhand, is a laborer who works with his hands and arms. See Galarza, *Merchants of Labor*; Craig, *The Bracero Program*; and Calavita, *Inside the State*, for overviews of the Bracero Program. On the exclusion of women from the Bracero Program, see Shelton, "Mexican Labor Migration to the United States," 116–19.

14. This figure represents the number of contracts issued. The total number of braceros is much lower because many workers signed on year after year, and they appear in the statistics multiple times. Statistics cited are from Galarza, *Merchants of Labor*, 79, and Craig, *The Bracero Program*, 50, 63.

15. Gamboa, *Mexican Labor and World War II*, 58; Cárdenas, "Los Desarraigados," 164; Kerr, "Mexican Chicago," 299–301.

16. Galarza, *Merchants of Labor*, chapter 17. Quote is on pp. 183–84.

17. Valdes, *Al Norte*, 102.

18. Gamboa, *Mexican Labor and World War II*, 113.

19. Scruggs, "Texas and the Bracero Program, 1942–1947," 263.

20. Juan García, *Operation Wetback*, 225–28. Quote appears on p. 225.

21. Text of entire speech appears in Kiser and Kiser, eds., *Mexican Workers*, 164–66.

22. Immigration and Naturalization Service, *Statistical Yearbook, 1996*, table P.

23. Immigration and Naturalization Service, *Statistical Yearbooks* (1969, 1979, 1989, 1996).

24. *New York Times*, February 4, 1997, A3.

25. For concise reviews of the research on the impact of immigrants see Center for Immigration Studies, "The Costs of Immigration," and González Baker, Cushing, and Haynes, "Fiscal Impacts of Mexican Migration to the United States." An interesting defense of immigrants coauthored by conservative columnist Linda Chávez appears in a recent issue of *Reader's Digest*. See Chávez and Miller, "The Immigration Myth."

26. *Arizona Daily Star*, October 7, 1991.

27. *Arizona Daily Star*, March 3, 1990, 2A.

28. *El Paso Times*, September 20–29, 1993, 1A, and March 20, 1994, 1A; *New York Times*, October 1, 1993, A1, and September 14, 1994, A1. See also Fried, *Operation Blockade*.

29. *Los Angeles Times*, February 22, 1997, A3, June 24, 1998, A3, and June 2, 1999, A16; *Washington Post*, July 29, 1999, A1.

30. *Atlanta Journal-Constitution*, December 10, 1995, H4.

31. *Atlanta Journal-Constitution*, April 3, 1996, A1.

32. *New York Times*, July 22, 1997, A1; *Florida Times-Union* (Jacksonville), April 24, 1998, A1.

33. The report was published by the Center for Immigration Research at the University of Houston. *El Financiero International* (Mexico City), August 18–24, 1997.

34. Balderrama and Rodríguez, *Decade of Betrayal*.

CHAPTER 3. The Legacy of Oppression

1. Rosales, *Pobre Raza!* Statistics on p. 100.

2. De León, *They Called Them Greasers*, chapters 3–6.

3. *The Commonwealth Club of California Transactions* II:1 (March 23, 1926), 1–34.

4. Grant, *The Passing of the Great Race*; McDougall, Is *America Safe for Democracy?*; Brigham, *A Study of American Intelligence*.

5. Saunders, *Cultural Difference and Medical Care*, 128; Madsen, *The Mexican-Americans of South Texas*, 16.

6. Billington, *The Far Western Frontier*, 1.

7. Hollon, *The Southwest*, 175.

8. Banfield, *Big City Politics*, 76.

9. Juan García, "Hollywood and the West," 82. See also Pettit, *Images of the Mexican American*, 140–42.

10. Quoted in Delpar, "Goodbye to the 'Greaser,'" 35.

11. Woll, *The Latin Image*, 106–7.

12. Woll, *The Latin Image*, 1–2.

13. Richard, *Contemporary Hollywood's Negative Hispanic Image*, xxxix.

14. Lichter and Amundson, "Distorted Reality," 59.

15. Lichter and Amundson, "Distorted Reality," 66.

16. National Council of La Raza, "Out of the Picture," 23–24; *El Paso Times*, July 8, 1999, 13A.

17. Betten and Mohl, "From Discrimination to Repatriation," 374–75.

18. Laslett, "Historical Perspectives," 55.

19. Oppenheimer, "Acculturation or Assimilation," 432; Juan García, *Mexicans in the Midwest*, 194; Luckingham, *Minorities in Phoenix*, 40; Kotlanger, "Phoenix, Arizona," 431; Avila, "Immigration and Integration."

20. Luckingham, *Minorities in Phoenix*, 31.

21. González, *Chicano Education*, 13.

22. *Alvarado et al. v. El Paso Independent School District*. Field notes by Paul S. Taylor, undated. Plaintiffs' Exhibits 2A-2 and 2A-3.

23. *Alvarado et al. v. El Paso Independent School District, et al.* Field notes by Paul S. Taylor, undated. Plaintiff's Exhibit 2A-5.

24. Tijerina, *Mexican Americans in Lubbock County*, 41.

25. Kibbe, *Latin Americans in Texas*, 271–72.

26. *Look* 15, no. 7 (March 27, 1951), 36.

27. *Arizona Daily Star*, April 13, 1997, D3.

CHAPTER 4. Identity and the Struggle for Integration

1. González, *The Spanish-Americans of New Mexico*, 202–9. Quote on p. 205.

2. Quoted in Taylor, *Mexican Labor in the United States*, vol. 1 (Report #2: *The Valley of the South Platte, Colorado*), 213.

3. *San Antonio Evening News*, November 18, 1965, 8F.

4. Simmons adds that he encountered exceptions to this generalization. Simmons, "Anglo Americans and Mexican Americans in South Texas," 480.

5. Quoted in Simmons, "Anglo Americans and Mexican Americans," 479.

6. Quoted in Gutiérrez, *Walls and Mirrors*, 145.

7. *Wall Street Journal*, October 21, 1986.

8. *Arizona Daily Star*, April 20, 1997, B7.

9. Comments by immigrants critical of Mexican Americans are found in a number of the interviews conducted by Manuel Gamio in the 1920s. See Gamio, *The Life Story of the Mexican Immigrant*.

10. The full text is found in McWilliams, *North from Mexico* (1948), 225–26.

11. The first quote is by Calvin Veltman and the second by David López. Cited in Barrera, *Beyond Aztlán*, 73.

12. Mexican Fact-Finding Committee, *Mexicans in California*, 61.

13. From interview in Gamio, *The Life Story of the Mexican Immigrant*, 45–47.

14. Quoted in Romo, *East Los Angeles*, 141–42. Hostile statements against naturalization also appear in Reisler, *By the Sweat of Their Brow*, 113–15, 125.

15. *El Paso Times*, April 23, 1914, 9.

16. Santillán, "Rosita the Riveter," 122.

17. Letter from Alonso S. Perales to Congressman Paul J. Kilday, November 24, 1944. Reprinted in Perales, *Are We Good Neighbors?* 283–84. See also Pycior, *LBJ and Mexican Americans*, 53.

18. U.S. Department of Defense, *Hispanics in America's Defense*, 36.

19. From M. García, *Mexican Americans*, 210.

20. Morín, *Among the Valiant*, 280.

21. Griswold del Castillo, *La Familia*, 69.

22. Murgía, *Chicano Intermarriage*, 48; Santos Ramírez, "Matrimonios entre norteamericanos y mexicanos," 29.

CHAPTER 5. Travails of Making a Living

1. De León, *The Tejano Community*, 63–65. Quote is on p. 65.

2. McWilliams, *North from Mexico* (1948), 144–51. Quote is on p. 149.

3. Valdes, *Al Norte*, 9; Gómez-Quiñones, *Mexican American Labor*, 130. Sugar-beet companies in the Northwest also participated in the recruitment process. Gamboa, *Mexican Labor and World War II*, 14–15.

4. Taylor, "Mexicans North of the Rio Grande," 136–37.

5. U.S. President's Commission on Migratory Labor, *Migratory Labor in American Agriculture*, 130–31.

6. Reisler, *By the Sweat of Their Brow*, 80–81.

7. Quoted in Reisler, *By the Sweat of Their Brow*, 84.

8. Quoted in Mayer, "After Escalante," 447.

9. Quoted in Simmons, "Anglo Americans and Mexican Americans," 183–84.

10. Quoted in *The Reporter*, February 2, 1961. Reprinted in Moquin, ed., *A Documentary History of the Mexican Americans*, 344.

11. Galarza, *Farm Workers and Agri-business in California*, 30.

12. Carey McWilliams refers to a strike call given by one Juan Gómez in 1883 to several hundred cowboys in California as the "the first attempt to form a union of 'agricultural' workers in the United States." McWilliams, *North from Mexico* (1948), 190.

13. Gómez-Quiñones, *Mexican American Labor*, 79, 141–44; De León, *Mexican Americans in Texas*, 86, 104.

14. Quoted in Gómez-Quiñones, *Mexican American Labor*, 77.

15. McWilliams, *North from Mexico* (1948), 189–93; Gómez-Quiñones, *Mexican American Labor*, 131–41.

16. The UCAPAWA story is told in Ruiz, *Cannery Women*. Cited statistics appear on pp. 84–85.

17. Quoted in Griswold del Castillo and García, *César Chávez*, 70.

18. *New York Times*, March 31, 1997, A1, A9.

19. Reisler, *By the Sweat of Their Brow*, 3–4, 97; Taylor, *Mexican Labor*, vol. 2 (Report #2: Chicago and the Calumet Region), 32; Juan García, *Mexicans in the Midwest*, 6.

20. Quoted in Reisler, *By the Sweat of Their Brow*, 4.

21. Quoted in Vargas, *Proletarians of the North*, 35.

22. Smith, "Mexicans in Kansas City," 36.

23. Camarillo, *Chicanos in a Changing Society*, 206–7, 213.

24. Clark, "Mexican Labor," 479; Juan García, *Mexicans in the Midwest*, 8–9.

25. Martínez, "Hispanics in Arizona," 101.

26. Clark, "Mexican Labor in the United States"; Mexican Fact-Finding Committee, *Mexicans in California*, 81, 95; Barrera, *Race and Class in the Southwest*, 86–89.

27. Taylor, "Mexican Women in Los Angeles Industry in 1928," 112–13; Ruiz, *Cannery Women*, 15; Vargas, *Proletarians of the North*, 134–36.

28. Vargas, *Proletarians of the North*, 134.

29. Santillán, "Midwestern Mexican American Women," 83.

30. Rosales and Simón, "Chicano Steel Workers," 267–68; Vargas, *Proleterians of the North*, 95–96.

31. Mexican Fact-Finding Committee, *Mexicans in California*, 92.

32. Mexican Fact-Finding Committee, *Mexicans in California*, 94.

33. Mexican Fact-Finding Committee, *Mexicans in California*, 92–93.

34. Santillán, "Rosita the Riveter," 115–16.

35. Coyle, Hershatter, and Honig, *Women at Farah*, 65. On the Farah conflict and other garment strikes in El Paso and San Antonio from the 1950s to the 1970s, see Ledesma, "Unlikely Sisters," 137–219.

CHAPTER 6. Mixed Social Progress

1. Galarza, "Program for Action."

2. Quoted in McWilliams, *Brothers under the Skin*, 131.

3. Morales and Bonilla, "Restructuring and the New Inequality," 4.

4. De la Garza, et al., "Mexican Immigrants, Mexican Americans, and American Political Culture," 232.

5. Data from González, "Dreams of 'Buenos Dias'" (unpublished book manuscript).

6. Jaffe, Cullen, and Boswell, *The Changing Demography of Spanish Americans*, 91–93, 135–37.

7. American Council on Education, *Minorities in Higher Education, 1994*, tables 3, 5, 9, 16.

8. O'Hare, "The Rise of Hispanic Affluence," 40–42.

9. *Hispanic Business*, November 1992, 57, 60.

10. *Hispanic Business*, January 1997, 38.

11. *Hispanic Business*, April 1999, 22.

12. Excerpted from biographical essay in *Hispanic Business*, November 1994, 42.

13. Excerpted from biographical essay in *Hispanic Business*, November 1994, 38.

14. *Los Angeles Times*, November 10, 1996, A3.

15. See Pitt, *The Decline of the Californios*; Griswold del Castillo, *The Los Angeles Barrio*; Camarillo, *Chicanos in a Changing Society*; De León, *The Tejano Community*; Sheridan, *Los Tucsonenses*.

16. Juan García, *Mexicans in the Midwest*, 17.

17. Martínez, *The Chicanos of El Paso*, 12; Sheridan, *Los Tucsonenses*, 184–85, 235–36.

18. González, *The Spanish Americans of New Mexico*, 159.

19. *Hispanic Business*, May 1994, 60.

20. *Hispanic Business*, February 1997, 25, 42. Other data gathered by *Hispanic Business* suggest that only a small minority of these board members and executives were Mexican Americans.

21. Boyle, *Los Capitalistas*.

22. Miranda, *A History of Hispanics in Southern Nevada*, 50–51; Boyle, *Los Capitalistas*, 102.

23. Sheridan, *Los Tucsonenses*, 94–96.

24. M. García, *Desert Immigrants*, 82–83.

25. Stephens, "The Women of the Amador Family," 270; *Handbook of Texas* (1992), author's files.

26. Taylor, *Mexican Labor*, vol. 2 (Report #2: Chicago and the Calumet Region), 168.

27. *El Paso City Directory, 1928*, 899–994.

28. Getty, "Interethnic Relationships," 110.

29. U.S. Bureau of the Census, *Economic Censuses, 1987: Survey of Minority-Owned Business Enterprises*, table 3; *Hispanic Business*, December 1991, 28.

30. *Hispanic Business*, March 1993, 34–60.

31. *Hispanic Business*, May 1998, 33–38. Quotation and profile of Ms. Pohl appear on p. 38.

32. Millman, *The Other Americans*, 20–23, 54.

33. Millman, *The Other Americans*, 119, 333.

34. Millman, *The Other Americans*, 108.

35. *Arizona Daily Star*, January 15, 1990, 4A.

36. U.S. Department of Education, *The Condition of Education, 1997*, 66, 94.

37. *The Chronicle of Higher Education*, March 7, 1997, A35, and May 29, 1998, A32; *New York Times*, April 23, 1997, A19.

38. *The Chronicle of Higher Education*, April 2, 1999, A36–38; *New York Times*, November 24, 1999, A1, A18; *San Francisco Chronicle*, April 4, 2000, A15.

CHAPTER 7. Community and Political Power

1. Menchaca, *The Mexican Outsiders*, 19–24; Weber, *Foreigners in Their Native Land*, 148; Pitt, *The Decline of the Californios*, 158, 271; Griswold del Castillo, *The Los Angeles Barrio*, 158–59.

2. Quoted in Sheridan, *Arizona*, 174.

3. Sheridan, *Arizona*, 174–79.

4. Quote found in Ellis, ed., *New Mexico*, 206.

5. Montejano, *Anglos and Mexicans*, 143; Shelton, *Political Conditions among Texas Mexicans*, 11.

6. Montejano, *Anglos and Mexicans*, 146–47; Lay, *War, Revolution, and the Ku Klux Klan*, 101, 115.

7. The following New Mexicans served in the U.S. Congress between 1919 and 1935: Benigno Cárdenas Hernández (1919–1921), Nestor Montoya (1921–1923), and Dennis Chávez (1931–1935).

8. Lochtin, "Hispanics, Women, and Western Cities," 312; Jensen, "Disfranchisement Is a Disgrace," 25.

9. Officer, "Sodalities and Systemic Linkage," 55.

10. Sheridan, *Los Tucsonenses*, 169–75.

11. Pycior, *LBJ and Mexican Americans*, 29.

12. Membership data taken from Márquez, *LULAC*, 36. For LULAC's involvement in educational issues in Texas, see San Miguel, *"Let All of Them Take Heed."*

13. Marín, "La Asociación Hispano-Americana de Madres y Esposas."

14. Simmons, "Anglo Americans and Mexican Americans," 219–92. Quote on p. 292.

15. Simmons, "Anglo Americans and Mexican Americans," 293–97; Martínez, *The Chicanos of El Paso*, 6, 18–21; quotation from McWilliams, "The El Paso Story," 46.

16. J. A. Gutiérrez, *The Making of a Chicano Militant*, 39.

17. Officer, *Arizona's Hispanic Perspective*, 144, 149.

18. D'Antonio and Form, *Influentials in Two Border Cities*, 142.

19. J. A. Gutiérrez, "La Raza and Revolution," 46.

20. Fincher, *Spanish-Americans*, 250–59.

21. For excellent surveys on El Congreso and AMNA, see M. García, *Mexican Americans*, chapters 6 and 8. Quote on AMNA appears on p. 200.

22. Pardo, *Mexican American Women Activists*, 5.

23. The TELACU story is ably told in J. Chávez, *Eastside Landmark*.

24. *Hispanic Business*, November 1994, 34; December 1996, 9; January 1997, 8; Montejano, ed., *Chicano Politics and Society*, xix; Lochtin, "Hispanics, Women, and Western Cities," 304; Skerry, *Mexican Americans*, 105.

25. Córdova, "Harold Washington and the Rise of Latino Electoral Politics in Chicago," 52; *Hispanic Business*, November 1994, 34.

26. *Newsweek*, November 25, 1996, 35; *Hispanic Business*, December 1996, 9; January 1997, 8.

27. *Arizona Daily Star*, November 8, 1998, A11; "Election '98: Results," NALEO Web site, naleo.org/CivicEducation/electionwatch.

28. *North County Times* (San Diego), November 17, 1996, A11; *Arizona Republic*, November 18, 1998, A1.

CHAPTER 8. Reflections

1. Martínez, "On the Size of the Chicano Population," 55; U.S. Bureau of the Census, *Censuses of Population, 1900–1990.*

2. Arreola, "The Texas-Mexican Homeland," "Mexico Origins of South Texas Mexican Americans," and "Mexican Texas."

3. U.S. Bureau of the Census, *Censuses of Population, 1900–1990.*

4. Steinberg, *The Ethnic Myth*, 97–101.

5. Pedraza-Bailey, *Political and Economic Migrants in America*, 1–2, 12–17, 41–52.

6. Steinberg, *The Ethnic Myth*, 273; U.S. Immigration and Naturalization Service, *Statistical Yearbook, 1996*, table 21; Borjas, *Friends or Strangers*, 321; Portes and Rumbaut, *Immigrant America*, 60.

BIBLIOGRAPHY

Note: This abbreviated bibliography includes sources cited in the notes as well as works consulted and found particularly valuable in their treatment of both general and specialized subjects addressed in this study. A comprehensive version of this bibliography is found online at www.uapress.arizona.edu.

Primary Sources

Alvarado et al. v. El Paso Independent School District, School Desegregation Suit, EP-70-CA-279, U.S. District Court for the Western District of Texas, El Paso Division (1975).

American Council on Education, Office of Minorities in Higher Education. *Minorities in Higher Education, 1994*. Washington, D.C.: Government Printing Office, 1995.

Clark, Victor S. "Mexican Labor in the United States." In U.S. Bureau of Labor Bulletin 78 (September 1908): 466–522.

Mexican Fact-Finding Committee. *Mexicans in California*. San Francisco: R & E Associates, 1970. (Originally published in 1930).

U.S. Bureau of the Census. *Census of Population. Persons of Hispanic Origin in the United States*. Washington, D.C.: Bureau of the Census, 1993.

———. *Census of Population* (reports for 1850–1990). Washington, D.C.: Bureau of the Census.

———. *Economic Censuses, 1987: Survey of Minority-Owned Business Enterprises. Hispanic*. Washington, D.C.: Bureau of the Census, 1991.

———. *Statistical Abstract of the United States, 1995, 1997*. Washington, D.C.: Bureau of the Census, 1995, 1997.

U.S. Department of Defense. *Hispanics in America's Defense*. Washington, D.C.: Government Printing Office, 1990.

U.S. Department of Education. *The Condition of Education* (reports for 1994 and 1997). Washington, D.C.: Government Printing Office.

U.S. Immigration and Naturalization Service. *Statistical Yearbooks* (for the years 1969–1997). Washington, D.C.: Government Printing Office.

U.S. President's Commission on Migratory Labor. *Migratory Labor in American Agriculture.* Washington, D.C.: Government Printing Office, 1951.

Newspapers, Magazines, and Other Periodicals

Arizona Daily Star
Arizona Republic
Atlanta Journal-Constitution
Backgrounder (Center for Immigration Studies)
Chronicle of Higher Education
The Commonwealth Club of California Transactions
El Financiero Internacional (Mexico City)
El Paso City Directories
El Paso Herald Post
El Paso Times
Florida Times-Union (Jacksonville)
Fort Worth Star-Telegram
Handbook of Texas (Texas State Historical Association, Austin)
Hispanic Business
La Luz
Look
Los Angeles Times
Modesto Bee
The Nation
New York Times
Newsweek
North County Times
The Reporter
Rocky Mountain News
San Antonio Evening News
San Francisco Chronicle
San Jose Mercury News
Southwest Voter Research Notes (Southwest Voter Research Institute)
Survey
USA Today
Wall Street Journal
Washington Post

Secondary Sources

Acuña, Rodolfo F. *Anything but Mexican: Chicanos in Contemporary Los Angeles.* New York: Verso, 1990.

———. *Occupied America: A History of Chicanos*, 3d ed. New York: Harper and Row, 1988.

———. *Sometimes There Is No Other Side: Chicanos and the Myth of Equality.* Notre Dame: University of Notre Dame Press, 1998.

Allen, James P., and Eugene J. Turner. *The Ethnic Quilt: Population Diversity in Southern California.* Northridge, Calif.: Center for Geographic Studies, 1997.

Almaguer, Tomás. *Racial Fault Lines: The Historical Origins of White Supremacy in California.* Berkeley: University of California Press, 1994.

Alvarez, Robert. *Familia: Migration and Adaptation in Baja and Alta California, 1800–1975.* Berkeley: University of California Press, 1994.

Anders, Evan. *Boss Rule in South Texas: The Progressive Era.* Austin: University of Texas Press, 1982.

Arreola, Daniel D. "Mexican Texas: A Distinctive Borderland." In *A Geographic Glimpse of Central Texas and the Borderlands: Images and Encounters*, edited by James F. Peterson and Julie A. Tuason, 3–9. Indiana, Pa.: National Council for Geographic Education, 1995.

———. "Mexico Origins of South Texas Mexican Americans, 1930." *Journal of Historical Geography* 19 (January 1993): 48–63.

———. "The Texas-Mexican Homeland." *Journal of Cultural Geography* 13 (spring/summer 1993): 61–74.

Arroyo, Luis L. "Chicano Participation in Organized Labor: The CIO in Los Angeles, 1938–1950. An Extended Research Note." *Aztlán* 6, no. 2 (1975): 276–303.

Avila, Henry J. "Immigration and Integration: The Mexican American Community in Garden City, Kansas, 1900–1950." *Kansas History* 20 (spring 1997): 22–37.

Balderrama, Francisco E. *In Defense of La Raza: The Los Angeles Mexican Consulate and Mexican Community, 1929–1936.* Tucson: University of Arizona Press, 1983.

Balderrama, Francisco E., and Raymond Rodríguez. *Decade of Betrayal: Mexican Repatriation in the 1930s.* Albuquerque: University of New Mexico Press, 1995.

Banfield, Edward C. *Big City Politics.* New York: Random House, 1965.

Barrera, Mario. *Beyond Aztlán: Ethnic Autonomy in Comparative Perspective.* New York: Praeger, 1988.

———. *Race and Class in the Southwest: A Theory of Racial Inequality.* Notre Dame: University of Notre Dame Press, 1979.

Barrera, Mario, Carlos Muñoz, and Charles Ornelas. "The Barrio as an Internal Colony." *Urban Affairs Annual Review* 6 (1972): 465–98.

Bean, Frank D., and Marta Tienda. *The Hispanic Population of the United States*. New York: Russell Sage Foundation, 1987.

Betten, Neil, and Raymond A. Mohl. "From Discrimination to Repatriation: Mexican Life in Gary, Indiana, during the Great Depression." *Pacific Historical Review* 42, no. 3 (1973): 370–88.

Billington, Ray A. *The Far Western Frontier, 1830–1860*. New York: Harper and Row, 1956.

Bixler-Márquez, Dennis, Carlos F. Ortega, Rosalía Solórzano Torres, and Lorenzo La Farelle, eds. *Chicano Studies: Survey and Analysis*. Dubuque, Iowa: Kendal/Hunt, 1997.

Blauner, Robert. "Colonized and Immigrant Minorities." In *Nation of Nations: The Ethnic Experience and the Ethnic Crisis*, edited by Peter Rose, 243–58. New York: Random House, 1972.

Bogardus, Emory S. *The Mexican in the United States*. Los Angeles: University of Southern California, 1934.

Borjas, George J. *Friends or Strangers: The Impact of Immigrants on the U.S. Economy*. New York: Basic Books, 1990.

Boswell, Thomas D. "The Growth and Proportional Distribution of the Mexican Stock Population in the United States: 1910–1970." *Mississippi Geographer* (spring 1979): 57–76.

Boyle, Susan Calafate. *Los Capitalistas: Hispano Merchants on the Santa Fe Trail*. Albuquerque: University of New Mexico Press, 1997.

Brigham, Carl C. *A Study of American Intelligence*. Princeton: Princeton University Press, 1922.

Bryan, Samuel. "Mexican Immigrants in the United States." *Survey* 28 (September 7, 1912): 725–30.

Calavita, Kitty. *Inside the State: The Bracero Program, Immigration, and the INS*. New York: Routledge, 1992.

Calvert, Robert A., and Arnoldo de León. *The History of Texas*. 2d ed. Arlington Heights, Ill.: Harlan Davidson, 1996.

Camarillo, Albert. *Chicanos in a Changing Society: From Mexican Pueblos to American Barrios in Santa Barbara and Southern California, 1848–1930*. Cambridge: Harvard University Press, 1979.

———. *Chicanos in California: A History of Mexican Americans in California*. San Francisco: Boyd and Fraser, 1984.

Cárdenas, Gilbert. "Los Desarraigados: Chicanos in the Midwestern Region of the United States." *Aztlán* 7, no. 2 (1976): 153–86.

Cardoso, Lawrence A. *Mexican Emigration to the United States, 1897–1931*. Tucson: University of Arizona Press, 1980.

Carlson, Alvar W. *The Spanish-American Homeland: Four Centuries in New Mexico's Rio Arriba*. Baltimore: Johns Hopkins University Press, 1990.

Center for Immigration Studies. "The Costs of Immigration: Assessing a Conflicted Issue." *Backgrounder* no. 2-94 (September 1994): 1–21.

Chacón, Ramón D. "Labor Unrest and Industrialized Agriculture in California: The Case of the 1933 San Joaquin Valley Cotton Strike." *Social Science Quarterly* 65, no. 2 (June 1984): 336–53.

Chapa, Jorge. "The Myth of Hispanic Progress: Trends in the Educational and Economic Attainment of Mexican Americans." *Journal of Hispanic Policy* 4 (1989–1990): 3–18.

Chávez, Ernesto. "Creating Aztlán: The Chicano Movement in Los Angeles, 1966–1978." Ph.D. diss., University of California at Los Angeles, 1994.

Chávez, John R. *Eastside Landmark: A History of the East Side Los Angeles Community Union, 1968–1993*. Stanford: Stanford University Press, 1998.

Chávez, Linda. *Out of the Barrio: Toward a New Politics of Hispanic Assimilation*. New York: Basic Books, 1991.

Chávez, Linda, and John J. Miller. "The Immigration Myth." *Reader's Digest* (May 1996): 69–73.

Córdova, Teresa. "Harold Washington and the Rise of Latino Electoral Politics in Chicago, 1982–1987." In *Chicano Politics and Society*, edited by David Montejano, 31–57.

Corwin, Arthur F., ed. *Immigrants — And Immigrants: Perspectives on Mexican Labor Migration to the United States*. Westport: Greenwood, 1978.

Coyle, Laurie, Gail Hershatter, and Emily Honig. *Women at Farah: An Unfinished Story*. N.p., 1979.

Craig, Richard B. *The Bracero Program: Interest Groups and Foreign Policy*. Austin: University of Texas Press, 1971.

D'Antonio, William V., and William H. Form. *Influentials in Two Border Cities: A Study in Community Decision Making*. Notre Dame: University of Notre Dame Press, 1965.

De la Garza, Rodolfo O., Angelo Falcón, F. Chris García, and John García. "Mexican Immigrants, Mexican Americans, and American Political Culture." In *Immigration and Ethnicity*, edited by Barry Edmonton and Jeffrey S. Passey, 227–50. Washington, D.C.,: Urban Institute Press, 1994.

De la Torre, Adela, and Beatriz M. Pesquera, eds. *Building with Our Hands: New Directions in Chicana Scholarship*. Berkeley: University of California Press, 1993.

Del Castillo, Adelaida R., ed. *Between Borders: Essays on Mexicana/Chicana History*. Encino, Calif.: Floricanto, 1990.

De León, Arnoldo. *Mexican Americans in Texas: A Brief History*. 2d ed. Arlington Heights, Ill.: Harlan Davidson, 1999.

————. *The Tejano Community, 1836–1900*. Albuquerque: University of New Mexico Press, 1982.

————. *They Called Them Greasers: Anglo Attitudes toward Mexicans in Texas, 1821–1900*. Austin: University of Texas Press, 1983.

Delgado, Richard, and Jean Stefancic. "Home-Grown Racism: Colorado's Historic Embrace — and Denial — of Equal Opportunity in Higher Education." *University of Colorado Law Review* 70, no. 3 (1999): 703–811.

Delpar, Helen. "Goodbye to the 'Greaser': Mexico, the MPPDA, and Derogatory Films, 1922–1926." *Journal of Popular Film and Television* 12, no. 1 (1984): 34–41.

Deutsch, Sarah. *No Separate Refuge: Culture, Class, and Gender on an Anglo-Hispanic Frontier in the American Southwest, 1880–1940*. New York: Oxford University Press, 1987.

Driscoll, Barbara A. *The Tracks North: The Railroad Bracero Program of World War II*. Austin: University of Texas at Austin Center for Mexican American Studies, 1998.

Duran, Livie I., and H. Russell Bernard, eds. *Introduction to Chicano Studies*. New York: Macmillan, 1982.

Ellis, Richard N., ed. *New Mexico Past and Present: A Historical Reader*. Albuquerque: University of New Mexico Press, 1971.

Escobar, Edward J. *Race, Police, and the Making of a Political Identity: Mexican Americans and the Los Angeles Police Department, 1900–1945*. Berkeley: University of California Press, 1999.

Esquivel Tywoniah, Frances, and Mario T. García. *Migrant Daughter: Coming of Age as a Mexican American Woman*. Berkeley: University of California Press, 2000.

Fincher, Ernest B. *Spanish-Americans as a Political Factor in New Mexico, 1912–1950*. New York: Arno, 1974.

Foley, Douglas E., Clarice Mota, Donald E. Post, and Ignacio Lozano. *From Peones to Politicos: Ethnic Relations in a South Texas Town, 1900 to 1977*. Revised and enlarged ed. Austin: University of Texas at Austin Center for Mexican American Studies, 1988.

Foley, Neil. *The White Scourge: Mexicans, Blacks, and Poor Whites in Texas Cotton Culture*. Berkeley: University of California Press, 1997.

Fried, Jonathan. *Operation Blockade: A City Divided*. Philadelphia: Community Relations Division of the American Friends Service Committee, 1994.

Galarza, Ernesto. *Farm Workers and Agri-business in California, 1947–1960*. Notre Dame: University of Notre Dame Press, 1977.

————. *Merchants of Labor*. Santa Barbara, Calif.: McNally and Loftin, 1964.

————. "Program for Action." *Common Ground* (Summer 1949). Reprinted in *A Documentary History of the Mexican Americans*, edited by Wayne Moquin with Charles Van Doren, 334–41. New York: Praeger, 1971.

Gamboa, Erasmo. *Mexican Labor and World War II: Braceros in the Pacific Northwest, 1942–1947*. Austin: University of Texas Press, 1990.

Gamio, Manuel. *The Life Story of the Mexican Immigrant*. Chicago: University of Chicago Press, 1931. Reprint, New York: Dover, 1971.

García, Alma M. *Chicana Feminist Thought: The Basic Historical Writings*. New York: Routledge, 1997.

García, F. Chris, and Rodolfo O. de la Garza. *The Chicano Political Experience: Three Perspectives*. North Scituate, Mass.: Duxbury, 1977.

García, Ignacio M. *Chicanismo: The Forging of a Militant Ethos*. Tucson: University of Arizona Press, 1997.

————. *United We Win: The Rise and Fall of La Raza Unida Party*. Tucson: University of Arizona Mexican American Studies and Research Center, 1989.

García, John A. "The Voting Rights Act and Hispanic Political Representation in the Southwest." *Publius* 16 (fall 1986): 49–66.

García, John A., Teresa Córdova, and Juan R. García, eds. *The Chicano Struggle: Analyses of Past and Present Efforts*. New York: Bilingual Press, 1984.

García, Juan R. "Hollywood and the West: Mexican Images in American Films." In *Old Southwest/New Southwest*, edited by Judy N. Lensink, 75–90. Tucson: Tucson Public Library, 1987.

————. *Mexicans in the Midwest, 1900–1932*. Tucson: University of Arizona Press, 1996.

————. *Operation Wetback: The Mass Deportation of Mexican Undocumented Workers in 1954*. Westport, Conn.: Greenwood, 1980.

García, Mario T. *Desert Immigrants: The Mexicans of El Paso, 1880–1920*. New Haven: Yale University Press, 1981.

————. *The Making of a Mexican American Mayor: Raymond L. Telles of El Paso*. Southwestern Studies no. 105. El Paso: Texas Western Press, 1998.

————. *Mexican Americans: Leadership, Ideology, and Identity, 1930–1960*. New Haven: Yale University Press, 1989.

García, Richard A. *Rise of the Mexican American Middle Class: San Antonio, 1929–1941*. College Station: Texas A&M University Press, 1991.

Gelbard, Alene H., and Marion Carter. "Mexican Immigration and the U.S. Population." In *At the Crossroads: Mexican Migration and U.S. Policy*, edited by Frank D. Bean et al., 117–44. New York: Rowan and Littlefield, 1997.

Getty, Harry T. "Interethnic Relationships in the Community of Tucson." Ph.D. diss., University of Chicago, 1950. Published, New York: Arno Press, 1976.

Gómez-Quiñones, Juan. *Chicano Politics: Reality and Promise, 1940–1990.* Albuquerque: University of New Mexico Press, 1990.

―――. *Mexican American Labor, 1790–1990.* Albuquerque: University of New Mexico Press, 1994.

―――. *Roots of Chicano Politics, 1600–1940.* Albuquerque: University of New Mexico Press, 1994.

Gonzáles, Manuel G. *Mexicanos: A History of Mexicans in the United States.* Bloomington: Indiana University Press, 1999.

González, Arturo. "Dreams of 'Buenos Días.'" Book manuscript, 1999. Author's files.

González, Gilbert G. *Chicano Education in the Era of Segregation.* Philadelphia: Balch Institute Press, 1990.

―――. *Labor and Community: Mexican Citrus Worker Villages in a Southern California County, 1900–1950.* Urbana: University of Illinois Press, 1994.

―――. *Mexican Consuls and Labor Organizing: Imperial Politics in the American Southwest.* Austin: University of Texas Press, 1999.

González, Nancie L. *The Spanish-Americans of New Mexico.* Albuquerque: University of New Mexico Press, 1967.

González Baker, Susan, Robert G. Cushing, and Charles W. Haynes. "Fiscal Impacts of Mexican Migration to the United States." In *At the Crossroads: Mexican Migration and U.S. Policy,* edited by Frank D. Bean et al., 145–76. New York: Rowan and Littlefield, 1997.

Gordon, Linda. *The Great Arizona Orphan Abduction.* Cambridge, Mass.: Harvard University Press, 1999.

Grant, Madison. *The Passing of the Great Race.* New York: Charles Scribner's Sons, 1916.

Griego, Richard, and Gilbert W. Merkx. "Crisis in New Mexico." In *Chicano: The Evolution of a People,* edited by Renato Rosaldo, Robert L. Calvert, and Gustav L. Seligmann, 385–92. Minneapolis: Winston, 1973.

Griswold del Castillo, Richard. *La Familia: Chicano Families in the Urban Southwest, 1848 to the Present.* Notre Dame: University of Notre Dame Press, 1984.

―――. *The Los Angeles Barrio, 1850–1890: A Social History.* Berkeley: University of California Press, 1979.

Griswold del Castillo, Richard, and Arnoldo de León. *North to Aztlán: A History of Mexican Americans in the United States.* New York: Twayne, 1996.

Griswold del Castillo, Richard, and Richard A. García. *César Chávez: A Triumph of Spirit.* Norman: University of Oklahoma Press, 1995.

Guerin-Gonzáles, Camille. *Mexican Workers and American Dreams: Immigration,*

Repatriation, and California Farm Labor, 1900–1939. New Brunswick: Rutgers University Press, 1994.

Gutiérrez, David G. *Walls and Mirrors: Mexican Americans, Mexican Immigrants, and the Politics of Ethnicity in the American Southwest, 1910–1986.* Berkeley: University of California Press, 1994.

———, ed. *Between Two Worlds: Mexican Immigrants in the United States.* Wilmington: Scholarly Resources, 1996.

Gutiérrez, José Angel. "La Raza and Revolution: The Empirical Conditions of Revolution in Four South Texas Counties." M.A. thesis, St. Mary's University, 1968.

———. *The Making of a Chicano Militant: Lessons from Cristal.* Madison: University of Wisconsin Press, 1998.

Guzmán, Ralph. "Mexican-American Casualties in Vietnam." *Congressional Record,* 91st Cong., 1st sess., October 8, 1969. Reprinted in *A Documentary History of the Mexican Americans,* edited by Wayne Moquin with Charles Van Doren, 371–73. New York: Praeger, 1971.

Haas, Lisbeth. *Conquests and Historical Identities in California, 1769–1936.* Berkeley: University of California Press, 1995.

Herrera-Sobek, María. *Northward Bound: The Mexican Immigrant Experience in Ballad and Song.* Bloomington: Indiana University Press, 1993.

Hoffman, Abraham. *Unwanted Mexican Americans in the Great Depression: Repatriation Pressure, 1929–1939.* Tucson: University of Arizona Press, 1974.

Hollon, W. Eugene. *The Southwest: Old and New.* Lincoln: University of Nebraska Press, 1961.

Hundley, Norris Jr., ed. *The Chicano.* Santa Barbara, Calif.: American Bibliographical Center and Clio Press, 1975.

Jaffe, Abram J., Ruth M. Cullen, and Thomas D. Boswell. *The Changing Demography of Spanish Americans.* New York: Academic Press, 1980.

Jensen, Joan M. "Disfranchisement Is a Disgrace: Women and Politics in New Mexico, 1900–1940." *New Mexico Historical Review* 56, no. 1 (1981): 5–35.

Kerr, Louise Año Nuevo. "The Chicano Experience in Chicago, 1920–1970." Ph.D. diss., University of Illinois at Chicago Circle, 1976.

———. "Mexican Chicago: Chicano Assimilation Aborted, 1939–1954." In *Ethnic Chicago,* edited by Melvin G. Holli, 269–98. Grand Rapids, Mich.: W. B. Eerdmans Publishing Co., 1981.

Kibbe, Pauline R. *Latin Americans in Texas.* Albuquerque: University of New Mexico Press, 1946.

Kingsolver, Barbara. *Holding the Line: Women in the Great Arizona Mine Strike of 1983.* Ithaca: IRL Press and Cornell University Press, 1989.

Kiser, George C., and Martha W. Kiser, eds. *Mexican Workers in the United States: Historical and Political Perspectives.* Albuquerque: University of New Mexico Press, 1979.

Kiser, George C., and David Silverman. "Mexican Repatriation during the Great Depression." In *Mexican Workers in the United States: Historical and Political Perspectives,* edited by George C. Kiser and Martha W. Kiser, 45–66. Albuquerque: University of New Mexico Press, 1979.

Kotlanger, Michael J. "Phoenix, Arizona: 1920–1940." Ph.D. diss., Arizona State University, 1983.

Lane, James B., and Edward J. Escobar, eds. *Forging a Community: The Latino Experience in Northwest Indiana, 1919–1975.* Bloomington: Indiana University Press, 1987.

Laslett, John H. M. "Historical Perspectives: Immigration and the Rise of a Distinctive Urban Region, 1900–1970." In *Ethnic Los Angeles,* edited by Roger Waldinger and Mehdi Bozorgmehr, 39–78. New York: Russell Sage Foundation, 1996.

Lay, Shawn. *War, Revolution, and the Ku Klux Klan: A Study of Intolerance in a Border City.* El Paso: Texas Western Press, 1985.

Ledesma, Irene. "Unlikely Sisters: Mexican-American Women in Strike Activity in Texas, 1919–1974. Ph.D. diss., Ohio State University, 1992.

Leyva, Yolanda Chávez. "Faithful Hard-Working Mexican Hands: Mexican Workers during the Great Depression." In *Mexican American Women: Changing Images,* edited by Juan R. García, 63–77. Perspectives in Mexican American Studies no. 2. Tucson: Mexican American Studies and Research Center, 1989.

Lichter, S. Robert, and Daniel R. Amundson. "Distorted Reality: Hispanic Characters in TV Entertainment." In *Latin Looks: Images of Latinas and Latinos in U.S. Media,* edited by Clara E. Rodríguez, 57–72. Boulder: Westview Press, 1997.

Lochtin, Roger W. "Hispanics, Women, and Western Cities: Setting the Pace—Political Emergence and the Renaissance of Western Exceptionalism." *Western Historical Quarterly* 29:3 (Autumn 1998): 293–316.

López y Rivas, Gilberto. *Los Chicanos: Una minoría nacional explotada.* México, D.F.: Editorial Nuestro Tiempo, 1971.

Lowenthal, Abraham F., and Katrina Burgess, eds. *The California-Mexico Connection.* Stanford: Stanford University Press, 1993.

Luckingham, Bradford. *Minorities in Phoenix: A Profile of Mexican American, Chinese American, and African American Communities, 1860–1992.* Tucson: University of Arizona Press, 1994.

Maciel, David R., and Isidro R. Ortíz, eds. *Chicanas/Chicanos at the Crossroads: Social, Economic, and Political Change.* Tucson: University of Arizona Press, 1996.

MacLachlan, Colin M., and William H. Beezley. *El Gran Pueblo: A History of Greater Mexico*. 2d ed. Upper Saddle River, N.J.: Prentice Hall, 1999.

Madsen, William. *The Mexican-Americans of South Texas*. 2d ed. New York: Holt, Rinehart, and Winston, 1973.

Maldonado, Carlos S. "An Overview of the Mexicano/Chicano Presence in the Pacific Northwest." In *The Chicano Experience in the Northwest*, edited by Carlos S. Maldonado and Gilberto García, 1–34. Dubuque: Kendal/Hunt, 1995.

Marín, Christine. "La Asociación Hispano-Americana de Madres y Esposas: Tucson's Mexican American Women in World War II." Renato Rosaldo Lecture Series Monograph no. 1, 5–18. Tucson: Mexican American Studies and Research Center, 1985.

———. "Mexican Americans on the Home Front: Community Organizations in Arizona during World War II." *Perspectives in Mexican American Studies* 4 (1993): 75–92.

Márquez, Benjamín. *LULAC: The Evolution of a Mexican American Political Organization*. Austin: University of Texas Press, 1993.

Martínez, Oscar J. *Border People: Life and Society in the U.S.-Mexico Borderlands*. Tucson: University of Arizona Press, 1994.

———. *The Chicanos of El Paso: An Assessment of Progress*. Southwestern Studies Monograph no. 59. El Paso: Texas Western Press, 1980.

———. "Hispanics in Arizona." In *Arizona at Seventy-Five: The Next Twenty-Five Years*, edited by Beth Luey and Noel J. Stone, 87–122. Tempe: Arizona State University, Public History Program and the Arizona Historical Society, 1987.

———. "On the Size of the Chicano Population: New Estimates, 1850–1900. *Aztlán* 6, no. 1 (1975): 43–59.

———. *Troublesome Border*. Tucson: University of Arizona Press, 1988.

Mayer, Vicente V. "After Escalante: The Spanish-Speaking People of Utah." In *The Peoples of Utah*, edited by Helen Z. Papanikolas, 437–68. Salt Lake City: Utah Historical Society, 1976.

Mazón, Mauricio. *The Zoot-Suit Riots: The Psychology of Symbolic Annihilation*. Austin: University of Texas Press, 1984.

McDougall, William. *Is America Safe for Democracy?* New York: Charles Scribner's Sons, 1921.

McKay, Robert R. "Texas Mexican Repatriation during the Great Depression." Ph.D. diss., University of Oklahoma, 1982.

McWilliams, Carey. *Brothers under the Skin*. Boston: Little, Brown, and Co., 1964.

———. "The El Paso Story." *The Nation* (July 1948): 46.

———. *North from Mexico: The Spanish-Speaking People of the United States*. New

York: Praeger, 1948. (Updated edition with new chapters by Matt S. Meier. New York: Praeger, 1990.)

Meier, Matt S., and Feliciano Ribera. *Mexican Americans/American Mexicans: From Conquistadores to Chicanos.* New York: Hill and Wang, 1993.

——, eds. *Reading on La Raza: The Twentieth Century.* New York: Hill and Wang, 1974.

Menchaca, Martha. *The Mexican Outsiders: A Community History of Marginalization and Discrimination in California.* Austin: University of Texas Press, 1995.

Metzgar, Joseph V. "The Ethnic Sensitivity of Spanish New Mexicans: A Survey and Analysis." *New Mexico Historical Review* 49, no. 1 (1974): 49–73.

Millman, Joel. *The Other Americans: How Immigrants Renew Our Country, Our Economy, Our Values.* New York: Viking, 1997.

Miranda, Malvin L. *A History of Hispanics in Southern Nevada.* Reno: University of Nevada Press, 1997.

Mirandé, Alfredo. *The Chicano Experience: An Alternative Perspective.* Notre Dame: University of Notre Dame Press, 1985.

Mirandé, Alfredo, and Evangelina Enriquez. *La Chicana: The Mexican American Woman.* Chicago: University of Chicago Press, 1979.

Monroy, Douglas. *Rebirth: Mexican Los Angeles from the Great Migration to the Great Depression.* Berkeley: University of California Press, 1999.

Montejano, David. *Anglos and Mexicans in the Making of Texas, 1836–1986.* Austin: University of Texas Press, 1987.

——, ed. *Chicano Politics and Society in the Late Twentieth Century.* Austin: University of Texas Press, 1999.

Moquin, Wayne, ed., with Charles Van Doren. *A Documentary History of the Mexican Americans.* New York: Praeger, 1971.

Mora, Magdalena, and Adelaida R. del Castillo, eds. *Mexican Women in the United States: Struggles Past and Present.* Los Angeles: University of California at Los Angeles, 1980.

Morales, Rebecca, and Frank Bonilla. "Restructuring and the New Inequality." In *Latinos in a Changing U.S. Economy,* edited by Rebecca Morales and Frank Bonilla, 1–27. Newbury Park, Calif.: Sage, 1993.

Morín, Raúl. *Among the Valiant: Mexican Americans in World War II and Korea.* Alhambra, Calif.: Borden, 1966.

Muñoz, Carlos Jr. *Youth, Identity, Power: The Chicano Movement.* New York: Verso, 1989.

Murgía, Edward. *Chicano Intermarriage: A Theoretical and Empirical Study.* San Antonio: Trinity University Press, 1982.

Nash, Gerald D. *The American West in the Twentieth Century: A Short History of an Urban Oasis*. Englewood Cliffs, N.J.: Prentice Hall, 1973.

National Council of La Raza. "Out of the Picture: Hispanics in the Media." In *Latin Looks: Images of Latinas and Latinos in U.S. Media*, edited by Clara E. Rodríguez, 21–35. Boulder: Westview Press, 1997.

Navarro, Armando. *The Cristal Experiment: A Chicano Struggle for Community Control*. Madison: University of Wisconsin Press, 1998.

Navarro, Carlos, and Rodolfo Acuña. "In Search of Community: A Comparative Essay on Mexicans in Los Angeles and San Antonio." In *Twentieth Century Los Angeles*, edited by Norman M. Klein and Martin J. Schiesl, 195–226. Claremont, CA: Regina Books.

Nelson-Cisneros, Victor B. "La clase trabajadora en Tejas, 1920–1940." *Aztlán* 6, no. 2 (1976): 239–65.

Officer, James E. "Sodalities and Systemic Linkage: The Joining Habits of Urban Mexican Americans." Ph.D. diss., University of Arizona, 1964.

———. *Arizona's Hispanic Perspective*. Tucson: University of Arizona Press and Arizona Academy, 1981.

O'Hare, William. "The Rise of Hispanic Affluence." *American Demographics* 12 (August 1990): 40–43.

Oppenheimer, Robert. "Acculturation or Assimilation: Mexican Immigrants in Kansas, 1900 to World War II." *Western Historical Quarterly* 16, no. 4 (1985): 429–48.

Orozco, Cynthia E. "Beyond Machismo, La Familia, and Ladies Auxiliaries: A Historiography of Mexican-Origin Women's Participation in Voluntary Associations and Politics in the United States, 1870–1990." Renato Rosaldo Lecture Series Monograph no. 10. Tucson: Mexican American Studies and Research Center, 1994.

Pardo, Mary S. *Mexican American Women Activists: Identity and Resistance in Two Los Angeles Communities*. Philadelphia: Temple University Press, 1998.

Paredes, Américo. *With His Pistol in His Hand*. Austin: University of Texas Press, 1958.

Pedraza-Bailey, Silvia. *Political and Economic Migrants in America: Cubans and Mexicans*. Austin: University of Texas Press, 1985.

Pedraza, Silvia, and Rubén G. Rumbaut, eds. *Origins and Destinies: Immigration, Race and Ethnicity in America*. Belmont, Calif.: Wadsworth Publishing, 1996.

Perales, Alonso S. *Are We Good Neighbors?* New York: Arno, 1974.

Pérez, Emma. *The Decolonial Imaginary: Writing Chicanas into History*. Bloomington: Indiana University Press, 1999.

Pettit, Arthur G. *Images of the Mexican American in Fiction and Film*. Edited and with an afterword by Dennis E. Showalter. College Station: Texas A&M University Press, 1980.

Pitt, Leonard. *The Decline of the Californios: A Social History of the Spanish-Speaking Californians, 1846–1890*. Berkeley: University of California Press, 1966.

Portes, Alejandro, and Rubén G. Rumbaut. *Immigrant America: A Portrait*. Berkeley: University of California Press, 1990.

Pycior, Julie Leininger. *LBJ and Mexican Americans: The Paradox of Power*. Austin: University of Texas Press, 1997.

Reisler, Mark. "Always the Laborer, Never the Citizen: Anglo Perceptions of the Mexican Immigrant during the 1920s. *Pacific Historical Review* 45, no. 2 (1976): 231–54.

———. *By the Sweat of Their Brow: Mexican Immigrant Labor in the United States, 1900–1940*. Westport: Greenwood, 1976.

Rendon, Armando B. *Chicano Manifesto: The History and Aspirations of the Second Largest Minority in America*. New York: Collier Books, 1971.

Richard, Alfred C., Jr. *Contemporary Hollywood's Negative Hispanic Image: An Interpretive Filmography, 1956–1993*. Westport: Greenwood, 1994.

———. *The Hispanic Image on the Silver Screen: An Interpretive Filmography from Silents into Sound, 1898–1935*. Westport: Greenwood, 1992.

Richardson, Chad. *Batos, Bolillos, Pochos, and Pelados: Class and Culture on the South Texas Border*. Austin: University of Texas Press, 1999.

Ríos-Bustamante, Antonio, and Pedro Castillo. *An Illustrated History of Mexican Los Angeles, 1781–1985*. Chicano Studies Research Center Monograph no. 12. Los Angeles: University of California at Los Angeles, 1986.

Romo, Ricardo. *East Los Angeles: History of a Barrio*. Austin: University of Texas Press, 1983.

———. "The Urbanization of Southwestern Chicanos in the Early Twentieth Century." *New Scholar* 5 (1977): 183–208.

Rosales, F. Arturo. *Chicano! The History of the Mexican American Civil Rights Movement*. Houston: Arte Público Press, 1996.

———. *Pobre Raza! Violence, Justice, and Mobilization among Mexico Lindo Immigrants, 1900–1936*. Austin: University of Texas Press, 1999.

Rosales, F. Arturo, and Daniel T. Simón. "Chicano Steel Workers and Unionism in the Midwest, 1919–1945. *Aztlán* 6, no. 2 (1975): 266–75.

Rothenberg, Daniel. *With These Hands: The Hidden World of Migrant Farmworkers Today*. New York: Harcourt Brace, 1998.

Ruiz, Vicki L. *Cannery Women, Cannery Lives: Mexican Women, Unionization, and the California Food Processing Industry, 1930–1950.* Albuquerque: University of New Mexico Press, 1987.

———. *From out of the Shadows: Mexican Women in Twentieth-Century America.* New York: Oxford University Press, 1998.

———., ed. *Las Obreras: The Politics of Work and Family. Aztlán* 20, no. 1–2 (1993).

Samora, Julian, and Patricia Vandel Simon. *A History of the Mexican-American People.* Rev. ed. Notre Dame: University of Notre Dame Press, 1993.

Sánchez, George J. *Becoming Mexican American: Ethnicity, Culture, and Identity in Chicano Los Angeles, 1900–1945.* New York: Oxford University Press, 1993.

San Miguel, Guadalupe Jr., *"Let All of Them Take Heed": Mexican Americans and the Campaign for Educational Equality in Texas, 1910–1981.* Austin: University of Texas Press, 1987.

Santillán, Richard. "Midwestern Mexican American Women and the Struggle for Gender Equality: A Historical Overview, 1920s-1960s." In *Mexican American Women: Changing Images*, edited by Juan R. García, 79–119. Perspectives in Mexican American Studies no. 5. Tucson: Mexican American Studies and Research Center, 1995.

———. "Rosita the Riveter: Midwest Mexican American Women during World War II, 1941–1945." In *Mexicans in the Midwest*, edited by Juan R. García, 115–47. Perspectives in Mexican American Studies no. 2. Tucson: Mexican American Studies and Research Center, 1989.

Santos Ramírez, Leopoldo. "Matrimonios entre norteamericanos y mexicanos en Sonora y Arizona. Manuscript, 1997. Author's files.

Saunders, Lyle. *Cultural Difference and Medical Care. The Case of the Spanish-Speaking People of the Southwest.* New York: Russell Sage Foundation, 1954.

Scruggs, Otey M. "Texas and the Bracero Program." *Pacific Historical Review* 32, no. 3 (1963): 251–64.

Shelton, Edgar G. *Political Conditions among Texas Mexicans along the Rio Grande.* San Francisco: R & E Associates, 1974.

Shelton, Laura. "Mexican Labor Migration to the United States, 1910–1936 and 1942–1964." M.A. Thesis, Temple University, 1996.

Sheridan, Thomas. *Arizona: A History.* Tucson: University of Arizona Press, 1995.

———. *Los Tucsonenses: The Mexican Community in Tucson, 1854–1941.* Tucson: University of Arizona Press, 1986.

Simmons, Ozzie G. "Anglo Americans and Mexican Americans in South Texas: A Study in Dominant-Subordinate Group Relations." Ph.D. diss., Harvard University, 1952.

Skerry, Peter. *Mexican Americans: The Ambivalent Minority.* New York: Free Press, 1993.

Slatta, Richard W. "Chicanos in the Pacific Northwest: An Historical Overview of Oregon's Chicanos." *Aztlán* 6, no. 2 (1975): 327–40.

Smith, Michael M. "Mexicans in Kansas City: The First Generation, 1900–1920." In *Mexicans in the Midwest*, edited by Juan R. García, 29–57. *Perspectives in Mexican American Studies* no. 2. Tucson: Mexican American Studies and Research Center, 1989.

———. *The Mexicans in Oklahoma*. Norman: University of Oklahoma Press, 1980.

Steinberg, Stephen. *The Ethnic Myth: Race, Ethnicity, and Class in America*. Boston: Beacon, 1989.

Stephens, Sandra L. "The Women of the Amador Family, 1860–1940." In *New Mexico Women: Intercultural Perspectives*, edited by Joan M. Jensen and Darlis A. Miller, 257–78. Albuquerque: University of New Mexico Press, 1986.

Stoddard, Ellwyn. *Mexican Americans*. New York: Random House, 1973.

Stuart, Gary L. *The Gallup 14: A Novel*. Albuquerque: University of New Mexico Press, 2000.

Suro, Roberto. *Strangers among Us: How Latino Immigration Is Transforming America*. New York: Knopf, 1998.

Takaki, Ronald. *Strangers from a Different Shore: A History of Asian Americans*. New York: Penguin Books, 1989.

Taylor, Paul S. *Mexican Labor in the United States*. 2 vols. New York: Arno Press and *New York Times*, 1970. Collection of reprints of many individual works on various topics originally published between 1928 and 1934.

———. "Mexican Women in Los Angeles Industry in 1928." *Aztlán* 11, no. 1 (1980), 99–131.

———. "Mexicans North of the Rio Grande." *Survey* 66 (May 1, 1931): 135–205.

Tijerina, Andrés A. *History of Mexican Americans in Lubbock County, Texas*. Lubbock: Texas Technological University Graduate Studies, 1979.

Torres, David L., and Melissa Amado. "The Quest for Power: Hispanic Collective Action in Frontier Arizona." *Perspectives in Mexican American Studies* 3 (1992): 73–94.

Valdes, Dennis N. *Al Norte: Agricultural Workers in the Great Lakes Region, 1917–1970*. Austin: University of Texas at Austin Center for Mexican American Studies, 1991.

———. *Barrios Norteños: St. Paul and Midwestern Mexican Communities in the Twentieth Century*. Austin: University of Texas Press, 2000.

Vargas, Zaragosa. *Proletarians of the North: A History of Mexican Industrial Workers in Detroit and the Midwest, 1917–1933*. Berkeley: University of California Press, 1993.

Vigil, Ernesto. *The Crusade for Justice: Chicano Militancy and the Government's War on Dissent*. Madison: University of Wisconsin Press, 1999.

Vigil, Maurilio E. *Hispanics in American Politics: The Search for Political Power*. Lanham, Md.: University Press of America, 1987.

Villarreal, Roberto E., Norma G. Hernández, and Howard D. Neighbor, eds. *Latino Empowerment: Progress, Problems, and Prospects*. Westport: Greenwood, 1988.

Weber, David J. *Foreigners in Their Native Land: Historical Roots of the Mexican Americans*. Albuquerque: University of New Mexico Press, 1973.

Weber, Devra. *Dark Sweat, White Gold: California Farm Workers, Cotton, and the New Deal*. Berkeley: University of California Press, 1994.

Woll, Allen L. *The Latin Image in American Film*. Los Angeles: University of California at Los Angeles Latin American Center, 1977.

Zamora, Emilio Jr. *The World of the Mexican Worker in Texas*. College Station: Texas A&M University Press, 1993.

INDEX